Predatory Globalization

Predatory Globalization

A Critique

RICHARD FALK

Polity Press

First published in 1999 by Polity Press in association with Blackwell Publishers Ltd.

Reprinted 2000

Editorial office:
Polity Press
65 Bridge Street
Cambridge CB2 1UR, UK

Marketing and production:
Blackwell Publishers Ltd
108 Cowley Road
Oxford OX4 1JF, UK

Published in the USA by
Blackwell Publishers Inc.
350 Main Street
Malden, MA 02148, USA

ISBN 0-7456-0935-X
ISBN 0-7456-0936-8 (pbk)

A catalogue record for this book is available from the British Library and has been applied for from the Library of Congress.

Typeset in 10 on 12 pt Times
by Best-set Typesetter Ltd., Hong Kong
Printed in Great Britain by MPG Books, Bodmin, Cornwall

This book is printed on acid-free paper.

For Dimitri, Noah, and Zeynep
  may their journeys be smooth and satisfying

  . . . Let go. Let fly. Forget.
You've listened long enough. Now strike your note.

Seamus Heaney, "Station Island" from *New*
Selected Poems 1966–1987

Contents

Acknowledgments

This puzzling phenomenon we call "globalization," for want of a better term, is evolving almost as I write these words. The speed of change is itself part of our historical circumstance that makes it a continual necessity to reassess our bearings. This is especially true in relation to the macro-trends of our time, which have been replete with satisfying and discomforting surprises. In these circumstances only a stubborn fool would have any confidence about anticipating what the future holds in store for us. It remains more important than ever under these conditions to evaluate this process so as to encourage the more hopeful possibilities, and to do so in a spirit that combines conviction and humility without undermining the will to act on behalf of a more humane future.

I have accumulated many debts to friends and colleagues in the course of writing this book over the course of the last five years, but I will refrain from enumerating them in detail. I will limit myself to what has been most persistent and relevant in relation to this particular endeavor.

As has been the case for several decades, my most abiding feeling of gratitude is to the Center of International Studies at Princeton University, which continues to provide a supportive, stimulating working atmosphere. I feel a particular kinship with the work and outlook of its current director, Michael Doyle, who shares many of the concerns and aspirations that animate this book. And, as has so often been the case over the years, I have been blessed by the superb assistance of June Garson, who combines intelligence, sensitivity, wit, and grace, and provides them all on a daily basis.

Much of my work on globalization has been influenced by conversations with like-minded colleagues in various parts of the world. Although less active than earlier, I feel a strong kinship with the core participants in the World Order Models Project, who have diverse approaches to globalization yet share a commitment to use knowledge for the sake of human betterment.

In formulating a political response to globalization, I have been particularly influenced by a series of friends with whom I have worked in various contexts, either on academic undertakings or in a more activist mode. This influence has been in the direction of rethinking the meaning of democracy in this era of globalization. I thank for their help particularly David Held, Mary Kaldor, Radha Kumar, Walden Bello, Yoshikazu Sakamoto, Daniele Archibugi, Lester Ruiz, Rob Walker, and Eqbal Ahmad.

The cultural context of globalization has also been of great importance to me in this period, and I am especially grateful for a series of conversations on various aspects of "reconstructive" or "restructive" postmodernism held in Scotland and known to the participants as "the Portrack Seminars." The extraordinary auspices were made possible by the generosity and commitment of Maggie and Charles Jencks, and the continuity of the discussions was achieved by a core group that consisted of Charles, Charlene Spretnak, David Ray Griffin, and myself.

Finally, I would mention two other sets of discussions that were influential in the shaping of my views. First are several meetings and workshops on the impact of globalization upon human rights and terrorism organized by JUST under the inspired leadership of Chandra Muzaffer in Malaysia. The second were of a quite different sort, a series of "Copenhagen Seminars" sponsored by the Danish Foreign Ministry as part of the follow-up to the 1995 Social Summit and given intellectual shape by Jacques Baudot, who exhibited great talent in assembling representative figures from around the world. What united the participants was a shared concern about human suffering and how to minimize social distress in a new era in which neo-liberal thinking seemed to prevail in official circles.

I have also had the benefit of a loving family. In partial acknowledgment of this I have dedicated the book to my three younger children who are close by, but I also want to mention my older son, Chris, and his family, who are distant in space, yet close in spirit. And most of all, my wife, Hilal, who has brought so much joy and warmth into my life; she *is* that romantic fantasy, a total partner!

I also want to thank Jean van Altena for her excellent editorial assistance, and the following publishers for permission to use and adapt previously published materials: United Nations University Press;

x *Acknowledgments*

Royal Institute of International Affairs (London); Carfax Publishing Limited; Macmillan Press Limited; St Martin's Press; and the *Australian Journal of International Affairs*; Faber and Faber Ltd for permission to quote from 'Station Island' from *New Selected Poems 1966–1987* by Seamus Heaney and Farrar, Straus and Giroux for permission to quote from 'Station Island' from *Opened Ground: Selected Poems 1966–1996* by Seamus Heaney (1998).

RICHARD FALK
Princeton, NJ

Introduction

For better and worse, "globalization" has become the most satisfactory descriptive label for the current historical era. Of course, it is important to clarify a particular usage of such a banner concept to the extent possible, if only to gain a bit of distance from trendy and manipulative invocations. The main preoccupation of this volume is with interactions between the strength of global capital and governments operating at the level of the sovereign state. Or put slightly differently, the overriding concern here is with the effects of economic globalization on the capacity of the state to contribute to human well-being, first of all in relation to territorial matters, but also with regard to such wider goals as peace, security, and sustainability.

The historical unfolding of economic globalization in recent decades has been accompanied by the ascendancy of a group of ideas associated with the world picture of "neo-liberalism." This ideological outlook is often somewhat coyly referred to as "the Washington consensus," which accurately highlights the "made in the USA" packaging of the neo-liberal scheme of things. This neo-liberal scheme points in the general direction of autonomous markets and facilitative states. Adherents of these ideas believe that they were responsible for promoting rapid economic growth in trade and investment, as well as for the spread of moderate patterns of governance, especially electoral democracy. In the last few years, as things went bad, there has been a sharpening disagreement within capitalist circles as to whether the banking and monetary systems should be insulated from periodic panic by large commitments of public funds in the form of bail-outs. This controversy also bears directly on whether the lessons of the financial crisis that has been unfolding since mid-1997 lend support to an expanded role for the International Monetary Fund as primary crisis manager. Or whether, on the contrary, the evidence of this recent period demonstrates that the IMF has been administering snake oil that has not only failed to rescue troubled economies but has actually aggravated the distress of society by its insistence on capital-friendly adjustments as the condition for receiving billions of dollars of bail-out funds. The shock troops of neo-liberalism seem sharply split on this one.

The characteristic policy vectors of neo-liberalism involve such moves as liberalization, privatization, minimizing economic regulation, rolling back welfare, reducing expenditures on public goods, tightening fiscal discipline, favoring freer flows of capital, strict controls on organized labor, tax reductions, and unrestricted currency repatriation. It is the cumulative adverse effects of these moves on human well-being that accounts for the title *Predatory Globalization*. It needs also to be understood that these ideological trappings are not intrinsic to economic globalization, which could have occurred and might still be redirected under a variety of ideational auspices other than neo-liberalism. The prevailing ideas are primarily a reflection of political preferences that are widely endorsed by dominant elites at a given time. By comparison, the phenomenon of globalization represents mainly material developments that reflect the expansion of technological capabilities to a global scale, as well as the de-territorialization of these capabilities due to informatics and the Internet. These developments could have been guided by alternative economistic and noneconomistic world pictures, including various shades of green Keynesianism, different types of neo-social democracy, and a large number of possible views on the political economy of governance – that is, on how best to handle the core relations between economic activity and society.

But my intention is not to provide one more critique of neo-liberalism. My objective is rather to call positive attention to a series of countermoves to neo-liberalism, especially those whose source is situated within civil society. The coherent ideological identity of these countermoves to globalization-from-above is in the process of formation and remains difficult to label. For my purposes in this book such activity can be tentatively and most descriptively associated with what has come to be called "cosmopolitan democracy." This provision of an overarching, although often implicit, orientation by reference to cosmopolitan democracy is meant also to encourage grass-roots participants and issue-oriented social movements to consider more directly the wider implications of their efforts, which may be overlooked due to a concentration on very local and specific circumstances.

This more positive part of the inquiry is directed toward the possible emergence of a new equilibrium of ends and means on a global scale in the trilateral relations between state, people, and capital. In essence, the argument is that "predatory globalization" has eroded, if not altogether broken, the former social contract that was forged between state and society during the last century or so. This contract urgently needs to be rewritten in light of current conditions, on behalf of the peoples of the world and to ensure a sustainable future. Unfortunately the state is not likely to be amenable to such a project in the present atmosphere, in which public policy is heavily conditioned by deference to the discipline of global capital. It would appear that only the massing of a variety of strong transnational social pressures on the states of the world could alter the political equation to the point where the state could sufficiently recover its autonomy in relation to the world economy. On this basis, the state could launch initiatives to restore its own legitimacy by way of negotiating a new globally conceived social contract between the citizenry and the representatives of business and finance. The purpose here would be to retain the material benefits of globalization without paying excessive social costs, a bargain that might eventually be negotiated to smooth the rough edges of early globalization.

These transnational pressures are generating a new kind of transnational politics that is referred to in this book as "globalization-from-below." This is an aggregate designation for the overall efforts of global civil society to restore the various social and political gains made during the latter stages of the industrial era, as well as to move consistently forward to establish the constitutive elements of cosmopolitan democracy as the political template for an inevitably globalizing world. The trend toward increasing interconnectedness on regional and global levels contains many benefits for society worldwide, especially if it can be combined with the opening of space for the protection of human rights, including the right of self-determination.

Criticism of globalization in its current embodiment is not at all a type of "closet Marxism" that is out, above all, to annihilate capital-driven forces – what is referred to here as "globalization-from-above." It is rather to work toward their containment and partial transformation by reference to widely shared world order values. By so doing, it would eventually be possible to promote more mutually beneficial outcomes for business and society that would at the same time be able to take a much increased account of what might be called "world order priorities." These priorities relate, first and foremost, to protecting the planet and its inhabitants from the ongoing gathering of destructive tendencies that currently threaten human well-being and the viability of the global commons through pollution of the oceans, rising water levels, a warming of the atmosphere, and release of an array of ultra-hazardous substances. They also extend to a concern about the rise of transnational crime and political violence of a sort that is difficult to regulate so long as one relies so heavily on the political will and coercive capabilities of traditional sovereign states. The imagination of government bureaucracies is ill-adapted to meet the disruptive, extraterritorial threats being mounted.

But such world order priorities also extend to affirming an ethos of human solidarity that maintains that as a matter of *right* there exists a duty to provide for the basic needs of all persons. It also crucially includes an extension of the democratic spirit of governance to all the various international and national arenas of authority and decision that together make up that integrated whole that we are beginning to treat as if it might indeed sometime become a genuine global polity, perhaps sometime early in the next century. This extension involves a reaffirmation of the roles of a strengthened and reformed United Nations system and of emergent regional institutions. These institutional ingredients of global governance are needed to encourage cooperative approaches to conflict and complexity. Important contributions to global governance can also be made by states, especially if they can be reempowered to exercise a *responsible sovereignty* that expresses an evolving balance between globalization-from-above and -below. States as currently oriented have been instrumentalized by the pull of global capital, so the prospect of their contributing positively to the quality of global governance depends on a prior process of de-instrumentalization. The idea of instrumentalization is meant as a contrast to that of autonomy with respect to the relations between capital and labor markets.

Human solidarity as a ground condition of global governance needs to be understood as fully consistent with civilizational diversity and the importance of inter-civilizational dialogue as the foundation for an acceptable normative (law and ethics) order. The appreciation of cultural differences is particularly appropriate in light of the earlier periods of Euro-centricism and Western normative hegemony. Acknowledging this, however, is not meant to immunize oppressive and exploitative behavior from accountability to universally legitimated standards. When rulers encourage genocidal practices or massive rape and torture, their acts are criminal violations of international law and qualify everywhere as crimes against humanity.

The manner whereby the cold war ended generated a short-lived triumphalism that encouraged supporters of the neo-liberal outlook to endow it with a quasi-theological stature. This mood was best captured by Francis Fukuyama's polemical caper about "the end of history," which became highly influential, if only briefly, because it seemed to rest the triumph of the market-oriented states on a philosophical and historical basis that promised its permanence. In the early 1990s the mainstream rejection of all criticism of markets and their operations by policymakers and the media was commonplace. What resulted was a dogmatic climate of opinion that virtually shut down the political imagination, presenting citizens of even the most established democracies with a strong dose of their own irrelevance. The convergence of political parties led to elections fought around images rather than issues, where style came to matter more than substance, leading pundits to affix the label "choiceless democracies" and critics to wonder whether electoral democracy and political parties were rapidly becoming dysfunctional. In such an atmosphere the globalizing juggernaut seemed inevitable and irresistible. It was treated by most leaders as an occasion for celebration resting on claims of having provided the longest period of sustained growth in human history, with benefits for the first time spread around the planet, including some of the previously most economically disadvantaged states. Whatever objections were advanced by progressive or populist forces were treated as emanating from the distant sidelines, and were quickly brushed aside as "socialistic" or "utopian," or simply as impractical assaults on "competitiveness," "efficiency," and "growth." A government had no real choice but to enter the playing field of global capitalism and play the game as well as it could. If a government refused to play or was disallowed for political and ideological reasons by the geopolitical gatekeepers, as was the case with the so-called rogue states, it tended to be confronted with capital flight, stagnancy, a loss of external support, and acute poverty. Supposedly, signs of impoverishment, environmental degradation, and widening gaps in income and wealth were to be overcome at some point by the not-so-tender mercies of the favored neo-liberal deity, easily recognized by its huge, but supposedly benign, if slow-moving, "invisible hand." The other, visible hand of this deity was blatantly harsh, counseling respect for the way the market sorted out winners and losers, and resisting, as inefficient and futile, efforts to soften the sufferings of those who were being bypassed by investors and speculators. This atmosphere of ideological closure in the early 1990s was as depressing as was the growing evidence of severe social and environmental harm resulting from the excesses of globalization-from-above. Such empty ideologizing was an especial disappointment after so many years of sterile East–West debate. It had been hoped that the end of geopolitical bipolarity would give rise to a surge of Western enthusiasm for a safer, cleaner, friendlier, and more empathetic world; but such a hope was quickly dashed on the shoals of neo-liberal individualism.

This dismal atmosphere was also reinforced by the most militant advocates of a supposedly radical and new politics deriving from the Internet that stressed the virtues of self-organizing systems. From such cyber-perspectives, the market enables real freedom, and the interfering state, whatever its character, erects a structural impediment that continues to cast dark shadows by holding stubbornly onto roles crafted in response to earlier technologies suited to bounded space and long durations of time. In political terms, this libertarian co-optation of information and computer technologies fostered a natural alliance between the most ardent geeks strung out along the electronic frontier and the more dynamic parts of the private sector that built new empires of wealth mainly through the manipulation of information and money. Both market and Internet are global in scope and outlook and have little inherent feeling of loyalty to national or territorial communities. Both regard the intrusion of borders and regulators of any kind on human activity as imposing unwelcome limitations on freedom and efficiency and as essentially artificial and anachronistic reminders of a spatially organized world.

Such a regressive political destiny for the worldwide web is fortunately by no means predetermined. The web also offers contradictory emancipatory resources as free goods to all those who are seeking to build networks of relations among activist social forces throughout the world. Potentially, these networks are visionary and dedicated to transformative political goals, offering the poor and vulnerable possibly their best hopes for the future. The worldwide web allows for an empowerment of globalization-from-below in a manner that seems presently difficult to subdue or ignore. Such empowerment could facilitate both the politics of resistance and transformation in a variety of circumstances.

At the same time, it needs to be stressed that the choices are by no means so stark, that the contrast implied by the counterposing of globalization-from-above and -below is at best a convenience that calls our attention to the main configurations of tension currently at work in the world. At worst, such a contrast may induce us to downplay the prospect for several hybrid and promising developments, such as the reemergence of compassionate states dedicated to human well-being and the international practice of responsible sovereignty. Such states would be the "postmodern" sequel to "modern" compassionate states – for instance, Sweden in the period of the cold war. Postmodern compassionate states would align themselves with progressive social forces in various specific settings and refuse to endorse the discipline of global capital if the results were to produce social, environmental, and spiritual harm.

There is another danger with such polarizing conceptions of what is beneficial and what is detrimental. It tends to encourage various forms of simplistic ethical classification. By such moral reasoning, all corporations and banks are demonized as socially harmful, while all civic associations are romanticized as beneficial. In the lifeworld, especially given the many contradictory tendencies at work, the realities are almost always more complex and more shaded and may quite often be counterintuitive. A private sector actor, whether for pragmatic or principled reasons, may to varying extents in particular circumstances turn out to be more benevolent than expected from the perspective of world order values. Contrariwise, voluntary civic initiatives may be quite regressive in their internal organization and social vision, and irresponsible or inconsequential in their undertakings. Simple examples can illustrate this growing complexity: corporate leaders pushing for restraint on further population growth, governments pushing for an anti-personnel land mines treaty, as opposed to aroused civic groups, which engage in violence against abortion clinics that serve the poor or champion the right of citizens to have easy access to assault rifles.

There is, then, nothing deterministic about globalization, with reference to either its ideological content or its normative goals. Not even its friends and foes are fixed. New coalitions are possible and promising. It is important at this stage to remain open and flexible with respect to opportunities to enhance the outlook for humane governance in all settings of social action.

At the same time, the historical flow of developments has generated some pronounced, and troubling, trends, and it is these that justify drawing such a sharp distinction at this time between globalization-from-above and globalization-from-below. The further benefit of the distinction is to direct our energies toward this ongoing, yet seldom acknowledged, fight for "the soul of the state." In its essence, the question being posed in the chapters that follow is whether the state will function in the future mainly as an instrument useful for the promotion and protection of global trade and investment or whether, by contrast, the state can recover its sense of balance in this globalizing setting so that the success of markets will not be achieved at the expense of the well-being of peoples. Such a recovery implies a creative synthesis in this new global setting informed by extraordinary technological innovations and can certainly not be achieved by a simple retreat into a social democratic past. The globalizing dynamic is powerfully embodied in the technological capabilities of the information era, and the main challenge facing all of us is to find ways to ensure that these technologies are deployed in response to ethical as well as market criteria, which include as central normative ideas sustainable development, human rights, and cosmopolitan democracy. These ideas must not be allowed to degenerate into slogans but should inform a continuous and multi-civilization critical evaluation of ongoing activities and programs of action for the future.

These possibilities for an opening of the policy debate have been greatly enhanced by the global economic crisis that has been deepening and spreading since mid-1997, with no clear end in sight at this time. This crisis has ended the mood of complacency about a recessionless future and eroded the dogmatic insistence that the guidance provided by listening to the market all but eliminated the need for politics and an attentive citizenry. The economic turmoil started in East Asia and was viewed restrictively as a subregional crisis at first. It was seen at this stage as a wonderful opportunity to spread the gospel of neo-liberalism through the interventions of the IMF. But when the crisis spun out of control and later spread to Japan and Russia, alarm bells went off throughout the world, and globalist reverberations were registered in the form of sharp downturns and swings in financial markets everywhere. The economistic medicine being administered by the IMF suddenly became controversial and was no longer treated as if it were a proven cure. All sorts of additional and alternative remedies abruptly became respectable and, most surprisingly, were often put forward from *within* the ranks of market-oriented elites. The intra-capitalist struggle for the revival of globalization-from-above is now in full swing.

But there has also emerged an excellent opportunity for civil society to reassert progressive influences on political life. This opportunity arises from the loss of confidence in the world picture that animates neo-liberalism. It is also fostered by the return to governmental leadership of left/center coalitions in many important countries that are mandated to move toward a more balanced view of societal/market relations. This new receptivity is helped, as well, by the inadequacy of United States leadership, its reliance on the old ways of coercive diplomacy and unilateral violence, its retreat from active internationalist involvement in many settings, and its regressive, inward-looking Congress.

Against such a background, the chapters that follow explore both the detrimental impacts of economic globalization and the creative initiatives that are emerging as responses in many settings.

Part I
Diagnosing the Challenge

1

Democratizing, Internationalizing, and Globalizing: A Collage of Blurred Images

Getting a Grip on "Reality"

The ending of the cold war both concluded an era of ideological rivalry and stripped away the illusion of consensus about the shape and direction of world order. Beyond the domain of cold war truisms that had prevailed between 1945 and 1989, there were increasingly evident analytic and explanatory difficulties: how to take conceptual account of the globalization of capital and communications; whether or not to treat the porousness of state boundaries with regard to drugs, illegal immigration, environmental degradation, unwanted ideas and threats, financial flows and banking operations, as posing a fundamentally new series of questions about the nature and effectiveness of sovereignty as the basic approach to the distribution of authority on a global basis; the extent to which generalized descriptive narratives about the economic/political/legal conditions of the peoples of the world homogenized crucial differences or illuminated vital affinities.

The position taken here is that the end of the cold war has made it easier to focus on structural trends and countertrends in international life and to set forth a normative critique, but that these challenges would have manifested themselves in any event. With the end of the cold war there has emerged an irresistible disposition to debate and reflect upon the future of world order. For this reason alone George Bush's advocacy of "a new world order" during the Gulf crisis of 1990–1 captured headlines that sent pundits of all persuasion rushing off to their personal computers. On the one side were those who welcomed this American project as a necessary step in the direction of "hegemonic stability," giving leadership and cohesion during a turbulent time of growing geoeconomic tensions. On another side were those who worried about a new exploitative, imperial order, sometimes sloganized as Pax Americana II, and what this might explicitly mean for specific regions, such as Africa, the Pacific, and Europe. And then there were those who expected a shift of policy emphasis from geopolitics to environmental protection. As Lester Brown put it: "The cold war that dominated international affairs for four decades and led to an unprecedented militarization of the world economy is over. With its end comes an end to the world order it spawned." Brown argues that the only foundation for hope about the future is to allow the struggle "to reverse the degradation of the planet" to "dominate world affairs for decades to come."[1] In a certain respect, these views had two misleading features in common: first of all, that the shape of the future depended on the decisions of the political leaders representing the most powerful state; secondly, that the North–South axis of relations was of no particular relevance to the future of the world order in the next phase of international relations.

This chapter proceeds on a different set of assumptions. To begin with, even at the level of state action, the future will be shaped by the inter-action among states, with the effectiveness of United States leadership likely to be limited in time and dependent on context. Further, since 1992 the US effort to provide a coherent vision of "the new world order" has faltered, as of early 1997, partly by default, partly by failure to carry off the Gulf War diplomacy in a manner that might have solidified Washington's claim to undisputed leadership, partly by evidences of US economic selfishness and domestic restiveness, and partly by conceptu-alizing the future in a militarist and unipolar framework that engendered an immediate backlash both at home and abroad.[2] In this regard, the shape and orientation of a new world order will emerge over the course of the next decade as an outcome of an intense political struggle among many contending actors and social forces. States will certainly play a role, with leading states exerting considerable influence; but a statist future will be modified by market forces of various kinds and by the democra-tizing struggles of peoples and their associations and movements in many local, national, regional, and global settings. This refocusing of inquiry gives rise to a counter-project to that of post–cold war geopolitics: namely, the strengthening of global civil society animated by an agenda of demilitarization, democratization, equitable and sustainable develop-ment, environmental protection, cultural pluralism, human rights, and global governance.

This perspective can be summarized as follows: the main statist/ market project of the North is to sustain geopolitical stability, which in turn calls for the continuous expansion of world trade, economic growth, and the suppression of nationalist and regionalist challenges emanating from the South – by force if necessary. This project of the North is more or less challenged by several oppositional tendencies in international society, including a variety of fundamentalisms that refuse to collaborate and a range of democratizing processes that conceive of human rights and justice, not stability, as the end of politics. One major uncertainty is whether those forces supporting the strengthening of global civil society can gain sufficient influence to qualify as a genuine "counter-project," rather than merely a societal tendency, confined to the margins of policy in the North and of little relevance to the South. In this regard, the internationalization of the state, assuredly a strong tendency, can be a vehicle for promoting either emancipatory or oppressive outcomes, and is likely historically to be perceived ambiguously and with contradictory interpretations about resisting, co-opting, and conditioning a given state on behalf of one or another project of global reform. That is, domestic and transnational forces – from society and market activity – will exert various kinds of pressure on the state, often at cross-purposes.

To develop this interpretation further, the existing world order is depicted from three complementary perspectives: the structure of the global political economy; the interplay between environmental degradation and environmentalism; the normative architecture of the planet.

The Structure of the Global Political Economy

Several characteristics of the global political economy shape the tactics and aspirations of progressive social forces: extreme hierarchy and unevenness of circumstances; acute deprivation and mass misery among the poor; erosion of autonomy at the level of the state as a consequence of the play of nonterritorial capital forces.

It is notable that several recent independent analyses of the global political economy invoke the imagery and language of apartheid.[3] Writing in the preface to a comprehensive and devastating critique of the global economic order, Arjun Makhijani asserts that "[t]he principal conclusion" of his book "is that the structure of the world economy is in its most essential respects like that of apartheid in South Africa – a kind of global apartheid."[4]

But it is a conclusion reached not only by Third World commentators and progressive observers in the North. Thomas Schelling, long notable as a war thinker who influenced the outlook of the United States strategic community during the formative period of the cold war, poses for himself the question about what model of authority at a state level might "an incipient world state resemble." Schelling asks: "If we were to contemplate gradually relinquishing some measure of sovereignty in order to form not a more perfect union, but a more effective legal structure, what familiar political entity might be our basis for comparison? I find my own answer stunning and depressing: South Africa" (that is, apartheid South Africa).

It is worth quoting Schelling's account of the empirical underpinnings for such a radical assessment:

> We live in a world that is one-fifth rich and four-fifths poor; the rich are segregated into the rich countries and the poor into the poor countries; the rich are predominantly lighter skinned and the poor darker skinned; most of the poor live in "homelands" that are physically remote, often separated by oceans and great distances from the rich.
>
> Migration on any great scale is impermissible. There is no systematic redistribution of income. While there is ethnic strife among the well-to-do, the strife is more vicious and destructive among the poor.[5]

Schelling notes the correlation between race and poverty, as well as the refusal of the richer countries to accept "economic refugees" from the poorer. He does not extend the comparison to the use of military force: namely, that the rich, light-skinned countries enjoy a decisive military superiority and engage in frequent interventionary operations against the poor, dark-skinned countries.

It is, of course, striking that even North–South military interventions in this century – and there have been more than 100 major ones – have been by the North in the South. Preserving this interventionary option undoubtedly contributes to the near hysterical reaction against Third World terrorism against Northern targets and the new insistence that darker-skinned countries not be allowed to acquire nuclear weapons. In the leaked Pentagon guidance document of 1992 it was argued as possibly necessary for the United States even to use military force to prevent North Korea, Iran, Pakistan, and India from acquiring nuclear weaponry; but no reference is made to the acquisition of such weaponry by Israel or South Africa, states with a militarist record in recent foreign policy, but governed by light-skinned elites. Double standards based on race are being extended in practice to the ultimate form of violence: nuclearism – in effect, a regime of "nuclear apartheid." Such a pattern is not explicitly or deliberately racist, but the *de facto* racism evident in practice contributes to the impression of a racially stratified world order.

There is one more element to be noted. Schelling, reverting to form as establishment guru, insists that the national security mandate for US policymakers is to preserve "the US as a free nation with our fundamental institutions and values intact . . . must include what we *possess* as well as what we *appreciate*. It includes our material standard of living."[6] Such an emphasis confirms the notorious insistence by George Kennan back in 1948 within a then secret Policy Planning Staff document that the main objective of the United States in the Pacific region after World War II was to ensure that a country with only 6 percent of the world population could continue to use 50 percent of the world's resources upon which its prosperity was based. The numbers may have changed, but the fundamental imbalances remain.[7] More recent figures reveal the same essential structure as 45 years ago. According to Daniel Kevles, "The nations of the industrial north have about 24 percent of the world's population but use about 80 percent of its processed energy and mineral resources. About 33 percent of those resources are used by the United States alone, which has only about 5 percent of the world's population."[8] In effect, the Kennan/Schelling analysis implies that a principal role of military force is unabashedly committed to the perpetuation of global apartheid! No mighty invisible hand is sustaining these structures, but rather, by their own acknowledgment, the mailed fist of strategic planners in the rich countries.[9]

Without implying an inflammatory comparison with South Africa, the South Commission orients its entire report on North–South relations around a similar assessment of the intolerable character of the current structuring of the global political economy:

> While most of the people of the North are affluent, most of the people in the South are poor; while the economies of the North are generally strong and resilient, those of the South are mostly weak and defenceless; while the countries in the North are, by and large, in control of their destinies, those of the South are very vulnerable to external factors lacking in functional sovereignty. . . .
>
> Were all humanity a single nation-state, the present North–South divide would make it an unviable, semi-feudal entity, split by internal conflicts. Its small part is advanced, prosperous, powerful; its much bigger part is underdeveloped, poor, powerless. A nation so divided within itself would be recognized as unstable. A world so divided within itself should likewise be recognized as inherently unstable. And the position is worsening, not improving.[10]

The South Report stresses "instability" rather than illegitimacy, possibly to communicate more easily with adherents of "the realist consensus," who are not inclined to regard normative factors as relevant determinants of international behavior by sovereign states. Of course, under certain conditions instability flows from illegitimacy, but under other conditions instability is more likely to arise from political efforts to oppose illegitimacy.[11]

It may be wondered why such an effort has been made to substantiate the plausibility of a mere metaphor. But let us reflect upon what it is we acknowledge by this metaphor of apartheid. Even during the most divisive period of East–West tensions there was a consensus at the international level that apartheid in South Africa was morally and legally intolerable; indeed, the UN General Assembly declared that apartheid was an international crime. Sanctions were imposed to reinforce this censure and may well have been a large part of the explanation for the dramatic repudiation of apartheid by the De Klerk leadership in the early 1990s. What has been criminalized at the global level and repudiated within South Africa is both descriptive of the global political economy in crucial respects and widely accepted as the basis of a legitimate world order, the safeguarding of which is implicitly and explicitly treated both as a central guideline for the foreign policy of the powerful and as grounds for military intervention in the South.

It hardly needs to be argued that such a manner of organizing the world economy is unacceptable to those social forces active in the work of creating a global civil society responsive to the goals earlier set forth. It also follows that the use of state power in the North to preserve such structures is an unacceptable basis upon which to establish world order; that, within the realities of "a global village," what is immoral and illegal when confined to the part is immoral and illegal when extended to the whole. Arguments of necessity and inevitability are no more appropriate here than in relation to torture or slavery. Besides, there are alternatives to global apartheid, and these possibilities are constantly being affirmed by representatives of dominant states and market forces, portraying a future freed from current miseries.

Reliance on the metaphor of apartheid is meant to be provocative, rather than fully explanatory. On a world scale, unlike in South Africa, the racist basis of the distribution of privilege and deprivation is neither formalized nor acknowledged. On the contrary, the international law of human rights, as endorsed by the white North, condemns all forms of racism. Beyond this, to stress race as the explanation of global stratification underestimates the relevance of class, gender, and imperial factors, as well as the related international division of labor based upon market forces. The elites in the North are prepared to collaborate with non-white elites if that facilitates economic gains in the South. Several Asian non-white economies, led by Japan, have broken out of a subordinate economic status as a consequence of building up a competitive edge with respect to goods and services traded in the world economy.

If these critical differences are appreciated, the global apartheid metaphor seems useful. It confronts the moral and political complacency of the North. It demands attention for certain disturbing racial features of perception and practice in recent international political behavior. It underscores the historical associations that arise as a consequence of Black Africa remaining the poorest and most tormented region of the world. The metaphor of global apartheid, then, represents a warning as well as a provocative line of critique, suggesting the urgency of taking far more serious steps to overcome the North–South cleavage.

The Race between Environmentalism and Environmental Degradation

Thirty-five years ago there was virtually no environmental consciousness aside from elements in privileged classes eager to preserve hunting, fishing, and wilderness areas. Also, locally, throughout the industrial revolution there were concerns about pollution of various kinds and about the tendencies for market and government to obscure or downplay health hazards. The great Norwegian playwright, Henrik Ibsen, wrote a timeless play on this theme, *An Enemy of the People*, at the end of the nineteenth century.

Over the last 20 years there has been an enormous surge of environmental concern. Public attention has ebbed and flowed. An initial wave of concern in the early 1970s focused on "the limits to growth," folding the perception of environmental danger into an overall conviction that industrial civilization was not sustainable given the interplay of resource use, decay of renewable resources (air, water, soil), food supply, and population density.[12] Books written at that time had in common a multidimensional view, but tended to share the conclusion that a civilizational or even a species survival crisis was imminent.

This initial mobilization of concern, well orchestrated by the Club of Rome in publicizing its famous study *The Limits to Growth*, generated a variety of responses. Mainstream industry and academia fought back, contending that the evidence didn't support such prophesies of doom, and that continuing economic growth was indispensable if political stability were to be maintained. The Third World reacted suspiciously to environmental alarmism during the 1970s, generally believing that to cut off a growth-based economy at early modernizing stages of development would deny poorer countries their best prospect of escape from the poverty trap. Governments tried, by and large, to mediate between contradictory pressures, expecting to deflect rising populist concerns about environmental quality by sponsoring the UN Conference on the Human Environment in 1972. The official intergovernmental event in Stockholm focused public concern, while the leading states resolved to limit their commitments to vague rhetorical assertions and the creation of a small, innocuous bureaucratic entity (the United Nations Environment Programme, UNEP). But the media, the counterculture of the late 1960s, and a fast-growing network of citizens' associations showed up in Stockholm to initiate a transnational environmental movement that has been expanding ever since.

The 1980s produced two significant developments: a consensus that environmental problems of long-range and global scope, especially ozone depletion and global warming, required massive adjustments at a behavioral level in all countries, or else dreadful effects on health and agriculture would occur; and a multilayered environmentalist movement, which gathered real political strength and employed sophisticated and varied tactics, with industry and government eager to establish their own environmentalist credentials. Perhaps the most startling conversion was "the greening of Mrs Thatcher," expressed by way of Britain's efforts to accelerate the phase-out of chlorofluorocarbons (CFCs) as evidence accumulated that the rate of ozone depletion was faster than even "the alarmists" had earlier predicted.

Surveying the legacy of these past two decades, a confusing and disturbing conclusion emerges. Environmental activism has had an extraordinary impact on mainstream politics and on state policy, including the formation of green parties in many countries and rapidly growing budgets and expanding memberships for militant environmental groups. The Brundtland Commission effectively contributed to the formation of a global consensus: the environmental crisis can be managed on behalf of sustainable development, but only if states cooperate as never before on behalf of the general planetary interest, and this will happen only if pollution is understood to encompass poverty, thus placing the economic burdens of adjustment on the richer countries and promising that Third World development prospects would not be diminished by efforts at environmental protection. Despite these achievements, by virtually every indicator of environmental quality on a global basis, the situation continues to deteriorate at a dangerous rate, with no signs of reversal in sight.

In June 1992, the UN Conference on Environment and Development (UNCED) took place, symbolically located in Brazil, with unprecedented fanfare (153 countries, 1,400 NGOs, 8,000 media representatives) but disappointing tangible achievements – no commitment to reduce carbon dioxide emissions, to preserve rain forests, to eliminate Third World debt, or to restrict population growth and consumptive habits, and no willingness to overcome the cumbersomeness of cooperation among states through the establishment of a powerful UN Environmental Protection Agency with revenue-raising and enforcement capabilities and a democratized authority structure that would enable real influence and participation by groups representing global civil society. What was achieved at UNCED is by no means negligible: the Rio Declaration, which contained 27 principles that provide a framework for environmental protection; a convention on climate change and another one on biodiversity, each signed by 153 countries; the adoption of Agenda 21, which, while not legally binding, is the most elaborate program for environmental protection ever developed (comprising 40 chapters, 800 pages), and establishment of a new body called the Sustainable Development Commission. Considerable networking among nongovernmental organizations (NGOs) also occurred at Rio to sustain a citizens' global presence in relation to further efforts to promote environmental protection.[13]

At this stage, world order is adrift in relation to the environmental challenge. An impressive response has, to be sure, occurred at all levels, including the state to an extent; but it is a response that falls dangerously short of the multiple, cumulative challenge. There is no evidence that the requisite political will exists in either statist or market settings. Other priorities impinge to keep environmental adjustments at the margins of policy. The prevailing attitude remains dominated by the growth/profits/trade dynamic, possibly accentuated by a prolonged global recession. A Japanese environmental minister captured the persisting mood when he said: "I think we should be growing and growing forever. It's my personal philosophy. Quite often materials, or amounts of materials available, and the degree of happiness have a very strong correlation, so I think the more we have, the better it is."[14]

Many factors are at work, including considerations of time and political habit. Political leaders are not held accountable for adverse impacts deferred to the future; the electoral cycle is not correlated with the time horizons of response to the most menacing dimensions of the environmental challenge; behavioral adjustment cuts directly against the grain of consumerism, the heart and soul of the capitalist ethos; the collapse of socialist alternatives, at least temporarily, generates a mood of virtual unconditional deference to market forces; even societal concerns emphasize immediate economic pressures – jobs and growth, which seem to create a trade-off between economic and environmental policy objectives; leaders of major states and their citizenry are easily diverted from the complexities and long time horizons of the environmental challenges. Geopolitics and materialist priorities remain opiates for elites and masses.

The world order dilemma is simple to express, difficult to overcome. States are challenged as never before by global-scale problems but lack the will to respond; the unevenness of human circumstances generates contradictory images of responsibility for causing the harm and the distribution of the burden of response. States are reluctant to facilitate coordination by establishing effective global governance mechanisms in relation to the environmental agenda. The tragedy of the commons remains tragic!

As with global apartheid, the probabilistic scenarios of environmental decay imply oppressiveness, especially in the form of shifting as much of the burden of environmental decay from North to South (relocating polluting industry – according to Lawrence Summers, then the chief economist of the World Bank, "I've always thought that under-populated countries in Africa are vastly *under*-polluted",[15] siting toxic dumps; exporting harmful pesticides and untested pharmaceuticals). More hopeful scenarios depend upon the greening of global civil society and its capacity to overcome the modernist preoccupations of a territorially constituted system of world order.[16]

Rethinking the Normative Architecture of World Order

Every world order system implies a complex normative architecture, partly explicit, partly tacit. For several centuries this architecture reflected the normative dominance of Westphalia logic, which was premised upon the primacy of the sovereign, territorial state. In effect, each state was entitled to exercise supreme authority within its own boundaries and respect the reciprocal rights of other states to do the same. Modern international law arose out of this premise of formal equality, which included the exclusive authority to participate in diplomatic relations with other states. Sovereignty was interpreted to mean that states were not subject to any legal duties other than those they had accepted voluntarily, or, according to some jurists, those founded on "natural law," which were binding independent of consent by the sovereign.

It is useful to recall that this formalized account of world order expressed a historical disposition to remove the religious affiliation of a political community from international contention. The Peace of West-phalia was, after all, a settlement of religious wars in Europe, known as the Thirty Years' War. The Westphalia approach also reflected the growing influence of secularizing trends in economic and political domains, which wanted both to centralize internal authority at the state level, and to evade the broader sorts of authority claimed and exercised by the Roman Catholic Church in feudal Europe. These secularizing trends were reinforced by developments in scientific thought, especially in the work of Galileo and Newton, reconceptualized as political theory by Thomas Hobbes.[17]

Of course, the Westphalia vision of the world was never descriptive of either normative claims or political reality, and the formulation of a world of equal sovereign states needs to be interpreted as a world order project (that is, a world to be created) and as a mystifying ideology (that is, a juridical masking of inequality).[18] The most subversive conceptual and normative challenges to Westphalian images subsequently arose from revolutionary ideas about reordering the shape of state–society and state–state relations, especially the rights of citizens, the accountability of leaders, and notions of class and racial solidarity. Some of these concerns have been incorporated into the normative framework of world order during recent decades, through the developments of the international law of human rights and the adoption of the Nuremberg Principles. These subversive challenges to the core Westphalian notion of territorial supremacy have been endorsed at a formal level by governments acting on behalf of states and thus do not in a technical sense violate the formal logic of state sovereignty; but their practical effect is to place constraints upon claims of territorial supremacy and sovereign prerogative. And what is most relevant from the perspective of this chapter is that democratizing social forces have been increasingly, if unevenly, effective in their capacity to erode statist forms of oppressive rule.[19]

In this century, the most notable shift in normative theory and practice has probably involved "the move to institutions."[20] First the League of Nations, then the United Nations, and, last in time but most ambitious in undertaking, the European Union. As will be argued in the next section, this move was both intentionally and inevitably ambiguous, being a gesture in the direction of qualifying sovereignty by deference to an emergent organized world community and a means to extend sovereignty by restricting within the narrowest limits the autonomous role of such institutions and by structuring participation beyond the state in a manner that ensured that only states were allowed membership. Both the League and the UN were largely a response to the failures of traditional diplomacy to prevent the two world wars and were not regarded as having any significant bearing on the scope of sovereignty except possibly in the war/peace domain. Article 2(7) of the UN Charter confirms this expectation by denying the organization any right to intervene in "domestic jurisdiction" except in the context of a Chapter VII peace and security undertaking.

To a large, yet variable, degree, these institutional developments are best conceived of as extensions of Westphalia logic, not alternatives. Only states are members; the principles of sovereign equality and non-intervention are affirmed; submission of disputes to the World Court is essentially voluntary. International institutions have so far been denied independent funding and have not been permitted to develop their own peacekeeping capabilities.

Yet there is a collective identity – the organized international community – that establishes a presence and performs roles that encroach upon the claims of sovereign rights. Limiting discussion to the United Nations, there is also embodied in the UN Charter an acknowledgment that geopolitics may be more important than sovereign status with respect to the crucial undertaking of collective security. Giving leading states permanent membership and a veto in the Security Council and confining the General Assembly to a recommendatory role represent a deliberate choice to give dominant states the authority to decide and the capacity to block. During the cold war this blocking dimension was continuously evident, confining the UN to the margins of the global peace and security agenda.

With the cold war over, the Gulf War disclosed both the potentiality and the danger of an effective, unblocked Security Council, providing both apologists and critics grounds for response. The former argue that the Gulf War has finally established the credibility of collective security, whereas the latter contend that the only thing the war established was the extent to which the UN lent its mantle of legitimacy to the geopolitical goals of the United States.

There is another aspect of normative architecture. Latent in existing international law are emancipatory ideas and commitments that await actualization. For instance, Article 28 of the Universal Declaration of Human Rights:

> Everyone is entitled to a social and international order in which the rights and freedoms set forth in this Declaration can be fully realized.

Is not this norm a powerful weapon to rely upon in the struggle to expose and transform global apartheid? Such a posture is reinforced by reference to the International Convention on the Suppression and Punishment of the Crime of "Apartheid," especially Article 1:

> The States Parties to the present Convention declare that *apartheid* is a crime against humanity and that inhuman acts resulting from the policies and practices of apartheid . . . are crimes violating the principles of international law, in particular the purposes and principles of the Charter of the United Nations and constituting a serious threat to international peace and security.[21]

Significant here is the fact that states have formally associated themselves, individually and collectively, with the legal conclusion that apartheid is criminal. The distance between criminalizing the part (and by implication defining it as "the other") and acknowledging that the whole resembles the part (and is by implication embodied in "the self") is considerable. For this reason, the metaphor of global apartheid challenges the dynamics of denial that have helped world opinion to ignore correlations of wealth, class, and race on a global scale.

The normative architecture of world order has not been completely static, although the main structures of statism have remained remarkably stable and have retained their centrality. The state has tamed challenges from peace forces that were mounted in the aftermath of world wars and has even weathered the early challenge posed by the alleged incompatibility between the new weaponry of mass destruction and the retention of statist control over war making. At this time, the most threatening challenges to the perpetuation of statism seem associated with the environmental agenda, although the most consequential may be connected with the globalization of capital and information, causing even powerful states to fail in their efforts to domesticate market forces and the dynamics of mass communication. In relation to these globalizing influences, those with democratic leanings are seeking to position themselves in a range of arenas from the very local to the planetary. One aspect of this democratic positioning is associated with the emergence and empowerment of global civil society as a bearer of a hopeful and progressive vision of the future of world order.

A central question being raised at this time is whether statist responses to these new forms of challenge are sufficient and to what extent these responses are a tribute to the growing significance of global civil society. The resilience of statism over the centuries is certainly remarkable, yet its capacity to adapt behaviorally and ideationally is being tested as never before, and not just from a single direction (until the 1970s world order challenges to Westphalia were almost exclusively motivated by fears about the recurrence of large-scale war).[22] Whether and to what extent the adaptive capabilities of the present framework of world order are sufficient will assuredly be a preoccupying drama at the close of the millennium and the opening decade or so of the next one, but so will the normative priorities of how the burdens of adjustment are distributed between North and South. The section that follows depicts some central dimensions of this cosmo-drama, which is better understood as a manifold of distinctly experienced cosmo-dramas.[23]

The Westphalian Cosmo-dramas

The intention here is to identify several settings in which the state is struggling to adapt. Reducing pressures on its claims to uphold the well-being of its citizenry increasingly requires credible control over aspects of the external setting. Often, of course, this impulse to extend control is a matter of the stronger projecting its power at the expense of the territorial supremacy of the weaker – for instance, carrying on the "drug war" in the supplying countries, while dumping toxic wastes and sub-par pharmaceuticals on those same countries. As the global realities become more integrated, the weaker inevitably hit back, desperation generating such phenomena as terrorist attacks and hordes of economic and political refugees.

What are at stake for the state are matters of legitimacy and competence, which are, of course, connected. Also, these cosmo-dramas often seem irrelevant to the circumstances of vulnerable, stateless peoples or oppressed minorities, who understandably conceive of their political emancipation as a matter of achieving full membership in the Westphalian world of territorial sovereign states with rights of full access to formal, international arenas. For the Palestinians, the Kurds, and the various "nations" of former Yugoslavia, any approximation to Westphalian statehood would be regarded as an occasion for celebration. At the same time, emancipation from ethnic oppression doesn't necessarily imply a Westphalian solution; indigenous peoples increasingly seek what is becoming known as "internal self-determination" – that is, accepting the boundaries of an encompassing state but negotiating a reliable social contract that defines autonomous spheres of political activity.[24] Note that, to the extent that internal self-determination arrangements are established, the territorial supremacy of the state is relinquished, and a process of refeudalization/retribalization is initiated, reversing the geometrical neatness of modernist maps of political reality.

While acknowledging that these ethno-nationalist struggles are also challenging the primacy of the state in a variety of ways, as yet largely undiscussed, the focus here is upon efforts by the state and states to safeguard their keystone roles in "the new world order." There are definite functional linkages with the problematic aspects of the internationalization of the state, as well as the virtual neglect of the main line of normative indictment (global apartheid). Four areas will be considered: market, nature, global governance, and information/popular culture.

Market

There are notable efforts by leading states, more or less deliberately, to avoid losing control over market forces. These efforts have been identified in different ways, but most characteristically by stressing the managerial task, as in the phrase "the management of interdependence." The most formalized expression of these mercantilist concerns has been the ritual of an annual economic summit bringing together the heads of state of the seven leading industrial countries in the North, the so-called Group of Seven, or G7. Not much tangible policy coordination has been achieved, but these sessions do give substance to claims that the world economy as a whole is being managed by and for the light-skinned minorities in the North without voices from the statist South and without participation by representatives of global civil society (GCS).

The more substantive managerial efforts are by way of the General Agreement on Tariffs and Trade (GATT) and international financial institutions. The main objective is to facilitate trade expansion in the face of protectionist pressures growing more severe as the struggle sharpens for market shares among the main centers of capital and business. In the present global setting, there is no effective economic hegemony of the sort provided by the United States in the post-1945 period, hence new mechanisms of coordination and compromise are needed to avoid unleashing a costly cycle of destructive competition resembling the cycle of the 1930s that generated both the Great Depression and the geopolitical drift that ended in strategic warfare. With the increasing complexity of the world economy and the advent of nuclear weaponry, a repetition of this earlier pattern seems totally unacceptable. Even the United States, now the lone superpower, will lose its credentials as leader if it cannot fashion effective global-scale managerial arrangements to avoid a crash of the world economy. The Uruguay Round of GATT negotiations was taken seriously beyond its obvious substantive effects, symbolizing the degree of managerial capacity. The Trilateral Commission, an initiative of élite business in the North in the mid-1970s, seemed mainly devoted to circumventing the inward-looking tendencies of the state so as to promote the coordinated interests of outward-looking sectors of capital; the main ideological thrust was to accord primacy to the efficiency of capital and subordinate deference to such internal priorities as welfare, environmental safety, and organized labor.

Another direction of response and adaptation involves ambitious projects of regionalization. Europe has, of course, moved furthest ahead, creating a magnetic field around Brussels that draws many disparate elements toward itself, and a zone called "Euroland" embracing the 11 countries that proceeded with monetary integration as of the start of 1999. The state can conceive of this type of regionalization as a means to participate beneficially in the world economy, maximizing the advantages of a big, continental market while minimizing the threats of competitive operations beyond the region. Yet the strong pull of regionalism may homogenize political economy at the state level, making franchise capitalists of us all. Sweden and Finland have been caught up in this regionalist whirlwind, finding no way to uphold their societal living standards except by eroding, and possibly abandoning, the distinctiveness of their own "models" of welfare and development. In this regard, the resilience of statism may also be its death knell, at least in the sense that one proud claim of Westphalian sovereignty was to be the guardian of economic, political, cultural, and ideational pluralism. In many ways the 1980s debate in the United Kingdom has highlighted the tension between adapting successfully to the globalization of capital by going the way of Brussels and retaining the traditional glories of autonomous statehood at the cost of further economic slippage. The Thatcherite contention was that the Eurofeds are bent on destroying the state to save it![25]

Part of this process of regionalizing the state is to win and retain popular support. Such support is solicited, first of all, by promises of economic reward, but also by assurances that the essential aspects of Westphalian sovereignty will not be jeopardized. Further, the regional framework offers to extend the protection of human rights and to facilitate more effective forms of environmental protection, and even to enlarge democratic space – the Strasbourg dimensions of the European Union. So far, at least, regionalism in the North has turned a blind eye to the global apartheid features of the world economy and has not pretended to offer any relief in relation to mass poverty in the South; at most, in the case of Europe, it has directed its gaze eastwards in relation to Europe and the former Soviet republics, or in the case of the United States (North American Free Trade Agreement) it has warily sought to include its Mexican neighbor in plans for trade expansion on a global basis.

Whether or not European innovations succeed in mediating between statist and globalizing pressures remains to be seen, but it will exert influence elsewhere in the world either as a positive model of adaptation and compromise or as some sort of failure, either because it cannot adapt or because the autonomy of distinct countries is undermined in a manner that produces some sort of populist backlash.

There is another kind of statist response to the dynamics of economic globalization. In a stimulating book, *The Work of Nations*, Robert Reich argues that traditional territorial statism will fail *functionally* because of globalizing market forces, but that what he calls "laissez-faire cosmopolitanism" will fail *normatively* because of its inability to benefit the lower four-fifths of the citizenry even in rich countries. Accordingly, Reich proposes "a third, superior position: a positive economic nationalism in which each nation's citizens take primary responsibility for enhancing the capacities of their countrymen for full and productive lives, but also work with other nations to ensure that these improvements do not come at others' expense."[26] By investing more heavily in frontier skills for successful participation in the world economy, problems of marginalization of the labor force will be minimized. In effect, educational sufficiency takes the place of disintegrating movements of organized labor. Such steps may help reduce the internalization of apartheid within richer countries – a process which is already well under way in North America and Europe, producing racial tension, widening income gaps, urban crime, drug cultures, AIDs, and proto-fascist backlashes.

At the same time, what Reich proposes seems to accept without serious questioning the background structures of global apartheid and unipolar geopolitics. It is a prescription of adaptation with particular relevance to rich and powerful societies, which face their own serious problems of adjustment due to globalizing pressures.

Nature

The environmental agenda is the greatest potential threat to the viability of the state and of the realist view of world order. Responding to the varying types of environmental decay that are of regional and global scale is complicated by causal factors (finding an agreed explanation for the harm and an adjustment policy), cognitive uncertainty (achieving a consensus about the seriousness of the threat), temporal dimensions (the

degree of urgency, the relationship to political horizons of accountability), geographical exposure (the length and height of coastline, vulnerability to flooding, latitude), financial responsibility (distributing the
adjustment costs, subsidizing the South), and behavioral impacts (regulating the acquisition and use of cars, restricting reproductive freedom).
From this partial and illustrative list of factors, the regulatory task of proceeding by way of agreement among sovereign states – that is, voluntary
patterns of cooperation and compliance – is seen to be daunting. Such
complexity is more serious because of the efforts by the North to shift
the effects of environmental deterioration to the South to the extent possible, perhaps symbolized by the audacity of the nuclear weapons states
engaging in testing in a manner that exposed indigenous peoples of
the Pacific to the highest health risks from fallout. In addition, many
influential people in the South continue to regard the environmentalist
approach as intended to deny their societies the material benefits of
modernity.

The resilience of the state is being tested as never before.[27] In certain
respects, the specific challenge of, and response to, ozone depletion provides support for both pessimists and optimists. Pessimists point to the
continuing process of depletion, indications of increasing adverse health
effects, the revelations that the rate of depletion is considerably higher
than earlier feared, and that the danger is in the North as well as the
South. A 1992 *Time* cover bore an eerie picture of a hole burning in a
normal sky with the caption, "VANISHING OZONE – THE DANGER
MOVES CLOSER TO HOME."[28] Optimists point to the impressive
regulatory response by way of the phase-out of the offending chemicals,
the development of commercially viable substitutes that involve no
encroachment on consumer uses, the negotiation of an encompassing
regulatory treaty supported by all leading states and placing the burden
of adjustment costs on countries in the North (the Montreal Protocol of
1986, as strengthened in 1990 and more so subsequently, as overall indications of a constructive response). However the debate is resolved, the
evidence supports the view that regulatory efforts have not yet arrested
the dynamics of deterioration.[29]

It would seem that the urgency and complexity of the environmental
challenge call for a supranational mechanism that has political and
financial independence, but only states could provide the resources and
the mandate. Their reluctance to move beyond the traditional modes
of diplomacy suggests the persistence of the realist mind-set and the
implied limits on regulatory effectiveness – a dependence on consensus,
volunteerism, and the absence of enforcement. The environmental challenge shows, then, both the resilience of statism, including its adaptive

impulses, but also the gap between the problems present and the solutions provided.

From a world order perspective, the central issue raised is how further environmental deterioration will affect political behavior. Given global apartheid, it is likely that some form of "environmental imperialism" will emerge, the rudimentary elements of which are already evident, and that "environmental refugees" will add to the planetary problems of facing human displacement. Anxiety about environmental decay is one of the main causative explanations for the emergence of a global civil society (GCS), and it is the information-disseminating and consciousness-raising activism of the transnational environmental movement that has pushed governments in the leading states as far as they have gone and that has put environmental policy on the mainstream political agenda.[30] The tactical sophistication of some GCS actors has increased impressively, exhibiting a willingness to resist militantly in certain arenas and to collaborate with governments, with international institutions, and even with multinational corporations in others. Japanese officials have called Greenpeace an organization of ecological terrorists because of its peaceful efforts to disrupt whaling on the high seas, while many governments have included Greenpeace and Cousteau Society specialists as advisors at formal meetings intended to administer the Antarctica Treaty regime.

Global governance

In market contexts, distinct corporate pressures are being brought to bear strongly upon governments to coordinate economic policy on a transnational basis. As discussed, this leads under certain conditions to mechanisms of regional governance. Jacques Delors has been emphatic in his insistence that regional economic governance must extend to other domains, including security and social policy, to be sustainable. In environmental contexts, GCS has generated a variety of pressures to induce a dramatic turnaround by state and business on the significance of the environmental challenge. At the same time, to the extent that regulatory claims entail enforcement authority and mechanisms to ensure autonomy, governments have been reluctant to respond; this reluctance becomes opposition when the environmental imperatives imply huge taxes on economic operations and deep intrusions upon consumer discretion. Corporate pressures are mounting for marketizing measures of environmental protection, as by enabling private sector actors to sell credits for maintaining pollution levels below agreed standards.

The political foundations for governance remain rudimentary, with renewed hopes being concentrated on strengthening the United Nations. It is notable that the UN, especially its main organs, is completely dominated by states and their formal representatives, with NGOs and GCS perspectives confined to the outer margins of the proceedings. Interestingly, both world federalists and geopolitically minded leaders can perceive the UN as a vehicle for their projects. The utopian mind-set perceives the UN as embodying the elements of a nascent world government, while the realist mind-set perceives the UN, especially the Security Council, as a selectively useful framework in relation to regional conflict resolution, large-scale North-to-South uses of force (as in the Gulf War), and, more recently, a variety of missions to bolster civic order in particular states. The UN has this dual potential and is inherently ambiguous with respect to progressive world order values, especially in the aftermath of the cold war.[31]

In an important respect, the UN, as a club of states, is an ideal framework for achieving structural adjustments in response to the erosion of competence at the territorial level of statist authority. In effect, states would delegate their authority outward so as to retain their overall claims to competence and legitimacy. To some extent this has already happened with regard to human rights and environmental regulation. But the retention of capabilities and discretion at the governmental level remains strongly embedded in the realist political consciousness and is part of the reason it is so difficult for realists to cope with the new deterritorializing realities of international life. But the various tendencies in GCS are also disabled, being skeptical about intergovernmental mechanisms and finding it difficult to mount effective educational and consciousness-raising campaigns. The NGO world is also hampered by the temptations of co-optation (speaking to statist power in a muffled voice so that the powerful will pretend from time to time to listen and heed) and incrementalism (concentrating on tinkering at the margins because the more ambitious requirements for governance are off the political agenda).

There are some signs of change. The Stockholm Initiative on Global Security and Governance was a report issued on April 22, 1991, under the title *Common Responsibility in the 1990s*. It was prepared and endorsed by prominent individuals possessing high degrees of credibility as present or former participants in the formal institutions of governmental authority. Its stress on "global governance" was a definite step towards consciousness raising about the functional need and political possibility of creating more effective regulatory authority at the global level; it was, perhaps, unduly influenced by both the recourse to, and abuse of, UN procedures during the Gulf crisis, being issued shortly after the cease-fire. The spirit of the Stockholm Initiative is indicated by the following: "We believe that the genuine common interest in a new global order of cooperation today is such as to rationally motivate nations to build a system of global governance."[32] Invoking "the spirit of San Francisco," the report calls for a process initiated by a global summit along the lines of Bretton Woods and San Francisco, as well as the establishment of an independent international commission on global governance along the lines of the Brandt, Brundtland, and Palme commissions.[33] Such proposals, coming from endorsers who are associated with feasible programs of global reform, do reveal a certain receptivity by states to a second surge of institution building, possibly correlated with the turn of the millennium. But they also reveal some dangers: that such initiatives can be diverted by geopolitical pressures, and that their implementation, if it happens, will be completely insulated from democratizing forces.

From the GCS perspective, several challenges exist: to evolve ideas about global governance to offset the plans of leading states and dominant market forces; to resist where necessary, to collaborate where possible, while being wary about co-option traps and dogmatic anti-statism. In these regards, the GCS approaches in the human rights and environmental areas provide helpful models. The added difficulty with respect to governance is the absence of concrete occurrences and the need to operate independently in large, government-controlled bureaucracies. Several interim approaches might help: an emphasis on strengthening international law by concrete undertakings (accepting the compulsory jurisdiction of the World Court, a Comprehensive Test Ban), working toward democratizing the procedures within the United Nations itself (giving the South more adequate representation in international institutions, creating "space" for participation by representatives of GCS), and imposing the discipline of constitutionalism on the UN system, especially the Security Council, as a counter to geopolitics (establishing a Security Council Watch that persuasively documents deviations from the Charter and that reports on "double standards" with respect to implementing Security Council decisions).

Information/popular culture

There are strong reinforcing linkages between the globalization of information/popular culture and the struggle to reshape world order in the aftermath of the cold war. At this stage, this dynamic of what might be called "cognitive globalization" is dominated by the United States and is image-oriented. Television is the basic technology, establishing post-modern ways of knowing as well as providing the substantive content of the good life. The roles of television are multiple and can be only hinted at here: facilitating the spread of franchise capitalism, glorifying the American life-style, legitimating the claims of geopolitics. These roles, in effect, are top-down expressions of the deep structures of global apartheid, despite a facade of liberal objectivity in relation to state and market.

The impacts of cognitive globalization are speculative, highly differentiated, and by no means fully discernible. One direction was evident during the initial phases of the Gulf War when CNN conveyed a carefully managed presentation of the war to the world; but another direction emerged after the war, when the plight of the Iraqi Kurds spoiled the impression of "smart weapons" directed with electronic precision against military targets. Television induces passivity, but it also can serve to convey political experience. Chinese students in 1989 were inspired by the successes of "people power" in the Philippines that they had witnessed on television a few years earlier; but so apparently were the Chinese rulers, who cracked down on the demonstrators in Tiananmen Square and elsewhere. Television brings Disney World and with it the dangers of "electropop fascism," but it also brings Madonna and others, who, despite commercialism, are mainly delivering subversive and anti-establishment messages of freedom, resistance, openness, empathy for victims, and racial equality.[34] Embodying these messages in the sinews of popular culture exerts great influence on popular attitudes in this TV age, especially given the growing distrust of moralizing politicians in many countries.

Global civil society has also depended on cognitive globalization for its growth and development, but mainly in the service of networking, relying on phone, fax, xerox, and personal computer. The greening of the imagination is the only potent challenge to the Americanized images of the market. Greenpeace has been imaginative in its appeal to visual sensibility, but its fields of operations have not challenged the structures of global apartheid and have questioned the persistence of militarism only in selective, environmentally related settings.[35] To the extent that GCS succeeds in challenging market and state it becomes "news" and plays its own role as an agency of influence on a global scale. Information/popular culture can serve the agenda of democratizing empowerment as well as operate as an instrument of disempowerment.[36] In the end, statism relies on violence in the form of militarized capabilities, whereas GCS relies upon information and conscience (that is, moral sensibility); in this complex respect, cognitive globalization is multiply contested, yielding contradictory interpretations of the future.

A Concluding Note

The Westphalian cosmo-dramas have been interpreted in relation to successive tidal waves of globalization. The primacy of the territorial state is being challenged as never before, making traditional realist inquiry strike even mainstream observers as increasingly archaic.[37] But the resilience of the state should not be underestimated, especially of those states capable of geopolitical ambitions on a regional and global scale. By aligning with market and other globalizing tendencies, the state may be reconceived, but not superseded, especially so long as market forces depend on militarism. To retain its ascendancy, the state must also co-opt environmentalist tensions, and this probably entails strengthening existing structures of global governance, including those associated with the United Nations. Somewhat paradoxically, to retain primacy, the state must give up many of its Westphalian attributes, especially those resting upon the claims and practices of territorial sovereignty.[38]

The forces of GCS are mainly oppositional, but as yet have been unable to contest the state seriously either in geopolitical settings of confrontation or with respect to the deep structures of global apartheid. During this formative period of empowerment, premised on the growth of critical social movements, the risks of co-option and demoralization are very high and pose a greater threat than direct oppression. For these reasons it is important for social forces that identify with global civil society to fashion their own visions of the future, visions able to compete with the designs and visions being developed in the think tanks of corporate, financial, media, and geopolitical elites. The advent of globalization need not be catastrophic, but its human prospects depend on struggle, resistance, and vision, which are best guided by an attuned, if diverse, embryonic global civil society.

There is some danger of demonizing state and market forces and romanticizing an emergent global civil society. Such polarization creates an interpretation of history that is over-generalized and simplistic. In some settings, state and market forces, especially when challenged by popular movements seeking greater economic and social justice, can serve the cause of human dignity, either by dissolving oppressive structures (the Soviet state under Gorbachev) or by overcoming the absolute depths of poverty, but usually at the cost of disturbing inequality. Global civil society is far from perfect. In some settings, unleashed social forces manifest regressive religious and political tendencies, as in the spread of fascist responses to foreigners, especially refugees, and in relation to societal support for capital punishment or rigid constraints on the reproductive rights of women. A nuanced appreciation of these contradictory patterns of influence will help us prepare for the challenges of a new millennium.

2

Co-opting the Sovereign State

In the interests of clarity, I would like to ground the inquiry of this chapter in the work of Hedley Bull and John Vincent as representative of the British version of realism in international relations. It is a convenient generalization to suggest that both Vincent and Bull felt conceptually and, what is more significant, normatively committed to an outlook that accepted "a society of states" as the only viable foundation of world order. As such, they were variously suspicious, and even somewhat scornful, of my more skeptical attitude toward statism, regarding my level of criticism as "utopian" or "salvationist" because it seemed to them to be advocating a post-statist type of world order as more desirable than the world of states that existed and – what was worse in their eyes – implying that a differently constituted and better world order might even be attainable in the near future under certain conditions.[1]

My concern is to use this realist backdrop as the basis for commenting upon the dubious triumph of globalization and its somewhat ironic implications for the future of the states system. I believe that the states system as the self-sufficient organizing framework for political life on a global level is essentially over: "it is history." Let me explain. The state remains the preeminent political actor on the global stage; but the aggregation of states – what has been called "a states system" – is no longer consistently in control of the global policy process. Territorial sovereignty is being diminished on a spectrum of issues in such a serious manner as to subvert the capacity of states to govern the internal life of society, and non-state actors hold an increasing proportion of power and influence in the shaping of world order.

I am not celebrating these developments as a vindication of my earlier views; far from it. In this respect my focus on the ascendancy of globalization is deeply ironic, because the post-statist world order that is increasingly becoming dominant even as I write is not at all what I had earlier favored as an alternative to statism. It is, rather, a new alignment of forces that is being crystallized by a constellation of market, techno-logical, ideological, and civilizational developments that have nothing in common with the alternative world orders that I and others had earlier proposed as normative projects, put forward in the form of rooted utopias within the framework of the World Order Models Project, and elsewhere.[2] The core of this normative project was, in contrast, based on embodiments of human aspiration responsive to world order values specified so as to emphasize the interplay of peace, economic well-being, social justice, and environmental sustainability. Instead – and this is part of the irony – the globalized world that is taking shape makes me, in central ways, nostalgic for the realities and potentialities for moral evo-lution of a society of states in the spirit of Hedley Bull: an orientation that Andrew Linklater has imaginatively interpreted in a recent paper devoted to matters of sovereignty and citizenship.[3] It should be realized that there is little, or no, normative agency associated with this emergent world order: it is virtually designer-free, a partial dystopia that is being formed spontaneously and in the process is endangering some of the achievements of early phases of statist world order.[4] I acknowledge that this emergent globalized world order is not altogether regressive in its effects; its operative logic is fashioning several dramatic improvements on what previously existed globally, especially through the remarkable transformation of a series of Asian societies as a consequence of sus-tained high economic growth and social orders that have been impres-sively redistributive as their economic pies have grown. However, even here the unresolved Asian economic crisis casts doubt on the durability of these gains. It no longer seems the case that these countries are achiev-ing benefits for an expanding proportion of their respective societies such that poverty and unemployment are contained and gradually elim-inated. Globalization also gives rise to a leveling dynamic that is making it possible for portions of North and South to cooperate and negotiate on the basis of far greater parity than in the past. Further, the weave of global economic interdependence works against the type of intense geopolitical rivalries among leading states that have accounted for most of the serious international wars that have occurred in the last several centuries.

Perhaps it would clarify matters at this stage if I were to refer more explicitly to the chapter title. I am contending that "globalization" has already won out in the sense that the language and imagery of a state-centric world have become anachronistic in crucial respects. At the same time, as is common with obsolete paradigms, it is the professional observers of international affairs who appear to be the last to know and resist stubbornly the mounting evidence that contradicts their "realist" world view. In this regard, it is almost amusing to note that realism has never been so professionally robust and ideologically dogmatic as now, when it appears to be languishing on its deathbed. How else to account for the seemingly endless fascination with the structural framework set forth by Kenneth Waltz or the ultra-realist constructions of reality by his star student and exponent, John Mearsheimer?[5] Much more than when I started out in academic life, it is difficult these days for young specialists in international relations to get past the academic gatekeepers at leading American universities unless they can demonstrate their unconditional, unto death, adherence to the outmoded postulates of realist orthodoxy. By comparison, at least in the United States, earlier academic resistance to Marxists during the cold war era was mild. These days Marxism has virtually disappeared as a serious strand of academic inquiry, and liberalism has become "a gentler realism," offering a pale, pacified, and generally contained "other," whether liberalism's gloss on realism is formulated by reference to human rights or support for somewhat stronger international institutions.[6] The most serious non-realist mode of inquiry these days is contained in the various strands of critical theory, which has been essentially deconstructive in its preoccupations, but is as agonistic as its realist adversaries to reconstructive thought or normative theorizing, especially by way of its rejection of metanarratives as such.[7]

What I am concerned about is the widespread reluctance at present to give academic credibility to those forms of inquiry that are dedicated to preferred futures for the organization of political life on the planet. The normative horizon of what is treated as serious inquiry into the future is foreshortened by realist orthodoxy, unless it happens to be presented in the guise of a challenge to geopolitical stability, as in the case of Samuel Huntington's "clash of civilizations" thesis. If conflict is highlighted, then an assessment of the future will be discussed endlessly, almost regardless of how thin the argument that is put forward.[8]

Of course, such attentiveness to conflict scenarios signals the degree to which realism (and its recent applications) remains, as always, a surrogate for geopolitics and specifically diverts attention from the continuing hegemonic project to extend Western, and in most instances American, dominance into the next century. Revealingly in the Huntington instance, what provokes discussion is the substance of the alleged challenge of Islam to the West, not the more fundamental contention being made in this chapter that a state-centric world order is being superseded by an emergent inter-civilizational world order. Taking Huntington's own words more seriously, "It is my hypothesis that the fundamental source of conflict in this new world will not be primarily ideological or primarily economic. The great divisions among mankind and the dominating source of conflict will be cultural."[9] It is essential to discern the ideological underpinnings of Huntington's conceptually presented argument, especially considering his earlier prominence in the Vietnam era as a counterinsurgency apologist and his continuing presumed closeness to the American foreign policy establishment.

It may help to situate Huntington's emphasis on the Islamic threat to realize that only a year before his notorious *Foreign Affairs* article, Huntington gave a lecture at Princeton in which he insisted on the inevitability of an imminent strategic clash with Japan, which was posited at the time as almost certain to lead to a future war, although possibly of the cold, rather than hot, variety.[10] In effect, Huntington has over the years been operating as a geopolitical therapist on special call to the Pentagon and has since 1989 been responding to the dangerous climate of depression that gripped the upper echelons of the American national security establishment when the full impact of the end of the cold war began to sink in, and the loss of a credible enemy was perceived as debilitating both to professional identity and to budgetary support. In effect, the extraordinary impact of Huntington's clash thesis was not a result of questioning world order fundamentals, but rather reflected the frenzied search for a new enemy of sufficient magnitude to fill the void created by the collapse of the Soviet Union and revolutionary Marxism. The specific policy implications drawn by Huntington have been widely criticized as irresponsibly encouraging the outbreak of culture wars. The amazing response to his article – a truly worldwide phenomenon – can be attributed partly to the sensitivity of his geopolitical proposals to the displacement of the states system, couching the emergent rivalry within an inter-civilizational rather than an interstate matrix.

The complementary side of this post-statist geopolitics is a renewed confidence in the capacity to project Western power successfully in relation to potential adversaries, and here one encounters not an acknowledgment of civilizational pluralism but an extension of the "unipolar moment" that was proclaimed in the aftermath of the Gulf War. Also writing recently in *Foreign Affairs*, Joseph Nye reaffirmed the hegemonic vision of world order on the basis of American mastery of the military applications of cyberinformatics, as follows: "In truth, the twenty-first century, not the twentieth, will turn out to be the period of America's preeminence. Information is the new coin of the international realm, and the United States is better positioned than any other country to multiply the potency of its hard and soft power resources through information."[11] What is being claimed for the United States is an overwhelming military capability that can be used with little risk and almost no human costs, explicitly invoking the Gulf War as a rudimentary foretaste; a similar, gentler version of this hegemonic interpretation of the future was expressed by Bill Clinton's former National Security Advisor, Anthony Lake, in a short essay, "For a Second American Century."[12] Returning to my main line of inquiry, there is present in this Huntington/Nye view of the future a geopolitical translation of the realist tradition in world order thinking into the idiom of the post–cold war world. Expressing this assessment differently, what is being advanced, partly analytically, partly ideologically, and partly normatively, is a dogmatically modernist view of international political reality.[13]

Let me briefly clarify what I mean by "modernist" in this setting of emergent globalization. I refer to the framing of international political life that was associated with the Enlightenment, broadly construed and somewhat over-generalized as resting on three pillars of interconnected ideas and convictions: the primacy of the territorial state; the secularization of political relations among states, including the prospect of technological innovation as enhancing the quality of life; and the globalizing mission by the West to dominate the non-Western world.[14] I am contending that each of these three pillars of modernism has been eroded in such a way as to deprive that statist orientation as a whole of its explanatory and structural authority in relation to world order theorizing.[15] The state persists as an important actor, of course, as indicated earlier, especially as the repository of ultramodern military technologies, and as such retains a crucial ordering role in most conflict situations. Increasingly, however, the state has itself been "globalized" or "internationalized"; that is, the policy orientation of the state has been pulled away from its territorial constituencies and shifted outwards, with state action characteristically operating as an instrumental agent on behalf of nonterritorial regional and global market forces, as manipulated by transnational corporations and banks and increasingly also by financial traders.[16]

Appropriately, these days, it is business elites that are declaring themselves most ardently to be citizens of Europe, or even global citizens, and thereby apparently most willing to forgo the specific identities of the nation-state; unlike more idealistic and cosmopolitan shifts in loyalty, which in the past have been associated with the advocacy of world government, this new type of global citizenship is pragmatic and has grown up without accompanying feelings of regional or global solidarity of the sort associated with a sense of community. It is questionable whether such globalist sentiments should be confused with traditional notions of citizenship, which implies a commitment to the well-being of the relevant community.[17] This new global orientation reflects mainly a cold, practical calculation of interest, reinforced by the capacity of franchise capitalism to light up the urban landscape throughout the world with McDonald's golden arches, a worldwide continental cuisine, five-star hotel chains, Benetton stores, homogeneous casual and formal dress codes, MTV, global Internet access, real-time uniform news dissemination by CNN and Sky News, and a capacity to be understood and entertained everywhere in the English language.

This partial instrumentalization of the state was evident in the Gulf War, properly regarded as the first postmodern war, where the extraordinary mobilization of military capabilities was responsive to severe global market anxieties about the price of oil and the future control of Gulf oil reserves. The visual portrayal of the war in real time made the war into a kind of simulation exercise that resembled a sophisticated arcade game in its early stages. Other relevant modernist concerns, such as the security of Israel, the stability of the region, and non-proliferation of nuclear weapons were also present, but the financing and scope of the war, including especially its self-limitation that allowed Saddam Hussein to survive while the social and military capacities of Iraq were devastated, reflected the primacy of a new set of largely hidden transnational factors associated with sustainable and profitable economic growth for an integrated world economy, but also a growing strategic indifference to state–society relations that belies and is at odds with pretensions to a serious foreign policy commitment to human rights and democracy.[18]

This indifference was underscored by the extent to which these same countries that had moved mountains to restore sovereign rights to the neo-feudal rulers of Kuwait waited near the sidelines ever so patiently for several years while ethnic cleansing and horrifying crimes against humanity were being committed in Bosnia, or while genocidal turmoil overtook Rwanda. The steps that were taken eventually as a result of public pressures were gestures of an ambiguous character, rather than serious political military initiatives: ambiguous sanctions, loosely implemented embargoes on arms, an underfunded war crimes tribunal – more responses to public pressure than efforts to protect the victims of gross abuse.[19]

The same line of argument can be approached from other angles. John Ruggie has noted that the dynamics of globalization are gradually disembedding the domestic social contract between the state and society which had become integral to the program of welfare capitalism and social democracy.[20] In effect, there is currently no sufficient countervailing power to offset the drive of business and finance to subordinate social policy to economistic criteria of profitability and efficiency in the use of capital. As a result, international corporations and banks report profits while downsizing and outsourcing operations, shifting production units to the Pacific Rim and elsewhere. It is a pattern that causes the stock market to rise to record or near record levels while the life of lower- – and middle- – class people in many settings continues to stagnate, or even deteriorate, with reduced wages and salaries along with cutbacks in public services. In this process, structural pressures of regional and global scope shape national policy to such an extent that credible political parties in democratic states adopt convergent party platforms that are all variations on the single theme of "neo-liberalism." This convergence of pressures on the state is particularly damaging and discrediting to those who favor the type of compassionate forms of governance associated with American liberalism or European social democracy. What this means is that, temporarily at least, in such a world order Sweden can no longer be Sweden! The humane or compassionate state is being phased out, although unevenly and incompletely.

Let us consider this altered character of the state from one further angle, continuing the focus on this eroded pillar of territorial sovereignty. In his important book on sovereignty and the modern state, *The Sovereign State and Its Competitors*, Hendrik Spruyt concludes that the statist world of modernity arose out of an organizational competition between states on the one side and city-leagues and city-states on the other. The state won out over these rivals for organizational preeminence in late medieval Europe. According to Spruyt's well-argued and documented appraisal, "States won because their institutional logic gave them an advantage in mobilizing their societies' resources."[21] I think we are living at a time when states are losing their organizational advantage in the provision of public goods, with the revealing exception of security, though only then if security is conceived in the narrowly artificial terms of military/police activities.[22] Elsewhere the pressure on public goods, whether involving labor rights, health care, social safety nets, higher education, support for the arts, or environmental protection, is prompting fiscal reductions, resulting in societal atmospheres of increasing austerity, despite overall indicators of continuing prosperity as measured by share prices, salaries for media celebrities and sports stars, and end-of-the-year bonuses for CEOs. Indicative of this new era has been a new pattern of labor relations, with traditional areas of industrial activity being mainly on the defensive, while worker militancy and "strikes" occur sporadically in privileged domains: millionaire athletes in soccer, baseball, basketball, and hockey seeking larger portions of the revenue pie from billionaire team owners, a phenomenon that arises not from the money paid by sporting fans in the stands, but mainly from the sale of national and international TV rights. Those sectors of labor that have been most afflicted by globalization in the form of layoffs and stagnant wages, victims of corporate restructuring to sustain profitability and competitiveness in this global era, have been surprisingly passive, undoubtedly reflecting their feelings of impotence, a sensed inability to mount effective challenges due to their declining political strength and economic leverage.

This loss of territorial focus by the state is reinforced by the manipulation of financial traders, by the flows of ideas and information, migrants, popular culture, drugs, life-styles, pollution, and organized crime. In this fluid setting, various transnational networks of social activists exhibiting a generally diminishing regard for the boundaries of sovereign states have also taken shape.[23] Rejection of these globalizing tendencies in its purest form is associated with, and expressed by, the resurgence of religious and ethnic politics in various extremist configurations. Revealingly, only by retreating to pre-modern, traditionalist orientations does it now seem possible to seal off sovereign territory, partially at least, from encroachments associated with globalized life-styles and business operations, and even then only with considerable materialist sacrifice and, for this reason, probably in a manner that is sustainable only for brief periods. Even in a setting of religious and ethnic resurgence, the primary identification is more often civilizational than territorial. Ayatollah Khomeini was emphatic in his insistence that the movement he was leading was an "Islamic revolution," not an "Iranian revolution." But elsewhere, as with the Bharatiya Janata Party (BJP) in India and the Likud in Israel, the religious vision is bound up with strong versions of statist nationalism. In other words, the territoriality of religious and ethnic nationalism is itself anti-modern in other respects, rejecting the second pillar of modernism: namely, its secularism, expressed by way of the separation of church and state, through its liberation of reason and science from any kind of accountability to, and regulation by, religious authority and its strong affirmation of the individual as the primary repository of socially constructed, as distinct from natural, rights.

There is also less operational content associated with the application of the doctrine of sovereignty to the practice of politics on the global level.[24] States, conceived as governmental units rather than as territorial entities, have increasingly been challenged from within and below, as well as from without and above.[25] The rise of identity politics associated with ethnic and religious affinities has recently challenged the authority and legitimacy of many secularist traditions associated with multiethnic states. Separatist tendencies operating under the rubric of "the right of self-determination" have been threatening the perception and reality of the state as a single unified actor at home and abroad and have had divisive impacts on even such a supposed bastion of moderation as Canada. Instead, a kind of neo-medievalism in international society, of the sort that Hedley Bull briefly anticipated two decades ago, has made claims of sovereignty less descriptive of the way problems are solved and social aspirations achieved.

Robert Jackson wrote a provocative book some years ago in which he contended that many of the ex-colonial states, especially those in Africa, were in effect unrealized, non-autonomous actors; he downgrades these with the epithet of "quasi-state," arguing further that these quasi-states are hopelessly seeking to make their way in interaction with "real" states.[26] My argument carries this logic of quasi-states further in both directions: all states, no matter how militarily potent and economically formidable, have become to a significant degree "quasi-states" while "real states," if these persist at all, are a hopelessly endangered species of political animal whose reality is subject to various forms of doubt.

Turning now more directly to the second pillar concerns of the modern with the dynamics of secularization, here too significant challenges are evident, although not so dramatically and self-evidently as in relation to territoriality and sovereignty. This is a complicated area, partly reflecting the widespread and variegated religious resurgences occurring in virtually every important civilizational space. There are crucial elements in this mixture. The development, and use of, and reliance on, the atomic bomb, nuclear weaponry, and nuclear powers (especially in the aftermath of the Chernobyl meltdown) have raised deep and persisting questions about whether science and technology, unmediated by some kind of spiritual tradition, are after all benign vehicles for innovation and progress, and even whether over time technological innovation linked to the market is compatible with the security and well-being of peoples. Culturally, the 1960s raised the question of whether the machine was not gradually impairing the quality of individual and collective life, setting a large question mark against the word *modernity*, politically, ethically, and philosophically. In the 1990s these issues remain on the agenda of social concerns, but tend to be phrased more powerfully in relation to computers, the emergence of superhuman artificial intelligence, the almost limitless claims made on behalf of virtual reality and genetic engineering, and the blurring of the line between human activity and machine mechanism, a process that Mark Dery has summarized effectively as "cyborging the body politic."[27]

Another challenge came from nature, no longer merely a backdrop to human adventure and conquest, but a realm to be brought under progressive dominion so as to minimize danger and maximize control. The modern thrust was in the direction of limitless growth and exploitation; but nature has revealed a formidable ability to hit back against human society in devastating ways, disclosing limits to the carrying capacity of the earth. In addition to the emergence of severe uncertainties about social risks, long-term effects are casting dark shadows over the future by way of unchecked global warming, expanding ozone depletion, water contamination, polluted commons, demographic pressures, and an array of specific environmental breakdowns producing immediate and local harm.

For several decades it has been evident that environmental consciousness has the capacity to generate mitigating policies and adjustments, but does not possess the leverage to induce drastic modifications in human behavior if such turn out to be necessary to achieve sustainability. The modernist confidence in human autonomy is thus deeply challenged by environmental risks; but the sustainability of a world order that lacks strong governance capacities and a collective will based on feelings of human solidarity is also put in question in relation to ultimate concerns about survival. These structural difficulties are now exacerbated by the influence being exerted by neo-liberal tendencies to downsize government, rely on the rationality of the market to signal social and physical dangers and induce corrective action, and trust in the enlightened self-interest of the private sector to protect the global commons and preserve the earth as a going concern.[28] In these domains, sovereignty, in the sense of a refusal to be accountable on a supranational level, imposes additional difficulties for any sort of global standard setting, allowing life-style orientations and economic development choices to proceed without external accountability and beyond the reach of any regulatory authority, even if the implications for the world over time appear to be ecologically catastrophic. Such risks are not figments of a doomsday imagination, but arise from such concrete phenomena as the existence of extensive radioactive waste dumps, the destruction of portions of the Amazonian rain forests, and the early stages in populous Asian countries of mass introduction of automobiles relying on internal combustion. The probable scale of these activities is so great, and the means of control so trivial and belated, that there is little that can be done beyond fervently praying that warnings will somehow be heeded and curative steps taken early enough to prevent full-scale bio-regional collapse. In effect, neither rationality, so prized as an attribute of the modern sensibility, nor reliance on secular politics provides any solid ground for hope regarding the human capacity to deal successfully with a range of unmet, mounting world order challenges.

Despite widespread psychological denial, the subliminal recognition of these vulnerabilities partly explains a widespread malaise among Western youth expressive of feelings of helplessness. The apocalyptically pessimistic lyrics of Nirvana's Kurt Cobain, coupled with his suicide, are best understood as a cultural scream of anguish in reaction to this disturbing prevalence of collective mechanisms of denial and escape in the face of continuing and mounting planetary danger. As a result, the modernist belief in the future, especially in the West, is disappearing as a cultural dimension and seems to be giving way to an array of post-modernisms and fundamentalisms that call into question the very possi-bility of coherent understanding or disinterested public action. Under these conditions various states are responding with differing degrees of success to the challenges arising from religious resurgence, identity pol-itics, regional and global market forces, transnational cyberpolitics, and the accelerating mobility of capital, people, and images.

The third pillar of modernity was its implicit civilizational arrogance in privileging the West in relation to non-Western societies. This has been most dramatically evident in the essentially genocidal meeting between European settler migrants and the indigenous peoples situated through-out the non-Western world. In the Americas alone the most reliable assessments now suggest that as many as 50 million natives died during the first century of large-scale European settlement. Zygmunt Bauman writes relevantly that "[m]odernity was not merely Western Man's thrust for power, it was his *mission*, proof of moral righteousness and cause of pride. From the point of view of reason-founded human order, tolerance is incongruous and immoral."[29] Modernity induced confidence, even arro-gance, as it spread its influence around the world. The dynamics of de-Westernization that started with the collapse of the formal colonial system, but are going forward now in the shape of the assertiveness of non-Western civilizational claims, particularly those being made on behalf of Islam and Asia, have undermined the universalism of the modern era. As a result, globalization coexists with civilizational plural-ism and various forms of political fragmentation, superficially contra-dictory pressures that have in common a move away from centering political action on the control of government in sovereign states.

To summarize, globalization has undermined the certitudes associated with proclamation of a state-centric world. At the same time, globaliza-tion has helped to conceal the emergent locus of real power in relation to the shaping of global economic policy. Leaders of states are constrained by these structural forces, although to varying degrees, and seem to be receptive to the interpretation of global market priorities as perceived through the prism of neo-liberal ideas. In paradoxical fashion, the Marxist account of the relation between economic and political power seems persuasive only after Marxism has lost its capacity to win adherents to its world view.

These developments pose a series of dangers that can be understood societally, politically, and ecologically, as well as ethically and cognitively. There is a loss of democratic control over the course of history. Polarization of society tends to deepen, and there are many victims who are left in the cold, ranging from the homeless in the streets of affluent societies to virtually the whole of sub-Saharan Africa. Beyond this, the creative and empathetic sides of governance are challenged and in retreat.

To avoid any impression of determinism arising from this analysis, it may be useful to take brief note of three directions of response that could avoid many of the negative policy implications of the argument:

- A global social contract that provides for basic human needs and regulatory uniformity, resembling the achievements of social democracy and the labor movement at the level of the state. The social agencies capable of bringing about such results are the backlash in Western societies experiencing rollback and downsizing and the greater social flexibility of Asian countries that have reached thresholds of development that give a higher priority to social demands.

- The strengthening of tendencies connected with world order values, transnational social forces dedicated to human rights, environment, gender consciousness – and peace – what I have called globalization-from-below, with an emergent capacity to balance the influence of globalization-from-above through the regulation of the global economy and by way of accountability for those beyond the reach of the regulatory operations of states; also the opening of pathways toward a cosmopolitan or transnational democratic ethos of renewal.[30]

- The inevitable push towards law and governance on regional and global levels as a result of greater complexity, interconnectedness, and fragility of human activity. Such tendencies could be accelerated by environmental breakdowns and failures of technology that rouse public consciousness.

The normative possibilities for international society that John Vincent and Hedley Bull foresaw and helped nurture are now more compelling than ever, but the substantial displacement of a statist world makes it necessary to recast such aspirations, as well as to rethink our conceptual tools for the framing of world order. Globalization has intermingled our categories of thought, discouraged the projection of "imagined communities" on a global scale, and eclipsed the image of global governance by way of a society of states. At this point, what we require minimally are visions of the present and future that can better encompass reality than "realism," as well as proposals and tactics for bridging the normative and ideological gaps between the ascent of economic globalization and the descent of human well-being in established societies.

3

On the Political Economy of World Order

The dominant tendencies of political life during the last several years are disclosed by the crowds of exultant young people pouring through gaping holes in the collapsing Berlin Wall and by the thousands of corpses of massacred Rwandans piled up by the side of the roads in and around Kigali: on the one side, exhilarating triumphs of nonviolent movements of democratization and, on the other, terrifying relapses into barbarism and genocide. Unfortunately, both are signature occurrences during these final years of the millennium, and each has recurred in a variety of formats. Against such a background, the defining political challenge of this era is to work towards a world order that would promote and sustain continuous projects of democratization, while consigning the dreadful ordeals of collective violence and genocidal cruelty to the annals of historical memory.

Movement in this direction depends on two sets of interrelated developments, neither of which is currently on the political horizon. The most immediate task, highlighted by the failure of the United Nations or leading states to halt ethnic cleansing in Bosnia, is to find the will and the means to oppose those forms of extremism – whether nationalist, religious, or ideological – that rely on massive violence to eliminate "the other" so as to purify their territorial space. The second, less focused task is to establish a regulatory framework for global market forces that is people-centered rather than capital-driven. My emphasis in this essay will be upon this latter objective.[1]

Any hope of reaching such goals in the present global setting and of purifying their political space depends on resituating the sovereign state, making governments less responsive to the priorities of global market forces and more receptive to the needs and aspirations of the peoples of the world, especially those who are most economically, socially, and politically deprived. Vaclav Havel has said that the Czech Republic should be judged by how it treats gypsies – that is, its most vulnerable inhabitants. This test can be set globally by considering the fate of indigenous peoples struggling to maintain their physical, cultural, and economic survival, or of the international treatment of the most troubled states in sub-Saharan Africa.

Michael Mandlebaum writes: "The world is ready for government, or rather it is ready for more international governance than ever before. But the UN is not a world government and it will not become one. The instruments of order are sovereign states. But there is no effective method of extracting resources from states to pay for governance."[2] This observation aptly expresses the tension between the normative/functional pressure to achieve political integration at a global level and the effective refusal by states to succumb to this pressure. This typical formulation of the ordering dilemma misleadingly posits an either/or relationship between the state and world government. As such, it overlooks the undertakings of states through the World Trade Organization, the annual economic summits of the leading industrial countries (the so-called Group of Seven), and the activities of international financial institutions (the IMF and the World Bank) to move towards the establishment of global economic governance to promote market goals of efficiency, stability, and growth. It also ignores regional developments that have evolved furthest in Europe but are also evident in North America and the Asia–Pacific region and that disclose a range of world order alternatives other than world government. At present, there is virtual paralysis when it comes to structural reform of a political character at the global level, which keeps in being an increasingly dysfunctional system of world order with respect to peace and security, as embodied in the United Nations, the interplay of leading sovereign states, and the emergent network of actors responsible for global economic governance.

Posing the Challenge: Resituating the State

World order for several centuries worked towards a universal system of governance that relied mainly on the capacity of sovereign, territorial states to serve the well-being of their inhabitants and to cooperate with each other sufficiently to uphold shared interests. By stages war was repudiated by governments and public opinion as a legitimate and effective instrument of statecraft, and the rise of human rights and their protection began to pose formidable obstacles to the maintenance of oppressive internal rule. The collapse of colonialism in the past half-century contributed greatly to the plausibility of this vision, effectively according rights of self-determination to the previously dominated and exploited non-Western peoples of the world. The decisive role played by human rights in the successful struggle against Communist rule in Eastern Europe and the Soviet Union during the 1980s seemed a further confirmation that the states system was ascending new heights in its evolution. Optimism for the future was also embodied in the widely endorsed belief that democratically oriented states would be moderate in their relations with one another and benign with respect to their own population, and that the spread of democratic governance was thus tantamount to establishing an ever more peaceful world.

Yet, despite these encouraging tendencies, the structural and normative foundations of world order seem increasingly unable to provide minimum human security for many of the peoples of the world. The state is being subtly deformed as an instrument of human well-being by the dynamics of globalization, which are pushing the state by degrees and to varying extents into a subordinate relationship with global market forces. Partly in reaction to these developments and partly as a result of the shortcomings of secularism as a source of human fulfillment, the state is also losing its capacity in many settings to provide the social, economic, and physical ingredients of security within its own borders, often giving way to a variety of extremist challenges that provide, if nothing else, a cause worth fighting for, or surrendering entirely to cynical readings of human purpose: religious fanaticism, ultranationalism, ethnic hatreds, warlordism, large-scale criminality.

In the face of such pressure, many states have been rendered virtually helpless, or – in some instances, worse – complicit, incorporating these destructive types of political orientation into their own governing process. This has led even some of the most admired governments gradually to dilute welfare and security programs serving their own citizens, recasting their claim for legitimate authority on a willingness to escalate the internal war against their own people beneath the banner of "law and order," often a euphemism for reliance on capital punishment, a larger, better-armed police force, and bigger prisons. In some instances, state power has been captured, or at least intimidated, by anti-secular, extremist, and gangster elements. Those who are not included are often exposed to a terrible fate, which can culminate in genocide or expulsion. Such developments are undermining the confident expectations of only a few years ago that democracy was a global tidal wave that would, by its own force, emancipate societies from such destructive threats.

Exacerbating this decline in the capabilities and legitimacy of the state is an apparent ideational vacuum. There are no commanding ideas of a progressive or humanist character coming forth in response to these various forms of deterioration. Socialist and other utopian conceptions of human well-being have been discredited as part of the end game in the cold war. The result has been that even moderate ideas of social democracy have been put on the defensive. Additionally, the globalized media disseminate variants of materialism through their uncritical emphasis upon economic growth and consumerism, goals which, if mindlessly pursued, are sure over time to erode the ecological and cultural foundations of life on earth.

The changing role of the state will remain the main arena of global reform for the next decade or so, although the content of this reform is likely to remain contested and unresolved. At present, the main reformist leverage is being exerted by global market forces shifting governmental allegiances from a territorial locus to one of finance and trade. But there are other reformist projects at work, seeking to make the state both more responsible to territorial concerns and more responsive to transnational initiatives in support of human rights, democratization, and the demilitarization of international relations.

This work of restoration need not rewind the clock of development or knowledge. The globalization of production and distribution cannot be reversed and is as much a consequence of the global reach of technology as it is of the expansionist compulsions of the market. Only a neutralizing counter-globalism arising out of comparably transnational societal initiatives can give the state the political space it needs to strike a better balance between the well-being of its own people as a territorial community and fulfillment of its emergent role and identity as an agency for the protection of the global commons and the promotion of human (as distinct from merely national) interests. It is the social construction of this other globalism, largely through the cumulative impact of democratizing efforts, which can be identified as either "rooted utopianism" or "global realism."

The success of this vast and vital normative project depends on critique, vision, mobilization and activism across borders, the engagement of large numbers of people, and their perseverance in struggle. The focus of political energy needs to be the achievement of "humane governance" at all levels of political interaction, from the family to the world. It is not enough to offer elaborate blueprints for governance at the level of region or world. More crucial at this time is a convincing account of the potential agents of renewal, social forces that could bring into being such an altered set of political conditions and thus, by being so empowered, exert an influence on state action and political leaders from the perspective of priorities set out to express a global ethos embodying widely shared human values.[3]

The state-centric world of Westphalia was based on neglect of the whole, according primacy to the *parts*, conceived as self-regulating, sovereign economic and political units that defended widely acknowledged territorial boundaries. Most important, changes in the size and arrangement of the parts was mainly expressed *spatially*, by altering maps, and generally came about as a result of warfare. Market-driven globalism subordinates the part to the whole on the basis of calculations such as profit margins, comparative efficiencies of production and distribution, and growth prospects, registering change in relative standing mainly by statistical measures of economic performance.[4] In contrast, people-driven globalism subordinates the part to the whole on the basis of human values, including such goals as ecological sustainability, alleviation of suffering caused by changing patterns of production and consumption, establishment of communities that uphold the security and economic and social rights of all their inhabitants, and a reduction of violence at home and abroad. Well-being is a matter of quality, not quantity. Because neither world nor regional governments are viable political projects for the foreseeable future, the state is almost certain to retain its pivotal role as political actor, both ceremonially and substantively, continuing as enforcer and mediator in relation to contending social forces and as the major, yet increasingly contested, source of political identity. A central question arises therefore from this analysis: *How can the state be pulled back from its current tilt toward market-driven globalism and led to manifest a greater degree of receptivity toward people-driven globalism, thereby over time achieving a new political stasis that supports the kind of institutional and legal superstructure that could underpin humane governance for the planet?*

Breaking the Connection between States and Peoples

Decades of encounter between East and West, both ideological rift and arms race, deflected the political imagination of both leaders and citizens from a series of more fundamental developments: the globalization of capital, communications, and popular culture, the decay of the global commons, the double menace of acute demographic pressure – non-sustainable, high-energy life-styles in the richer countries of the North and the growth of numbers in the poorer countries of the South – and, finally, the failure of secularism (reason, science, progress, materialist values, statist loyalty) to supersede religion and ethnicity as the dominant source of political identity.

The complex tensions between territorial sovereign states and global integrative/local disintegrative processes are converging in concrete circumstances to constrain the capacity of governments to promote effectively the well-being of their own citizenry, even to the extent of undermining popular support in some societies for the maintenance of a unified state. Without an acceptance of the political legitimacy of its territorial units a state-centric system of world order is continuously put in question, provoking a variety of ultranationalist movements for state-shattering forms of self-determination as well as almost everywhere generating a corrosive distrust of government and contempt for politicians. This assessment is confirmed by the current unpopularity of most elected political leaders in many important countries, as well as by prominence being accorded the view of Samuel Huntington that the locus of conflict is shifting from inter-state struggle to what he calls "the clash of civilizations."[5]

Such a focus on the civilizational level at least has the virtue of explaining, in part, the displacement of the state and the rise of identity politics, including the dialectical response to global market forces by way of revival of traditional values. What is objectionable about Huntington's adoption of a civilizational perspective is its programmatic effort to rally the West into a conflict-oriented mode of response to other world civilizations, especially Islam, and thereby to reconstitute geopolitics after the cold war around a new logic of ideological confrontation.

In one respect Huntington is giving an indirect rationale for the reorientation of the Western state, ignoring its role on behalf of global market forces by associating its altered mission with the defense of "the West." Such a formulation has the ideological virtue of concealing from those being victimized the capitalist agency of the state, and providing a more generic justification for the role of military power in the new world order – namely, to identify strategic interests and to avoid "irrelevant" conflicts without seeming to embrace global imperialism.[6]

A further serious indication of structural collapse is the absence of hopeful alternatives. A shout of despair is being emitted by the youth of the world, through its embrace of drugs and crime, often articulated in its most captivating and influential form of expression: popular music. The recent trends in rock lyrics manifest a mood of despair, not merely a repudiation of reigning cultural values or even countercultural defiance, but the sense that nothing personal or public is worth the effort of staying alive for, much less engaging in struggle to transform the social order for the sake of a better tomorrow.

The April 1994 suicide of Kurt Cobain, lead singer and songwriter of Nirvana based in Seattle, has reverberated deeply in global youth culture, partly because his death was foretold by his music, and partly because his message utterly denies authenticity to any reading of the world offering an alternative to opting out.[7] What is especially frightening about this cry from the young in our midst is the refusal of mainstream society to comprehend Cobain's suicide as anything more than an isolated reminder of the destructive effects of a permissive life-style and drugs – at most, a personal tragedy. Such an assessment of personal destruction is, of course, correct; but it is incomplete. It fails to appreciate that Cobain's stance toward life represented an important act of witness, a lyric insistence that the culture is failing the young, and that we may all be living quite unconsciously in a failed (or failing) culture. The likening to "failed states" is deliberate: this culture imparts no will to live because it engenders little meaning beyond the accumulation of money and because it celebrates as victories the achievements of one-sided violence, as in the aftermath of the Gulf War. These factors may help to account for the opting-out phenomenon.

These comments refer to the United States in particular, but the United States has acted as both the main influence in establishing a global popular culture and as the guardian of the global market. The cult associated with the music and life of Kurt Cobain, although emanating from Seattle, was global in scope and impact. This hypothesis of cultural failure helps us explain, by contrast, the unpopularity of political leadership and the inability of the political imagination to revive "faith" in secular authority. Yet not only secular authority is losing its grip!

The Roman Catholic Church's extraordinary recent reaffirmation of its gendered view of divinity and its persisting opposition to reproductive rights in the face of population pressure is suicidal in its own way, an opting-out that is a virtual repudiation of life on earth by one of the most revered institutional actors on earth. In face of such a failed culture, the extremist revival of nationalism and religion becomes more understandable, providing a less discredited foundation for living (and dying). In one sense, the exclusivism of these absolute creeds that deny validity to those who fall outside the pale of privileged identity is a distorted expression of a collapsing modernism.[8] The reemergence of tradition is, then, a kind of pre-modern backlash to the pressures being exerted by a faceless globalizing postmodernism in which the homogenizing and consumerist impacts of the market negate every particular identity and highlight the unbridgeable gulf between winners and losers in the world to come.[9]

Possibly, the inability to live up to the expectations created by the end of the cold war and the Soviet collapse is reason enough to explain the acute cultural malaise in the West that has emerged during the last five years. After basing explanation of the dangers of international relations for so long on Soviet aggressiveness and the continuous threat of an ulti- mate, apocalyptic war associated with the nuclear standoff, it was natural to look forward to a more moderate and constructive era of international relations that would spontaneously take shape, ensuring a soft landing in the next millennium.

Indeed, the collapse of the Soviet empire has ended for the foresee- able future any prospect of a war-threatening conflict among the richest and most powerful states. This is certainly not the end of history, but it is a weakening, at the very least, of the geopolitical glue that gave modern statecraft its coherence. We barely know how to think about security and power in a world of states that lacks a rivalry among leading states. The Gulf War, posing threats to oil pricing and supplies, as well as to the secu- rity of Israel, suggested the possibility that strategic interests of great magnitude could be so seriously threatened in the post–cold war world as to justify recourse to large-scale warfare. Such an undertaking was made more palatable by a series of factors: the formation of a coalition of states that included Islamic states in the region, a mandate from United Nations Security Council, a media campaign to demonize Saddam Hussein, and, perhaps most of all, a decisive victory on the desert battlefield that dramatically reasserted Western hegemony.[10] But the Gulf War was an anomaly, arising from a colossal miscalculation on Iraq's part back in 1990, and is unlikely to recur in such a congenial format.[11]

What is far more characteristic of this post–cold war setting is the daunting challenge of failed states and severe humanitarian disasters such as famine and chaos in Somalia, ethnic cleansing and other crimes against humanity in Bosnia, brutal militarism in Haiti, and sys- tematic massacre in Rwanda. Here we confront realism at work: a glob- alized media unavoidably mobilizes public concern through visual portrayal of extreme adversity, yet territorial states are governed by rel- atively insulated bureaucracies and, with their main gaze directed at keeping global market shares and containing various types of domestic disaffection, they are not inclined to perceive their national interests as threatened.

This array of nonstrategic challenges has encouraged leading govern- ments to dump such issues on the already overburdened United Nations, not as in the Gulf War to enhance the legitimacy of a geopolitical response, but now as a result of geopolitical indifference. This shift in geopolitical gears has occurred without any corresponding willingness to endow the UN with the enhanced capabilities it would need to play such a larger role in international political life on a successful basis. The result is to discredit the UN just at the very historical conjuncture when its enhanced capabilities are most needed and most plausible. A more ambitious UN would seem to follow from the absence of sharp disagreements among states of the sort that severely restricted international cooperation between 1945 and 1989 and in light of the impressive practical case for global-scale governance (not government).[12] Any further UN empowerment is exceedingly unlikely at this point. If enhancement comes at all, it is likely to arise from an appreciation by global market elites that more stability depends on global governance, which would then be supported for reasons of market efficiency and hence deemed worth the investment, possibly even in forms that cut the umbilical cord that binds the UN in a dependent relationship to its leading donor members. But market-driven potency for the UN would be far from a panacea, and would quite possibly intensify the worst ecological consequences of a stateless (or nonterritorial) geopolitics and aggravate the plight of the most economically disadvantaged societies.

A main contention in this essay is that the institutional framework available for cooperative action at the global (and regional) level is increasingly being manipulated by global market forces, and that not even the most powerful state is in a position to mount consistent effective opposition to protect specific territorial concerns, especially with respect to the protection of its own most vulnerable sectors, including the poor and various categories of workers. In this capital-driven, non-territorial world order, economic growth, as measured by trade and investment and promoted by consumerist advertising, achieves an almost absolute priority within the domain of public policy.

The ground rules of this new globalism are being set by patterns of corporate and banking practices and by the activities of currency traders, given some institutional presence in the form of the World Trade Organization, by the Bretton Woods international financial institutions, especially the IMF and the World Bank, and by a variety of regional frameworks. Increasingly, party affiliations and policy differences at the state level are being cast aside by this imperative to accommodate global market preferences regardless of domestic political orientation (thus Mitterand's France, Deng's China, and Clinton's United States have been market-oriented states, despite having leaders with an apparent social democratic or socialist ideological background). In such a setting of neo-liberal consensus, the only significant "dissent" comes from a resurgent right wing that places a renewed emphasis on territoriality and various expressions of the politics of identity – that is, aligning the state with indigenous national, ethnic, and religious identities, in opposition to more inclusive approaches in relation to minorities and refugees. This is a deformed modernism in that it rejects reason, science, rights – the normative foundations of modernism – while cleaving to conservative modes of exclusivity and territorial roots, including the organizing principles of a world of distinct sovereign states. The capital-driven postmodern fix is to relocate the normative foundations at regional and global levels – that is, with minimal political and legal accountability or community bonding beyond the boardrooms of transnational corporations and banks.

If managing the world economy is the primary task now being assigned to states, then the residual geopolitical job is to provide security for this process. This means addressing threats to the dynamics of integration at the global level. Seen from this angle, the Gulf War was "a perfect war" for the new age.[13] Similarly, denying nuclear weaponry to states that resist economic globalism becomes a strategic undertaking that is now invoked at the UN level to justify interventionary diplomacy beneath the banner of "non-proliferation," as in relation to North Korea. What makes this understanding so suspect is its overt embrace of double standards in the form of "nuclear apartheid," retaining nuclear weapons for the managers of the global system, who happen to be the five permanent members of the Security Council, but disallowing nuclear weaponry to those states that seem most inclined to challenge economic globalism, especially the so-called backlash states.[14]

This inability of states to cope with economic globalism, either through regulation of the operations of corporations, banks, and traders or by protecting citizens and societies from the trauma of fluctuating currencies and volatile financial markets, is being reinforced by the inability of those same states to provide a unifying political framework for the people living within their boundaries. The basic modern idea of a territorial sovereign state that would serve as an agency of reason and science and a focus for political identity and loyalty is being appropriated or opposed by different noneconomic modalities that take the ugly form of ethnic outbursts and religious extremisms. Often recourse to ethnic politics and ultranationalism is a tactic by opportunistic politicians unable to find a solution for a country's economic decline, as has been alleged in reference to Slobodan Milosevic's rise to power in post-Tito Yugoslavia. As such, the state either is discredited by its portrayal as an instrument of alien decadence (via fundamentalism) and ethnic passion and/or religious fanaticism is stirred up to provide feelings of unity that hide oppression. Secularism as the ideological foundation of a more inclusive and tolerant political authority cannot provide the basis for territorial unity under these conditions. A variety of destructive developments has ensued: theocratic states that violate elementary human rights; corrupt and inept states that cannot control mobsters and organized crime; failed states that cannot provide food and minimum order for their populations. As earlier argued, possibly most insidious of all, politics is being defined by a domineering culture that does not provide its members with a sense of their worth, thereby becoming not only materialist in its appetites but also supportive of various forms of social pathology, including widespread suicide among the young.

Imprisoning Imagination: The Realist World View

The necessary emancipation is Hegelian in character, a matter of ideas appropriate to the historic occasion. What is required is the formation of a consciousness that is politically relevant to the inevitable transition to globalization in *some* form. Without the ideational stage setting, structural solutions will not seem politically feasible or may be misappropriated by oppressive, anti-ecological tendencies.

Despite its anachronism for reasons set forth, a powerfully entrenched world view called here for convenience "realism" continues to hold sway in foreign offices and within the academic establishment, especially among those experts who interconnect with those who shape global policy. Realism is conflict-oriented and state-centered, dismissing law and morality as encumbrances upon the rational calculation of national interests, which should be associated as objectively as possible with the power and wealth maximization of a given political actor and not be deflected by sentimental considerations associated with adherence to the norms of law and morality.[15] To the extent that the territorial "part" is now being dominated by the global "whole," the overriding task for government is to adapt to, co-opting if possible and subordinating as necessary, territorial pulls based on vulnerability to stronger regional and global economic actors.[16] Yet, to the extent that most distressed societies fracture violently, mixing cultural, political, ethnic, economic, and environmental breakdowns, the phenomenon of mass migration poses a threat generally discussed as a problem of "refugees."

By several twists of irony, in late 1994 the Clinton presidency intervened successfully in Haiti. The claim made to support this intervention concentrated on the restoration of democracy and human rights, but not far in the background was the understanding that the only politically acceptable way to avoid a politically unacceptable influx of Haitian refugees into the United States was to restructure the political situation in Haiti. Note that the earlier debate in 1992 about a possible Haitian intervention was resolved negatively by the angry claim of US politicians that it was not worth losing a single American life to restore the democratically elected Jean-Bertrand Aristide to power, despite the earlier Governor's Island agreement reached with the Haitian military to do just that.[17]

A similar pattern is associated with the recent emphasis of the UN High Commissioner for Refugees (UNHCR) and the US government on forcible repatriation and related efforts to keep internally displaced persons from crossing borders and becoming thus counted as "refugees." In other words, enforced territoriality becomes a realist solution to the human pressures on "successful" states to escape the human spillovers from catastrophic conditions in failed states. In essence, the emergent world order after the cold war is shaping up in the short run as an attractive, yet competitive, globalism for the benefit of the rich and an oppressive statism to keep the poor in check.[18] Over the medium term such a perspective is harmful to all, as the consumerist ethos is likely to overburden the environment in several non-sustainable ways, and the fracturing of political community will expand the orbit of chaos further and further, provoking disruptive societal behavior and repressive governmental responses, thereby "preparing" many societies for outbreaks of religious and ethnic fanaticism and "nurturing" a variety of neo-fascisms.

Locating Rooted Utopianism in the Postmodern Era

To oppose the kind of dreary human future that is being shaped by this lethal interplay of realism, globalism, and exclusivism will depend in the short run on reorienting the outlook of the state sufficiently to strike a new balance between the well-being of peoples and the success of markets. Such a repositioning of the state can occur only if transnational democratic forces can fashion a strong enough global civil society to offset some of the influence exerted by global market forces. Such a prospect is here identified as "rooted utopianism," a horizon of hope and aspiration that currently appears beyond reach, yet is supported by a series of developments which, if sustained and deepened, will alter our sense of what is possible in the political domain. Encouraging such an outlook is the confirmation of rooted utopian outcomes that appeared nowhere on the radar screen of the realist political imagination: the largely nonviolent collapse of Communist rule in the Soviet bloc; the peaceful reunification of Germany; the negotiated repudiation of apartheid in South Africa and the emergence of multiracial constitutionalism presided over by an African co-recipient of the Nobel Peace Prize. Each of these developments remains fragile, having unleashed severe cross-currents; yet each is suggestive of the extent to which the *actual* range of possibilities for the future far exceeds the *realist* calculus of plausibility.

In his early years as Soviet leader, at the height of his influence and before the Soviet Union began to unravel, Mikhail Gorbachev depicted the basis for normative restructuring of world order: elimination of nuclear weapons by the year 2000, endorsement of a less war-oriented approach to security put forth in the form of proposals for "comprehensive security," increased UN autonomy, compulsory jurisdiction of the World Court over international disputes, global procedures and institutions to protect the environment, and deference to international law in the shaping of foreign policy. Such a program for reform was rooted in a state-centric framework of world order, actualizing its cooperative potentialities on the basis of an extension of rationality and Enlightenment values to a new set of global conditions. Despite Gorbachev's prestige and persistence, this aspect of "new thinking," significantly, never evoked a serious response from either the United States government or from other political leaders and did not have much impact on world public opinion. Drastic global reform even *within* the states system seemed of little interest as compared to efforts to liberate the countries of Eastern Europe from the Soviet yoke, the moves toward democracy and restructuring within the Soviet Union, and the search for a resolution of East–West confrontations in different regional settings. Reform at the level of global institutions was a non-starter, a manifestation of structural rigidity at a time of structural obsolescence.

At the close of the cold war there was a brief flourish of neo-Wilsonian idealism, promoted avidly during 1990–1 by George Bush's call to establish a "new world order" in response to Iraq's conquest of Kuwait. Bush briefly championed internationalism in the guise of a new confidence in the organized global community, essentially the UN Security Council, to serve as the foundation for global security on behalf of all peoples. This flourish took a historically potent, if ambiguous, form, but, once the immediate geopolitical mission of reversing Iraqi aggression and restoring Kuwaiti sovereignty was achieved, the wider world order pretensions of the Gulf War were quietly abandoned.[19] Especially in retrospect, the UN role in the Gulf War has been widely interpreted as providing little more than a legitimating cover for geopolitical maneuver.

Still, the hope has lingered in liberal circles that the UN could become the organized focus for a global security system that was collective in its character, premised more on the guidelines of international law and less on the manipulations of geopolitics (ambitions of leading military powers and economic interests being defined by the global centers of financial policy). Bill Clinton's initial presidential campaign promised an upgraded foreign policy emphasis on the UN, packaged as "assertive multilateralism"; but, chastened by Somalia, the Clinton presidency has backed away from any emphasis on UN-centered global security. Such a reformist impulse to create a stronger UN informed several influential initiatives, most notably the report *Our Global Neighborhood* issued by the Independent Commission on Global Governance. Discussions about UN reform planned for the fiftieth anniversary year were extremely muted in light of disappointments with the UN's performance in Bosnia and the rightward lurch of US politics. To the extent that UN reform has been discussed at all, orientation has again deferred to geopolitics, this time by limiting relevant debate on the expansion of permanent membership of the Security Council to whether the financial superpowers should be added and, if so, with or without a veto.[20]

Under present conditions of world order the UN is unlikely in the near future to play an enhanced role in international life, either in relation to keeping the peace, regulating the world economy, furthering development, or protecting the environment. Such possibilities are effectively blocked by market-driven globalism, which specifies the scope of the strategic interests to be pursued by dominant states and excludes from the definition of "strategic" issues of humanitarian or ecological concern. In this regard, a curtailed, rather than an enhanced, UN is the likely outcome for the years ahead, as the current array of challenges arising from humanitarian crises and implosions of state authority (black holes that generate maelstroms of chaos and massacre) could only be addressed by the serious commitments of resources. Such a commitment would imply a new people-oriented definition of "strategic" and a conception of human security that accorded primacy to the stability and well-being of the whole, as distinct from present preoccupations with the stability and prosperity of those powerful and affluent parts that make economic globalism appear robust.

Rooted utopianism is not astrology or channeling. It rests on solid evidence of grass-roots globalism, as well as on the democratizing resources and potentialities of the Internet that have been slowly emerging over the course of the last 25 years. There has been a real impact with respect to the protection of human rights and environmental quality and, more recently, with support for a more people-oriented approach to development and world economic policy. Such grass-roots info-power is countering the extraordinary business and media capacity to manipulate information for profit, relying on its own formidable networks of electronic empowerment. This movement of social forces, with a transnational democratizing outlook, is groping towards a new synthesis of scientific knowledge, religion, and politics, a reconstructive postmodernism that will extend and deepen the virtues of secularism to a world of diversity and difference, yet celebrate manifestations and experiences of the sacred. Most of these initiatives are preoccupied with specific sites of struggle and aspiration, whether preventing ecological destruction in the Philippines or Thailand, safeguarding whales, avoiding harmful economic dislocations beneath the banner of free trade, or insisting that demographic balance be achieved on the basis of full protection of the reproductive rights of women. In this sense, the local and the global are so interlinked as to be indistinguishable.[21]

Rethinking citizenship is crucial.[22] The citizen, unlike the subject of a monarchy or an authoritarian political order, is a participant in the polity. The quality of participation establishes whether or not a polity possesses a vital, as distinct from a formalistic, democratic character. If elections seem to avoid issues, to leave the electorate bored and indifferent, and if political parties converge on a consensus, then other modes of participation need to be identified and, if necessary, invented, to avoid the atrophy of civic virtue. Such phenomena of revitalization may help overcome the loss of ethical concerns as a result of the virtual disappearance from political life of a socialist alternative. Such a background encourages the reinvention of citizenship in the form of participation in civic initiatives of various sorts, including transnational attempts to promote human rights and peace, as well as to protect the environment, limit population growth, and seek the regulation of global market forces. In this regard, from the perspective of an emergent global civil society, the idea of a citizen pilgrim arises: participating in time, on a journey to a preferred future, a pilgrimage that loosens spatial connections, conceives of the planet as a unity, and associates loyalty with the nonviolent struggle to create a better world, not only for others, but for subsequent generations – a shift in loyalty from space to time.

In this setting the hyper-modern bonds with the pre-modern, reestablishing community across space without regard to boundaries, envisioning the future, relying on electronic resources of community (a monastic withdrawal from a vulgar public realm) as tools of pilgrimage. In this reconstructive postmodern world view, it is important to keep the democratizing priority in mind, and not validate an electronic vanguard for the benighted masses as a new opiate of revolutionary emancipation.[23] For this reason, among others, it is crucial to give highest priority to the struggle to reorient the outlook of the state, establishing a people-driven politics capable of regulating the global marketplace on behalf of human interests and for planetary benefit.[24]

4

A Regional Approach to World Order

This chapter seeks to assess the actual and potential contributions of regionalism to the achievement of such world order goals as peace, social justice, human rights, and democracy.[1] This assessment proceeds by way of discussing, in an introductory section, several main features of the global setting that have become prominent in the early aftermath of the cold war. Against this background, four possible roles for regional actors are depicted: containing negative globalism (basically associated with the adverse impacts of global market forces); mitigating pathological anarchism (the breakdown of minimum order and decency in state–society relations arising from extremes of either excessive control and abuse by the state or pervasive and dangerous chaos arising from the weakness or breakdown of governance capacity at the level of the state); promoting positive globalism (reinforcing the global capacity to achieve desirable world order goals); and promoting positive regionalism (achieving these goals at a regional level through the strengthening and orientation of regional structures of governance).

The intention here is to propose one type of research agenda with respect to the regional dimensions of world order. Necessarily, such an effort is preliminary, focusing on issues of conceptualization and offering a broad, normative perspective that differentiates what is negative (to be avoided or overcome) from what is positive (to be achieved or enhanced), but hopefully in a manner that usefully prefigures further and more detailed inquiry.

Background Considerations

Of course, many of the fundamental tendencies reshaping world order do not derive from the cold war, especially the complex dynamics of globalization. However, the preoccupations of the cold war, its East–West axis of interpretative logic, made it more difficult to appreciate the impact of globalization, including the various phenomena of backlash being generated. When the Berlin Wall was breached in November 1989, this ultra-stable geopolitical scaffolding provided by bipolarity, especially with respect to Europe since World War II, disintegrated before our eyes. The immediate reaction was to exaggerate the discontinuity, neglecting underlying forces for change that were having a transforming impact in any event, such as weaponry of mass destruction, technological innovation, environmental decay, economic integration, and a global communications net, with the cumulative effect of diminishing the functional competence and normative self-sufficiency of sovereign states.[2]

The end of the cold war definitely encouraged a greater emphasis on globalization, especially its human implications, and on such adverse reactions and contradictory trends as fundamentalism, a vehicle for religious and ethnic extremism. How regionalism of varying attributes fits within globalization is a central world order concern for which evidence and interpretation are necessarily inconclusive. This uncertainty is magnified by the diversity of regional settings and of the varying degrees to which economic, political, and cultural life has been regionalized. Almost any generalization about regionalism seems suspect and must be qualified.

There is one important exception to these admonitions of conceptual caution. It is persuasive to claim that regionalism as a perspective in this historical period is a promising focus for both empirical and normative inquiry: that regionalism identifies emergent trends and structures and clarifies a distinct array of prescriptions and strategies. Following Hettne's assessment, the provision of world order in the near future is unlikely to be provided to nearly the extent, as during the cold war, by hegemonic state actors.[3] Indeed, I would go further, contending that the weakening of the state, in general, is producing various adverse types of societal vulnerability to the integrative tendencies in the global economy and is partly responsible for the intensity and incidence of pathological forms of anarchy that are of a different character than the type of structural anarchy that Hedley Bull so influentially depicted.[4]

Thus, the regional alternative to statism seems potentially compensatory, in terms of the quality of world order, for both the erosion of hegemonic stability and addressing the more acute forms of pathology that are afflicting the weak state. These background conditions are linked to the ending of the cold war, especially the collapse of bipolarity and the loss of a capacity to maintain order within bloc limits;

also relevant is the inherently far more limited ordering role of unipolarity as a sequel to bipolarity has not lived up to expectations. This results partly from the contemporary perception by political leaders of a greatly diminished domain of strategic interests, but also from the internal pressures exerted by the citizenry on government to address domestic priorities. More concretely, the Gulf War epitomized the post–cold war perception of the persistence of hegemonic stability. After all, here was a hegemonic undertaking that succeeded fully in instrumentalizing the United Nations in the process, even generating illusionary claims of "a new world order" legitimized through collective security mechanisms.[5] Since 1991 it has become evident that "the unipolar moment" was indeed of brief duration, and its idealistic embodiment in a serious commitment to collective security by way of the UN was quietly abandoned.[6]

Why were the crises in Somalia, Bosnia, Haiti, and Rwanda treated as so much less deserving of a global community response than the invasion of Kuwait? The paramount explanation is, of course, oil, but also the security threat posed by a militant Iraq, already possessing chemical and biological weapons, and likely to possess nuclear weapons and delivery systems within years, to a strategic ally – namely, Israel – as well as to a strategic region, the Middle East.[7] It is unlikely that the Gulf crisis would have occurred in a bipolar world in which the dynamics of mutual deterrence induced greater prudence in relation to challenges directed at obvious strategic interests, as well as more effective control by superpowers over the initiatives undertaken by secondary states such as Iraq. But it is also unlikely that the internal tensions in Bosnia and Somalia would have spiraled out of governmental control, as each country was of strategic importance within a cold war setting, thus warranting the expenditure of lives and resources by superpowers to maintain a given alignment. At the same time, the causal significance of the cold war is by no means uniform with respect to the collapse of minimum internal order; Lebanon spiraled dangerously out of control in the decade following the outbreak of civil strife in 1975, and superpower intervention failed in the major test cases of Vietnam and Afghanistan. There is a temptation, in other words, to exaggerate the ordering achievements of bipolarity and deterrence during the cold war era.[8] These achievements did seem considerable in Europe, but not necessarily elsewhere.

What is somewhat different, however, is the circumscribing of the domain of strategic interests on the part of intervening states in the North, particularly the United States. The outcome in Somalia, and even in Haiti and Bosnia, has been widely regarded as a matter of virtual indifference, so long as the external effects are minimized. These external effects relate to "containment" in its post–cold war meaning: that is, discouraging not the expansion of the rival superpower/ideology, but the spread of disorder and violence via a wider war (Bosnia) or the massive generation of refugees (Bosnia again, but Haiti more centrally, where the prospects of even a relatively small number of black Haitian refugees coming to the United States was resisted as strategically intolerable).[9]

The UN has been reinstrumentalized since its moment of prominence in the Gulf during 1990–1, resuming its role as marginal player, while being somewhat unfairly accused of "failing." Unlike in the cold war, when failure was explained as a consequence of stalemate, it is now more damagingly seen as an expression of a feeble "political will." Yet it is here that enhanced roles for regional actors seem plausible, this possibility being highlighted, although ambiguously, by reliance on some military action by NATO in 1994 to curb the persisting excesses of the Bosnian Serbs. It is ambiguous in that NATO had earlier floundered, and its temporary revival owed as much to the electoral success of Zhirinovsky in December 1993 (reminding Europe that the Russian bear might prowl again) as it did to the alleged moral shock of a mortar shell that killed civilians at a market on a February day in Sarajevo.

But security concerns are not the only world order context. The play of economic forces is at least as important, even if not as visually captivating in a media sense. The transnational economic calculus is also being reshaped in contradictory ways by the ending of the cold war, above all by the weakening of alliance and bloc ties of the bipolar variety as a result of the decline in global threat perception. Such a decline in globalization of security arrangements makes regional security and political economy factors generally more significant, yet not at all in a uniform manner. This decline is offset in a contradictory manner by the rising globalization of the world economy, stimulating tactics for participation and protection, both types of reaction bearing on regionalist prospects in this period. The pattern of differing influences and perceptions bearing on the role of regionalism is complex and confusing.

Europe and Asia–Pacific are currently the critical arenas for assessing the world order roles of regionalist configurations. The collapse of the blocs and the widening of Europe have definitely slowed the deepening of the European Union and have possibly deferred political integration indefinitely. So many factors are at work that causal inferences will always be open to argument and inconclusive. Yet there is an apparent contrast between Europe and Asia with respect to regionalist development. In Asia, the US is not needed as much as during the cold war, allowing economic priorities to gain precedence, especially when combined with new feelings of cultural potency and identity.[10] Similarly, the US, no longer concerned with geopolitical alignment, is prepared to insist on more favorable trading and investment relations, creating special post–cold war tensions that invite a turn toward regional and bloc approaches. Whether this sets the stage for "the clash of civilizations" is doubtful; but it does shift economic and political concerns from the old geopolitics of Westphalia to the new geopolitics of inter-regional relationships as mediated by the Group of Seven (reconstituted at Naples in 1994 as the Group of Eight, provisionally including Russia in its ranks).[11] This dynamic has been further intensified by the monetary integration of 11 European countries as of the start of 1999.

A focus on strategic considerations as explanatory ignores the complex and concealed politics of instrumentalization: who is instrumentalizing whom in relation to what? The Westphalian model of world order assumes that states are, more or less, the exclusive agents of instrumentalization. In a globalized world economy, states are themselves increasingly instrumentalized by concealed, external forces such as markets and profit margins, and their instrumentalization is expressed by way of a weakening of commitment to such foreign policy goals as human rights and environmental protection and by the reroutinization of tasks and capabilities entrusted to the United Nations. This reorientation of policy by states is exacerbated by the weakening of organized labor as a domestic and transnational factor and by the discrediting of socialism (and its main operating modes) as a normative challenge to capitalism. Such an analysis supports an argument in favor of "resituating the state" – that is, strengthening its capacity to mediate between market drives and populist social forces.[12] The relevance of regional actors is evident, but far from consistent or self-evident: what is most uncertain can be phrased by reference to the theme of instrumentalization. Formal regional structures are still being constituted overwhelmingly by state actors as members; but to what extent are the regional approaches being taken by states themselves the unacknowledged secondary effects of their instrumentalization by the global marketplace?[13] Within regional frameworks, hegemonic relations of varying sorts can be established, as seems to be the case with respect to Germany in Europe, and certainly on the part of the United States in the setting of the North American Free Trade Agreement (NAFTA), and, more generally, throughout the Western Hemisphere.

There are many dimensions of regionalism worthy of exploration and analysis at this time: four, in particular, seem to illuminate the character of the unfolding, yet still inchoate, post–cold war world order. In discussing these world order dimensions, emphasis is placed on a distinction between "positive" and "negative" as pertaining to global and regional configurations of influence and authority. "Positive" refers to desired objectives such as the reduction of political violence, the attainment of economic well-being, the promotion of human rights and benevolent governance, the protection of ecological diversity, and the safeguarding of health and renewable resources. "Negative" refers to the negation of these goals through warfare, poverty, racism, ecological decay, oppression, chaos, and criminality. In the lifeworld positive and negative aspects are intertwined, and a given set of conditions associated, say, with global market forces or authoritarian government may generate positive, as well as negative, outcomes. Economic growth, even if it generates a non-sustainable consumerist ethos, may also alleviate poverty and despair, just as milder forms of authoritarianism, while cruel to their opponents, may nevertheless provide effective leadership.

In the discussion that follows, for the sake of analytic clarity, this interplay of elements is put aside, and the discussion seeks to identify four world order concerns (two negative, two positive) that can be associated with the emergence of regional frameworks of political action alongside state and global frameworks.

Clarifying the main links between regionalism and the "containment" of negative globalism Negative globalism refers here to the conjuncture of largely non-accountable power and influence exerted by multinational corporations, transnational banks and financial arenas, and their collaborators with the ideology of consumerism and a development ethos weighted almost entirely toward returns on capital mainly achieved by maximizing growth (no matter how often qualified, yet predominantly rhetorically, by the modifier "sustainable"). In essence, the main regionalist tendencies are simultaneously both reinforcing this drift toward negative globalism and creating resistance and alternative mitigating options, including the promotion of positive globalism. (That is, the democratizing of global institutions, creating accountability and responsiveness to more democratic social forces and establishing procedures for wider participation by representatives of diverse peoples. Also relevant here is the promotion of human rights, including economic and social rights, and a capability by the UN and other international institutions to contribute more effectively to global security than is predicated upon a consensus among currently ascendant geopolitical and geoeconomic forces.)[14] It should be acknowledged that the neo-liberal ideology informing global market forces disseminates constructive ideas about freedom and the rule of law, as well as destructive notions about greed and materialism.

Strengthening of regional frameworks to help meet the challenges being posed by several manifestations of pathological anarchism The latter refers to breakdowns of order associated with political normalcy and effective patterns of governance, leading to sustained violence that includes genocidal outbreaks and other crimes against humanity, as well as chaotic conditions producing massive displacements of people from their traditional places of residence.[15] These geopolitical "black holes" attract interventionary responses, but not of a reconstructive variety, as the recent tragedies in Somalia, Liberia, Sudan, Bosnia, and Rwanda illustrate in different ways. Existing agencies of intervention, whether under the auspices of leading states or the UN Security Council, have failed in both preventive and reactive modes, although some reductions in suffering have been achieved to the extent that the intervening mission is defined in purely relief terms.[16] Can regional frameworks make selective contributions, and if so, under what circumstances? The failure of Europe in relation to Bosnia has had the short-term effect of weakening regional sentiments, except possibly through reviving, at least temporarily, the post–cold war fortunes of NATO.[17]

Facilitating a renewal of positive globalism as a world order project through the medium of enhanced regionalism The implications of the first two points are essentially negative tendencies, which can, to some extent, be diminished or redirected by certain forms of regionalization. Positive globalism conceives of a governance structure for the world that is of an aspirational character, one that promotes sustainability, human rights, development (especially in relation to poverty and other forms of deprivation), and demilitarization (reducing warfare and arms races and sales).[18] Given concerns about homogenization, cultural diversity, and excessive centralization, the encouragement of stronger regional institutions might operate both as an alternative to and complement of positive globalism, thereby providing the peoples of the world with a vision of a desirable world order.

Considering the normative achievements of regionalism in terms of its contributions to the well-being of the peoples living within its framework This conception of positive regionalism as an end in itself is quite distinct from the evaluation of regionalism as a constituent element in a structure of global governance, and it has been most fully explored, of course, in the setting of Europe, especially in the encounter between Eurocrats of various hues and Euroskeptics. But it has relevance as well to visions of a better future in Africa, Latin America, and Asia.[19]

Against this background, it is possible to explore in a tentative and preliminary manner the possible contributions of regionalism to an improved quality of world order, assessing improvement by reference to widely shared and explicitly specified world order values.

Containing Negative Globalism via Regionalism

Negative globalism refers to the adverse effects of economic and cultural integration at the global level. The integrative dynamic is not inherently negative, but it is having a series of adverse effects, given the current world order context. These effects include insensitivity to human suffering, insufficient attention to ecological sustainability, tendencies toward polarization (widening gaps between and within countries and among regions) and marginalization (virtual exclusion of countries, regions, and ethnic minorities from developmental progress).

Negative globalism also instrumentalizes the state through mounting pressures to conform to globalizing priorities that give governments little political space. States are co-opted or subordinated, weakening impulses to regulate on behalf of the common good. In this regard the world economy, as a totality, bears certain resemblances to the early capitalist period when market forces prevailed to the extent that labor was exploited in a variety of ways (long hours, low wages, unsafe conditions, no job security, and no protection in old age or in the event of emergencies). At the state level, social movements helped to create a better equilibrium between state and market, corporate and banking power being balanced to varying degrees by organized labor and by a socialist option. Of course, the evaluation of this equilibrium was controversial, diverse, and dynamic, varying from country to country and over time.

The state in democratic societies mediated between market and social forces until this role was partially superseded by the imperatives of "competitiveness" in the wider settings of the regionalization and globalization of economic life. This process was complex and contextual, reflecting many factors, including the relative efficiency and productivity of the labor force and managerial methods, the extent to which labor protection was entrenched, the degree to which competition for markets was being mounted by low-wage societies, the overall impact of the Soviet collapse on the socialist option, and the shifting class and ideological composition of civil society.

What seem beyond debate are two factors that underpin negative globalism:

The successful resistance of market forces in relation to the establishment of global regulatory regimes that restrict market and banking practices with respect to an enforceable code of conduct. The elimination of the UN Centre of Transnational Corporations in the late 1980s was an expression of the influence exerted by market forces; part of this success was associated with the instrumentalization of leading capitalist states, operating as agents of negative globalism, virtually taking the resistance option off the domestic political agenda, despite its importance for the citizenry.

The downward pull on standards of well-being exerted elsewhere by the comprador market practices in the most dynamic sectors of the world economy, especially South Asia. This downward pull is accentuated by the increasing mobility of capital and by the relative failure of states with higher standards of well-being to negotiate from strength and conviction. In other words, labor reforms in China, Indonesia, and elsewhere would reduce the incentives to relocate or invest on the basis of unevenness in the treatment of workers, thereby diminishing the downward pull on welfare and labor in countries with higher levels of business regulation. The issue is complex because severe inequality in standards of living is being selectively reduced by the capacity to increase exports from some poorer countries and may depend for a period on achieving competitiveness on the basis of lower production costs, especially labor.

Regionalism has not yet emerged as a counter to negative globalism. On the contrary, its main drive to date has been to facilitate more effective participation on a global level, either by protectionist policies or by achieving export competitiveness. The impact may again result in some leveling down of well-being and environmental standards, at least on an intra-regional basis. Sweden, to prepare for its participation in the European Union, has had to roll back aspects of its exemplary welfare system, reducing taxes and cutting some services. Regionalism has helped Europe aggregate capital and maintain technological parity with the United States and Japan and therefore avoid the fate of moderate marginalization in relation to the globalized market.

In Asia–Pacific, although the experience varies from country to country and over time, regionalism has been seen almost exclusively as a means to accelerate growth of trade and investment, avoid marginalization, and combine capital, resources, labor, and market without regard to statist boundaries. The "regionalism" of Asia, especially recently, has not been based on the whole region or even on whole countries, but on privileging high-growth segments of society, leading to the emergence of so-called regional states.[20] Of course, it is misleading to assimilate the reality of states in the full Westphalian sense into the terminology of regionalism. The analogy is suggestive, but only if assessed critically in terms of its actual properties of control over a territorial domain that encompasses a clearly demarcated region. The notion of state implies an effective governmental center, clear and generally accepted boundaries, and a status that is accepted beyond the region in diplomatic relations. Europe, as the most developed region institutionally, has not yet clarified its boundaries: will Turkey be part of Europe? Surely, the East European countries will be included, but what of Russia and the Ukraine? And does "Europe" include the space of countries that remain formally separate as Switzerland and Norway have chosen to do?

The economic achievements of regional arrangements of different sorts are impressive in many respects, but *not* in relation to the containment of negative globalism – at least, not yet. Indeed, the contrary conclusion is more illuminating: that regional formations, especially with respect to the three main trading/investing blocs, have served to consolidate the negative features of global economic integration. This consolidating role has been played out by removing economic policy from the realm of domestic politics, an aspect of weakening the state as a mediating actor between territorial concerns, especially of those being marginalized, and global market forces. It is confirmatory, as well, that regionalism has not taken hold in those settings that are being most marginalized by the world economy and, further, that religious extremism in Islamic countries has produced a partly voluntary, partly involuntary, delinking from the world economy.

There are additional kinds of evidence. Recent efforts by the US government to build support within the citizenry for NAFTA were distinctively bipartisan at the level of elite politics. President Clinton was able to mobilize all five living presidents for the signing ceremony, a show of bipartisanship that would be neither possible (degree of consensus) nor necessary (extent of societal opposition) on any other issue of policy. Also, it seems anomalous that a president representing the Democratic Party would so unconditionally support NAFTA, given its Republican lineage and the hostile attitude of almost every labor union and of most liberal constituencies (environmental, church, and social activist). But it is not a true anomaly. It is an expression of the instrumentalization of state power in the strongest of states in relation to the priorities of economic globalism. Such an assessment is confirmed by the Zapatista revolt of Mexican Indians, centered in Chiapas, which began in 1994 and was timed to coincide with the formal start of NAFTA, expressing this awareness that economic regionalism and negative globalism were being reinforced at the expense of the most vulnerable ethnic and economic sectors of Mexican society.

Negative globalism is also – possibly preeminently – embodied in the World Trade Organization (WTO) arrangements of the Uruguay Round of the General Agreement on Tariffs and Trade (GATT), which create the institutional and political foundations for what has been described as the basis for an "economic autocracy" by their critics.[21] Both the modes of negotiation and the efforts to avoid full constitutional review, as would be appropriate if the latest GATT arrangements were regarded as a treaty requiring ratification, are expressive of this dynamic of instrumentalization. Within the United States the executive branch is most responsive, by and large, to these globalist pressures, while the Congress remains more influenced by local and territorial factors, more resistant, as a result, to the pure allure of nonterritorial influences. Such a GATT framework, elevating the priority to be accorded unencumbered trade, also operates to ensure conformity at the regional level, making an electoral choice of social democracy almost impossible to implement in practice.

Mitigating Pathological Anarchism

Labeling internal deformations of state power as "pathological" implies a conception of normalcy in the relations of state and society that has broken down; to associate this normalcy with the anarchy of international relations is to stress the structural point that institutions of global governance are very weak.[22] "Pathological anarchism" refers to acute political disorder: genocide, severe crimes against humanity, large-scale famine, substantial breakdowns of government.

In the long Westphalia period of international relations, pathological anarchism was essentially ignored unless the strategic interests of leading states were seriously threatened. Such threats were rarely perceived unless the governmental actor in question embarked upon expansion at the expense of the existing distribution of power informing world order. The response to Nazi Germany and the Stalinist Soviet Union are paradigmatic in both respects: appeasement or, at most, containment with respect to the pathological behavior, but willingness to risk everything to prevent territorial expansions that seek to revise the hierarchy of relations that inform world order. It is not that the pathological dimension is irrelevant. Indeed, especially in relation to democratic societies, the pathological character of a rival is relied upon to mobilize the resources and commitments needed to conduct warfare or to practice containment credibly.

The corollary point is that if the pathology does not pose external threats, it will be tolerated.[23] This has been demonstrated again in the period since the end of the cold war in the much discussed instances of Somalia, Bosnia, Haiti, and Rwanda. Perhaps the situation is more ambiguous: the historical memory of the Holocaust has encouraged the sentiment of "never again," particularly in Europe, and this has generated interventionary pressures in relation to Bosnia; the CNN factor selectively lifts the veil of ignorance from the occurrence of acute distress and induces public support for constructive responses; the entrenchment of human rights in international law has eroded the sovereignty arguments that abuses within states are of no concern externally. As a result, there have been responses to the recent instances of pathological anarchism, but of a half-hearted character as compared to the response mounted to reverse Iraq's aggression against Kuwait. These responses, collaborations between the UN and leading states, especially the United States, have provided a measure of relief for elements of the afflicted populations, but have not challenged the core pathologies. What has been relied upon has been diplomacy, sanctions, relief operations, and pinprick assertions of military power. The sum of these efforts is *less* than its parts!

To the extent that responses have moved toward more serious levels of commitment, this has resulted from boundary-transcending impacts such as the prospects of a wider war in the Balkans and the outflow of refugees causing destabilizing effects in important state actors (US, Germany, and France). These possible developments convert pathological anarchism into an occasion for strategic concern (justifying large allocations of resources and risks of loss of life), raising the stakes in the event that containment fails. Also, in relation to refugees, the alternatives of repatriation or deterrence may both fail, leaving only the option of military intervention. Such an interpretation of the situation in Haiti during the summer of 1994 has made some commentators write of intervention as "inevitable."

Enter regionalism: both states and the UN have failed to address pathological anarchism effectively. Could this failure be overcome, in some circumstances, by the empowerment of regional institutions? Could NATO act in the former Yugoslavia to challenge Serbian "aggression," restoring order and a unified, multiethnic Bosnia? Could the Organization of American States (OAS) bring constitutional democracy to Haiti? Could the Organization of African Unity (OAU) act in relation to Somalia, Rwanda, Burundi, Sudan, or Liberia?

These questions return us to the theme of instrumentalization. To the extent that regional actors are effective in peacekeeping or peace enforcement, it is because they are carrying out the policies of their leading members: states – especially, of course, hegemonic states. Further, to the extent that these leading states have themselves been instrumentalized by negative globalism, there is not much prospect that the pathological challenges posed within an organized region will produce a response different in kind from that issuing from the global level. In essence, the conception of strategic interest will not be very different, except for its geographical and cultural proximity. If regional capabilities include impressive military assets, then if strategic interests are deemed present, as has seemed weakly to be the case from time to time in relation to Bosnia, then the availability of NATO to act is definitely a potential factor in any move to challenge the core pathology. Nullifying this potentiality is the extent to which proximity may fracture collaborative possibilities, each major state perceiving its interests in handling the crisis in a distinct manner and being distrustful of its rivals; such rivalry has been operative in relation to Bosnia from the outset, varying in intensity over time.

The major conclusion to be drawn is that regional communities have not evolved to the point where their institutional ethos or capabilities are sufficient to address pathological anarchism in a manner comparable to the efforts made by competent and constitutionally moderate states in relation to pathologies embedded within their own polities. States, too, are not always effective, sometimes accommodating, containing, collaborating, and sometimes being instrumentalized from below by the pathology, or even having the pathology capture legitimate state power (as Hitler did in Germany in 1933). Can (should) regional actors be encouraged to take on these ordering tasks, especially the protection of those most victimized by pathological anarchism, as part of a commitment to both implement human rights and maintain regional peace and justice? The dilemma posed here seems quite fundamental: to be effective and autonomous (that is, non-instrumentalized), regional institutions would have to become cohesive and capable of commanding loyalty, thereby coming to resemble in certain respects a state of Westphalian lineage. But such an evolution would seem likely on a global level to stimulate inter-regional conflict among regions of greatly different resource bases and civilizational identities, making it more credible that "a clash of civilizations" would indeed ensue as the sequel to the cold war.

Promoting Positive Globalism

There are two intersecting traditions at work: first, anxiety that effective global governance cannot avoid encroachments on human freedom unless it avoids centralism; a regionalized world order is one approach to reconciling the quest for global governance with a concern for constitutional equilibrium and, to a lesser extent, with the preservation of cultural diversity.[24] The overriding goals in this outlook are so ambitious – transforming statism, ignoring globalization – in relation to the flow of events and horizons of aspiration, that evolution of this possibility has scarcely been under serious consideration in academic circles. A more moderate expression of this view is somewhat more influential, in the form of an advocacy of "subsidiarity" via regional institutions as a way of allocating downward from the UN, particularly with respect to security issues, and thus in the context of delimiting the UN role. Such an approach borrows from the European experience, which evidently borrowed from a Vatican doctrinal tradition. This approach is meaningful, of course, only to the extent that viable regional institutions exist, which is not the case, with the possible exception of Europe and in extremely limited respects Central and South America and Africa.[25]

The second approach here is to view regional institutions as complementary and subordinate tools of global governance, shaped within the UN and contributing in various settings to either effectiveness or legitimacy or some combination of these. The UN Charter seems to envisage such a relationship in Chapter VIII.[26] Since effective regional governance has so often in international history meant interventionary diplomacy by a hegemonic state, and hence geopolitics, it has been viewed with suspicion by those disposed toward more law-oriented modes of governance. The revival of practice and advocacy of spheres of influence is suggestive of a post–cold war pattern that acknowledges the failures of the UN in the setting of pathological anarchism; but it can hardly be properly identified as a variant of "positive globalism."[27] Conservatives often lend credibility to the view that international institutions add elements of constitutional moderation to traditional modes of interventionism and discretionary geopolitics, conceiving of recourse to the UN or a regional actor as confusing, hypocritical, and superfluous.[28]

At this point, it is difficult to credit regionalism with being more than an occasional instrument for the assertion of hegemonic control that, depending on circumstances, can be viewed as either legitimated by collective procedures or not. The US intervention in Panama in 1989 was carried out despite the refusal to accord it legitimacy at either the regional or the UN level, whereas intervention in Haiti enjoyed both regional and UN blessings. There is some difference; yet in both contexts intervention is essentially a hegemonic initiative (shaped in Washington, with respect to time, goals, modalities, and battlefield control).

Regionalism in relation to the emergence of positive globalism remains a latent potentiality. The Charter gives ample space for complementary regional roles in peacekeeping settings, and in Article 52(3) expresses a favorable disposition toward resolution of disputes at a regional level, thereby seeming to endorse subsidiarity. Again, context matters; Castro's Cuba is under more intense hegemonic pressures as a regional pariah than it is in the UN setting.[29] It would seem that the virtues of regionalism in relation to positive globalism are, at present, mainly speculative. Its more serious relevance would arise as a derivation from the emergence of positive globalism, not currently in the offing.

Promoting Positive Regionalism

Regionalism has achieved positive results in relation to specified world order values in several substantive sectors and various geographic settings, most significantly, of course, in Europe, but also in Asia–Pacific, Latin America, Africa, and the Middle East.[30] The most impressive of these achievements involve promotion of human rights, including revolutionary sovereignty-eroding procedures, as embodied in the European framework and to a lesser extent within the Inter-American setting;[31] mitigation and resolution of conflicts via diplomacy, mediation, and regional linkages; promotion of environmentalism; innovations in transnational cooperation and institutionalization; and experimentation by way of the Maastricht Treaty, with innovative extensions of political identity by way of the conferral of European citizenship.[32]

Perhaps, most significantly, regionalism has protected the peoples of Europe against deteriorating standards of living and the prospects of gradual marginalization. This protection has been somewhat controversial because of its tendency to build pressure by way of competitiveness to conform to the requirements imposed by negative globalism. The latter has contributed both to high levels of unemployment and to static, or even falling, real wage levels in Europe and North America. An assessment is not a simple matter. To the degree that regionalism has been instrumentalized by negative globalism (as argued earlier), then it forms part of an overall global structure of dominance that is leading to acute marginalization for certain nations and regions, sectors deemed inefficient and uninviting if considered either as producers or consumers. The geographic distribution has some North–South features, but the burdens of marginalization are not so neatly configured, given the rise of South and East Asia and parts of South America. This disregard of marginalization is exacerbated by the ideological consensus in support of neo-liberal economism in elite circles and reinforced by the abandonment of socialist and welfare-oriented perspectives by even the leading Social Democratic parties in Europe.

With respect to economic regionalization, the most important recent steps have involved Europe, North America, and Asia–Pacific. The cumulative impact on peoples within and outside these more integrated trading blocs is, as yet, conjectural and intensely contested. Whether the characterization "positive regionalism" is appropriate cannot be determined until more evidence on effects has been gathered. A worst-case assessment would suggest that regionalism is serving as a cover for the re-entrenchment of relations of privilege and domination that were challenged during the revolt against colonialism. A best-case scenario would attribute inequality in benefits and burdens to the short run, with a more equitable, sustainable, and democratic global economic order emerging in response to grass-roots and other challenges mounted against negative globalism.

In the Asia–Pacific region, the internal dimension of regionalism is to take early, mainly informal, and *ad hoc* steps toward economic cooperation and coordination, viewing the Association of Southeast Asian Nations (ASEAN) especially as possessing a potential for expansion and further institutionalization in the post–cold war era. These steps are reinforced by a new Asian cultural assertiveness, which both moves toward the affirmation of a regional identity and also represents a deepening of the decolonization process by its implicit repudiation of Euro-centricism.

In this regard, Asian–Pacific regionalism resists any renewal of Western hegemonic projects and helps explain Asian unity with respect to opposing doctrines of humanitarian intervention to correct abuses of human rights or to remove military rulers from power. As such, Asian–Pacific regionalism, even more than its European counterpart, may be moving toward limiting the Western, especially the United States, role, thereby encouraging a defensive dimension of regionalism.

A Concluding Note

More specific inquiries may help to clarify the impact of regionalism on world order values. This chapter has tried to conceptualize several main contexts in which regionalism has seemed dynamic in this post–cold war period, taking special account of hegemonic passivity on a global level (the disappearance of strategic, zero-sum rivalry, inducing a shrinking of perceived strategic interests; a rising sense of domestic opposition,

increased realization that power projection is expensive and often inconclusive in relation to "black hole" challenges), disappointment in the
limited capacity of the United Nations to provide a less hegemonic, yet
effective, world order, and the overbearing reality of globalization with
respect to markets, money, and information. Little ground for optimism
has been found with respect to regionalism as either a counter-
hegemonic democratizing influence or as a source of a new kind of
benign hegemonic order (although the trend toward the reactivation of
spheres of influence is clearly evident in Russia's effort to provide leadership and exert control over the new states that were formerly Soviet
republics; and by the United States in relation to the Western Hemisphere, especially Central America, through a reassertion of the Monroe
Doctrine as an ingredient of foreign policy; and by France in relation to
Francophonic countries in North and sub-Saharan Africa).

From a world order perspective the role of regionalism is to help
create a new equilibrium in politics that balances the protection of the
vulnerable and the interests of humanity as a whole (including future
generations) against the integrative, technological dynamic associated
with globalism.[33] One kind of balance is being promoted by transnational
social forces connected with human rights and the environment, but
regionalism could be another. Both phenomena are, in part, reactions to
the displacement of the state, from without and within, and the decline
of sovereign territorial space as a domain of unconditional political
control. Regionalism, if democratically conditioned, might yet provide,
at least for some parts of the whole, a world order compromise between
statism and globalism that has indispensable benefits for the circumstances of humanity, as well as some new dangers.

A recurrent theme of postmodern thought is the stress upon unde-
cidability. The rational grasp of reality does not resolve difficult issues of
choice. The cynical view is that such a circumstance ensures that interests will prevail, and there is support for such a reading of the times, particularly given the rise and spread of crime and even the danger of
the gangster-co-opted state. A more hopeful view is that the tendencies
toward democratization and human rights can be focused in the years
ahead on the menaces of negative globalism and pathological anarchism,
and that regional arenas will be important as sites of struggle and as
exemplification of the play of opposed forces.

Part II
Substantive Dimensions

5

The Illegitimacy of the Non-Proliferation Regime

There is a consensus in United States policymaking circles that preventing the proliferation of nuclear weaponry is the top foreign policy priority of the post–cold war world. A typical assertion along these lines is that of Michael Mazzarr at the start of an article on American efforts to halt the North Korean nuclear weapons program: "Halting the spread of weapons of mass destruction has become, in the minds of many US officials and analysts, the dominant post–cold war US national interest."[1] Even in the setting of United States–Russian relations, the most important arms control goal has been articulated by a recent blue-ribbon panel of prominent specialists as "preventing nuclear anarchy," by which is meant "leakage" to others from "Russia's huge inventories of nuclear weapons and fissile material."[2] This preoccupation with proliferation also underlies the revival of support, this time with the surprising bipartisan backing by a Democratic president, of a defense shield that its proponents claim might sometime early in the next century provide protection against nuclear missiles launched by a country that had managed to acquire or produce a few nuclear warheads.

It is difficult to explain the priority accorded to non-proliferation policy in US government policy, partly because it is doubtful that the official rationale expresses the whole story. The external focus of proliferation concern, despite its articulation in general world order terms, is clearly where it has always been, on the acquisition of these weapons by Third World countries, but especially by that subset of countries currently perceived as hostile to the sort of international stability being promoted by the United States. For instance, virtually no notice has been accorded to Japanese or German acquisition of the technical capabilities to support a possible future mid-scale nuclear weapons program, despite their record of past militarism and the possibility of serious political tensions arising from their economic rivalry with the United States.

Michael Klare has persuasively argued that US non-proliferation efforts in recent years have been mainly directed against the so-called rogue states, a shifting classification currently consisting of Iraq, Iran, Libya, Syria, and North Korea.[3] Klare also emphasizes the extent to which non-proliferation policy is underpinned by domestic considerations. He contends that the recent emphasis on this "rogue doctrine," as he calls it, represents the best effort of the Pentagon to play a meaningful international security role, thereby justifying a high defense budget, in a global setting that now lacks any credible strategic threat.[4] Regardless of motive, the result of such a preoccupation is to associate danger to world order more than ever with the possibility that a specific group of Third World countries will acquire nuclear weapons (and/or other weapons of mass destruction).

In my view, this kind of selective – and somewhat myopic and hyped – focus on non-proliferation has several detrimental effects on world order and opportunities for peace and security that are especially unfortunate within the current historical setting.[5] Such lines of criticism are not meant to imply that proliferation of such weaponry is desirable or of only trivial significance, even on a highly selective basis, although there are ultra-realists who have made such an argument.[6] The spotlighting of non-proliferation, together with the inconsistent implementation of the alleged general concern, has the following serious adverse consequences: it deflects attention from the dangers of nuclear weaponry; it overlooks opportunities for, and beneficial contributions of, nuclear disarmament, particularly if directed at achieving an overall demilitarization of international security; it diminishes the legitimacy of world order; and it reflects a posture that contradicts the mandates of international law, international morality, the political consensus of states, and the dictates of world public opinion. The remainder of this chapter will consider these criticisms of the geopolitics of nuclearism – that is, the ways in which the boundaries between the retention and denial of the nuclear weapons status quo are being managed by the nuclear weapons states, especially under the aegis of the US government.[7]

The dangers of nuclear weaponry   The non-proliferation focus is premised on the monumental misconception that the greatest dangers of nuclear weapons arise from those that do not currently possess the weapons, or that possess a minuscule arsenal, as distinct from the nuclear weapons states that have arsenals containing hundreds, and in some cases thousands, of nuclear warheads, as well as sophisticated means to ensure their delivery over long distances. In contrast, the rogue states, even with a handful of nuclear weapons, would be inviting their own annihilation if they ever launched or even seriously threatened to use a single nuclear warhead. As was evident in the Gulf War, such states could be effectively destroyed without reliance on nuclear weaponry, given the superiority of the United States and its closest allies in conventional weaponry, an international condition that is being projected well into the next century.[8]

In the background is the historical reality that atomic weapons were used to close out a victorious war, an occasion justified by the argument of saving lives on the battlefield and shortening the ordeal of World War II. Such a justification for the use of this weaponry has been generally accepted by public opinion in the United States and suggests in the present global setting the danger of some new "Hiroshima Temptation" – that is, a set of circumstances in which battlefield conditions suggest a considerable military advantage deriving from the threat or use of nuclear weaponry in circumstances where no prospect of retaliation exists. Throughout the cold war era nuclear deterrence was mutual, even if not entirely symmetrical. As a result, the inhibition on use was reinforced by a strong survival motive; despite this, on a number of occasions, nuclear threats were delivered to Third World adversaries so as to influence negotiations. Without the inhibition on use provided by the prospect of retaliation or escalation, the pressures to rely on nuclear weaponry in future conflict situations could become great, especially given the recent expectations that future wars could be successfully fought with virtually zero casualties on the American side.[9]

It is difficult to anticipate future war scenarios, but it is likely that conflict patterns will not be projections of present alignments. Samuel Huntington sets out what he calls "highly improbable but not impossible" conflict spirals ending in inter-civilizational war between the West and either the Islamic world or China.[10] In such altered geopolitical circumstances, exacerbated by inter-civilizational tensions, it may be far more difficult than during the cold war to manage hostile relationships in accordance with the dictates of prudence. In such a setting it would seem less dangerous if nuclear weapons were not a policy option. Preventive disarmament may be more relevant to future security relations than preventive war has been to the security of states in the past.

Finally, a high moral and cultural cost is paid by the willingness of a state to rely on weapons of mass destruction as an active ingredient of security policy, as has been the case for the United States and its close allies ever since 1945.[11] Every serious moral inquiry into nuclear

weaponry has found it impossible to condone the indiscriminate and catastrophic features of such weaponry except as a tragic adjustment to the
paradoxical circumstances of deterrence – that is, reliance to discourage
use by others, aptly named a balance of terror.[12] In contrast to reliance,
a serious commitment to denuclearizing and demilitarizing would be
morally uplifting in a manner that would help overcome the ambivalence
toward mass violence that is now embedded in the political cultures of
American and other modern societies.

Suppression of the disarmament alternative   The preoccupation with
non-proliferation is coupled with a strong tendency to hold constant the
rest of the military landscape, save a partial receptivity to cost-saving and
risk-managing measures of arms control. Such an orientation toward
nuclear weaponry excludes any serious inquiry into the prospects for disarmament and other forms of demilitarization as a policy option. In
this respect, it sustains the commitment of the nuclear weapons states to
weaponry of mass destruction by keeping the issue entirely outside the
realm of serious political discourse. In recent reviews of security policy
by mainstream specialists, the possibility of disarmament is not even
mentioned, much less evaluated. As Sherlock Holmes reminded us, it is
often crucial to be attentive to the dog that doesn't bark!

From many viewpoints such a neglect is deeply unfortunate. To begin
with, the altered international political context would seem to favor
a phased disarmament process, especially as associated with nuclear
weapons. It is true that secondary and undisclosed nuclear weapons states
might turn out to have the greatest dependence on these weapons as they
often lack nonnuclear alternatives to achieve their principle security
goals. In this respect, leaders in France, the United Kingdom, Russia, and
Israel may at this point sincerely believe that nuclear weapons are *needed*
for purposes of national security. Such considerations would undoubtedly
complicate any move toward a world free of nuclear weaponry, but it
would not preclude it. Giving the United States the global role of being
the major proponent of nuclear disarmament and alternative security
might rekindle creative energies on behalf of a truly beneficial "new
world order" that would reestablish American credentials to play a leadership role on the global stage. It would be a healing and legitimating
posture with respect to most countries in the world and would remove the
stigma of nuclearism from American foreign policy. It would also liberate
financial resources and the energies of the scientific and engineering communities in a manner that might facilitate a societal recommitment to
such currently under-supported public goods as education, health, environment, urban renewal, and welfare.

Diminished legitimacy of world order and US leadership Structures of authority work best when their reliance on coercion is minimized. This means that their norms of behavior are accepted voluntarily and thus with a sense of their inherent reasonableness and fairness, which adds up to an acknowledgment of legitimacy. The role of legitimacy in achieving policy objectives is of particular importance in international society, given the absence of centralized and impartial third-party procedures of interpretation and enforcement.[13] When the legitimacy of a legal regime is weak, compliance depends on a mixture of self-interest and geopolitical enforcement by dominant state actors. When geopolitical means are relied upon, the tendency is to implement norms against adversaries and to overlook violations by friends, which accentuates an impression of illegitimacy by its unequal treatment of equals. Such generalizations are particularly applicable, as with non-proliferation, in relation to peace and security issues.

Thomas Franck has usefully identified legitimacy with "*a pull towards compliance with those addressed normatively.*"[14] The approach taken by the United States to nuclear weaponry undermines in fundamental respects the very possibility of legitimacy associated with the structure and practices of world order and encourages perceptions of hypocrisy with respect to alleged concerns over non-proliferation, terrorism, and weaponry of mass destruction. This criticism can be reinforced by reference, first of all, to the selectivity of concern exhibited in relation to countries suspected of having developed or obtained nuclear weapons.[15] At one end of the scale is Israel, a country that achieved a nuclear weapons capability without evoking any expression of opposition by nuclear weapons states, particularly the United States, and is generally supposed to have received various forms of external governmental assistance.[16] At the other end of the scale is North Korea and Iraq, whose sovereign rights have been challenged in fundamental respects, partly as a result of suspicions that a nuclear weapons program was under way. Such a discriminatory pattern of geopolitical enforcement could, in theory, be rationalized by reference to perceived threats of use or aggressiveness. But such a justification is not convincing with respect to non-proliferation. After all, it is Israel that has been involved in a series of wars with its Arab neighbors, has expanded its territorial claims considerably since its founding in 1948, and was widely reported to be seriously contemplating reliance on nuclear weapons if the adversity of the first few days of the 1973 war had persisted.

Nor can this discrimination be satisfactorily explained by the intensity of a perceived security threat. As has often been noted, international society remains primarily a self-help system in relation to security; the

United Nations promise of providing effective forms of collective security on behalf of victims of aggression has, with rare exceptions (for example, Kuwait, 1990; South Korea, 1950), been unfulfilled. In this regard, Israel's perceived vulnerability to hostile neighbors makes it reasonable for it to acquire the most destructive conceivable deterrent; but the same justifying conditions apply, with even greater persuasiveness, to the situation of North Korea. Israel has the benefit of having the United States as a powerful and committed ally and enjoys positive relations with a number of other countries, whereas North Korea has been confronted by a hostile United States and was on the receiving end of nuclear threats in the latter stages of the Korean War.[17] Indeed, especially since the end of the cold war, North Korea seems to have been confronted by a much more menacing security environment than that facing Israel, being isolated and seemingly on the brink of internal economic collapse, as well as faced with South Korea's oft-proclaimed ambition to achieve reunification under its aegis.

A further facet of the non-proliferation regime's illegitimacy is the failure by the nuclear weapons states to fulfill their part of the bargain embodied in the Non-Proliferation Treaty of 1968. In exchange for the commitment by nonnuclear states to renounce their option to acquire such weaponry, the nuclear weapons states in Article VI of the Treaty committed themselves "to pursue negotiations in good faith on effective measures relating to . . . nuclear disarmament, and on a treaty on general and complete disarmament under strict and effective international control."[18] This commitment, which implicitly gives a legal and political sanction to the ideal of a world without nuclear weaponry and to an overall posture of demilitarizing international security, has never been seriously implemented and, as such, appears to constitute a continuing fundamental breach of the underlying world order bargain that endowed the non-proliferation regime set up by the treaty with its original legitimacy.

This breach is further aggravated by the dynamics of geopolitical manipulation of the treaty regime, oscillating between the extremes of over- and under-implementation. As mentioned, Israel and, to some extent, India and Pakistan were allowed to proceed with their nuclear weapons programs on a covert basis, while North Korea was warned that any effort on its part to exercise its *legal* option to withdraw from the NPT would be treated as provocative and impermissible.[19]

Respected commentators from Third World countries have over the years consistently derided the non-proliferation emphasis and regime as part of an overall Western posture labeled "nuclear apartheid."[20] In their view, the retention of nuclear weapons, even in the setting of the cold war, was motivated primarily by hegemonic ambitions, especially as coupled with the insistence that Third World countries should accept their permanent exclusion from the nuclear club. In this respect, from a legitimacy perspective, non-proliferation is better understood as the subordinate goal for world order, while renunciation of a nuclear option and rejection of the weaponry by all states is the primary goal. The illegitimacy of the present world order is highlighted by the fact that since the end of the cold war and the removal of the main deterrence rationale for the weaponry, there has not been evident any disposition by the nuclear weapons states to initiate negotiations dedicated to the elimination of nuclear weaponry, or even to accept firm limitations on their own options to use nuclear weapons on a discretionary basis.[21] This failure is particularly notable in the 1990s, with the erosion of the rationale for mutual deterrence at a strategic level, and given the absence of any fundamental geopolitical cleavage in relations among major states. Its depth is further evidenced by the refusal to accord even lip service to Article VI obligations in mainstream literature on non-proliferation, which interprets the regime as being one-sidedly directed at preventing the spread of the weaponry rather than, as negotiated, based on the reciprocal obligation to roll back reliance on, and possession of, nuclear weaponry by the nuclear weapons states.

In relation to legitimacy, then, non-proliferation arrangements have an extremely low status, and are perceived, especially in the Third World, as hegemonic in character, a reflection of geopolitical preoccupations rather than of an impartial regime maintained for the global common good. This perception is underscored by the coding of status in world politics. The highest formal ranking in international society is provided by permanent membership on the United Nations Security Council. It is notable, in this regard, that the five permanent members are precisely the five declared nuclear weapons states. So considered, the symbolic language of world order is rather incoherent: nuclear weapons endow their possessors with entry to the highest level of the international hierarchy, but the effort to achieve possession is stigmatized as pernicious to a degree that warrants demotion to the lowest level, that of pariah status, and may prompt intervention or even preventive war.

Even at this late date several steps could be taken in the spirit of seriousness by the nuclear weapons states to reconcile their policies toward the weaponry with the alleged priority accorded the non-proliferation regime: a joint, multilateral declaration by nuclear weapons states to renounce unconditionally first-use options; a proposal, especially tabled by the US government, outlining a phased process of total nuclear disarmament; a commitment by all NPT parties to implement the treaty as written fully, without exceptions, and impartially; an announced willingness to put carefully drafted plans for genuine and complete disarmament on the table at the next NPT review conference or in some other appropriate forum.

Inconsistency with prevailing views of international law, international morality, political consensus of states, and world public opinion The retention of nuclear weapons by the nuclear weapons states, without the explicit adoption of a kind of minimalist use posture and in the absence of credible efforts to negotiate nuclear disarmament, seems clearly to violate prevailing norms and currents of opinion.[22] Recently, such a tension between law and practice was dramatically expressed in an Advisory Opinion of the International Court of Justice. The Opinion held by a strong majority that a minimal reading of international law suggests that nuclear weapons are generally illegal, except, conceivably, in circumstances of "extreme self-defense where the survival of a state" is at issue.[23]

Similarly, with respect to international morality, especially as expressed in Third World settings, it is virtually taken for granted that any form of reliance on nuclear weaponry is immoral. In this regard, the continuous testing and development of new generations of nuclear weapons systems and doctrine are interpreted as an immoral embrace of this weaponry. Scholarly observers over the years have also linked reliance on nuclear weapons with a genocidal mentality, which is to consider such forms of security as tantamount to ultimate depravity.[24] In the World Court case, the strongest denunciations of the existing pattern of nuclearism came from three anti-nuclear dissenting judges each hailing from a Third World country.[25] In addition, the decision strongly invokes the legal obligation to pursue nuclear disarmament in good faith, a conclusion that enjoyed the unanimous support of the fourteen participating judges and was backed by the recognition that it was highly unlikely that the nuclear weapons states would otherwise assent to an effective regime of prohibition directed at threats or uses of the weaponry.

A political consensus of states favors the renunciation of nuclear use options, the criminalizing of threats or uses, and the initiation of nuclear disarmament negotiations. This consensus is evidenced by a series of General Assembly resolutions which stretches back at least to 1963.[26]

International morality has always exhibited a strong anti-nuclear bias. The most authoritative inquiry into the moral status of nuclear weapons was contained in a famous Pastoral Letter issued in 1983 by the North American bishops of the Roman Catholic Church, which emphasized the obligation to seek nuclear disarmament in some feasible form as an urgent priority and gave an exceedingly reluctant and conditional approval to a posture of limited, second-strike deterrence given the realities of the cold war. Clearly, the burden of the letter was the inability to reconcile nuclear weaponry with the just war tradition.[27] Michael Walzer's influential assessment of this same set of issues reaches similar conclusions.[28] It is logically possible, of course, to ground an ethical argument on support for existing approaches to nuclear weaponry, thereby reconciling morality with prevailing strategic and policy perspectives; but it fails to achieve moral resonance outside the framework of nuclearist assumptions about the world.[29]

World public opinion opposes the existence of nuclear weaponry unconditionally. Whenever dangers of nuclear war have surfaced, strong manifestations of anti-nuclear sentiments have followed, prompting reassuring moves by the nuclear weapons states. Such an outlook is predominant in the Third World, as evidenced by both support for nuclear-free zones and grass-roots opposition to nuclear testing.[30]

Conclusion The current effort to implement the non-proliferation regime on a selective basis against certain pariah states is subject to a series of objections. The existing non-proliferation approach is harmful generally to the quality of world order and, in addition, distorts priorities with respect to non-proliferation itself, but, more significantly, in relation to its indirect acquiescence in the persistence of nuclear weaponry as a continuing feature of international life. The above analysis argues, in effect, that the existing non-proliferation regime – that is, the combination of the treaty and its geopolitical implementation – is currently seriously flawed. Two lines of solution are recommended: either implement the NPT as negotiated, thereby giving serious effect to the mandate to pursue nuclear disarmament, or heed the implications of the majority decision in the recent Advisory Opinion of the World Court and conform doctrine and practice to its views as to the narrow, conceivable legal use of nuclear weapons and the legal duty to seek negotiated nuclear disarmament. To go on ignoring these fundamental flaws of the nuclear status quo is to contribute to the wider conviction throughout the Third World of an illegitimate world order.[31]

6

The Quest for Human Rights

The Surprising Emergence of Human Rights in the Last Half-Century

A Westphalian conception of world order would appear resistant to the emergence of human rights, the latter being understood primarily as claims against governments to uphold certain standards of behavior in the treatment of their citizens.[1] The fundamental binding idea of the modern juridical framework based on territorial sovereignty is that governments are not subject to standards or procedures of external accountability in the treatment of their own citizens or others under their control without an official expression of prior consent.[2] And this jural thinking reflects the underlying Hobbesian view of an anarchic international society in which community and civic ties are absent, and morality and legality have little role to play.[3] This understanding of statist logic underpins "realist" schools of thought about international politics, with its stress on "national interests" as the only reliable guide for policymakers and leaders and its critical rejection of any higher morality in international life as a courtship with dangerous utopian illusions.[4]

Thus it seems natural to inquire as to why governments have voluntarily subverted an earlier unconditional sovereignty by participating in the creation by stages of an elaborate normative architecture that began to be explicitly constructed in 1948 with the formulation of the Universal Declaration of Human Rights, which has turned out to be one of the most seminal documents ever enunciated through the operations of the traditional intergovernmental dynamics of the "old multilateralism."[5]

The same sort of inquiry could be made with reference to the imposition of international criminal liability in the immediate aftermath of

World War II; of course, to the extent that the Nuremberg innovation was limited to the leaders of the defeated countries, the subversive impact seemed containable in its wider challenge to sovereign preroga- tives. The tension in this setting was between the impulse to avoid having the war crimes trials scorned as "victors' justice" and the threat posed to statism in the future by the idea of a generalized criminal accountabil- ity.[6] Interestingly, in direct contrast to their stance on human rights, both superpowers refrained from accusing their rival of violations of the Nuremberg Principles, although there were several situations during the cold war years in which such accusations would have been definitely plausible. The difference in treatment can probably be best explained by recognizing that governments could handle human rights claims, dis- counting them as hostile propaganda, whereas the war crimes accusa- tions would directly engage the reputations and legitimacy of the highest leaders, rendering diplomatic contact problematic, and in the case of the West, would play into the hands of extremist political opposition at home.[7]

It seems evident at the outset that no such subversive intention was being consciously promoted by formulating in more specific terms the generalized Charter mandate expressed in the Preamble and Article 1 to promote human rights. The drafters of the Universal Declaration were not heavyweight diplomats, but idealists briefly called in from the cold to take on a task that was viewed cynically or indifferently at the time by top leaders, a matter of trivial relevance to the conduct of govern- ment or diplomacy, whether human rights were conceived of as a matter of commitments to shape internal governance (directed at the self) or commitments to influence foreign policy (an instrument directed at the other). The advent of international human rights started off as mainly a public relations undertaking in a post–World War II atmosphere domi- nated by the United States, an interpretation, strongly supported by the *declaratory* character of the foundational document, signaling the absence of any American enforcement intent.[8] Additionally, some of the governments that proclaimed their endorsement of the Universal Dec- laration were, even at the time, administering public order systems that were tightly controlled and systematically oppressive; that is, there existed in 1948 a manifest contradiction between the norms being endorsed and prevailing patterns of behavior. Why, then, would such political leaders expose themselves to claims based on their failure to adhere to the norms that had been officially and previously endorsed within the legitimizing framework of the United Nations? The partici- pating governments and their leaders undoubtedly perceived these early moves to internationalize human rights in many different ways, but hardly anyone viewed such initiatives as a significant potential threat to the unobstructed exercise of sovereign rights.

Yet the historical setting of the late 1940s seems best to explain why the human rights project was launched within the UN framework so soon after the Organization was founded and despite the onset of East–West tensions. The general atmosphere of public opinion in the West, as shaped by the United States, emphasized the failure of the liberal democracies to heed Nazi internal repressiveness in the years of buildup to World War II, and it was widely regarded as important to posit an international humanitarian responsibility in relation to the reemergence of totalitarian abuses in the future. Further, the Communist countries were already battling the West for the ideological high ground with respect to issues of societal well-being and thus regarded diplomacy relating to human rights as an opportunity to challenge the Western emphasis on individual civil and political rights by championing and invoking the socialist emphasis on economic and social rights of a collective nature.[9] By contrast, the Communist governments were prepared to give lip service to the constitutionalism associated with civil and political rights. Their consistent view was that sovereignty, as an operational reality, insulated such societies from any type of meaningful accountability to external authority. There existed the added assurance that the absence of an active civil society in the socialist bloc meant that these norms could not be meaningfully invoked internally as a challenge to governmental dominance. Thus, human rights, at most, were regarded primarily by political elites as providing an arena for the exchange of propaganda charges on the plane of international relations. They were not perceived initially as posing a subversive threat to the supremacy of the state in relation to persons situated within territorial boundaries.[10]

Thus the initial impetus in support of human rights on a global level was facilitated by this dual recognition that the normative standards being adopted were either redundant or unenforceable. The liberal democracies were particularly intent on achieving redundancy, because of their worries about the potential activism of their respective citizenries. Authoritarian countries seemed surprisingly willing to subscribe to normative standards wildly inconsistent with their internal operating codes, presumably because of their dual sense that there was no prospect for either implementation from without or pressure from within. For liberal democracies the endorsement of human rights, in general, represented values associated with their convictions about the dignity of the individual, including even the less seriously embraced economic and social rights reflecting a then prevalent ethos of welfare capitalism. For authoritarian states, engaged in the active abuse of their citizens as a whole, an endorsement of human rights may have served as a convenient disguise in the wider world of states, where their legitimacy was under varying degrees of attack. Norms of human rights also functioned, in part, as moral claims in the ideological rivalry for the hearts and minds of peoples throughout the non-Western world that was at the center of the cold war.[11]

In the early decades of this process of internationalizing the protection of human rights, the Westphalian view of statism held sway and was reinforced by geopolitical structures and priorities, including the awkwardness of large overseas colonial empires. Further, the gradual ascendancy of the realist world view even in the United States, possibly the last partial idealist holdout among influential countries, minimized the impact of human rights on diplomacy. For instance, the West was far more concerned with maintaining strategic solidarity *contra* the Soviet bloc (and with the protection of foreign investment and a market-oriented climate) than it was with whether its allies abandoned authoritarian rule. Indeed, the United States often lent its overt support, and occasionally resorted to interventionary means, to stabilize the rule of anti–human rights regimes so long as their orientation was anti-Marxist.[12] And for Soviet bloc countries a combination of Soviet interventionary supervision and the suppression of domestic dissent effectively nullified any human rights impact upon the style and substance of rule.[13] What happened, then, during this initial 20-year period, was that the foundations were laid for a potential human rights culture; but the circumstances for its actualization in terms of improved political and material conditions for the peoples of the world were almost totally absent and were not generally foreseen. As a result, there was little academic interest in human rights during this period, and what did exist tended to be descriptive and moralistic.

Indeed, in this early period, what with the persistence of colonialism and the tendency of many authoritarian governments to affirm their commitment to human rights, an aura of hypocrisy surrounded the subject.

The Rise of Implementing Pressures

Various developments at different levels of social order gave human rights an increasing, if inconsistent and uneven, place in power calculations that were shaping the outcome of political struggles occurring in various parts of the world. First and foremost, was the anti-colonial movement, which in many settings throughout Asia and Africa challenged the most prevalent form of oppressive rule, intensified by its alien character, which subordinated the nationalist impulses of many non-Western peoples. The United Nations General Assembly, and later the nonaligned movement, gradually came to endorse these anti-colonial struggles, and this gave an enormous push to the substance of human rights as a world order achievement, even if not formulated explicitly as a matter of human rights.

Indeed, several crucial UN resolutions built a bridge between the dynamics of decolonization and the emergence of human rights as a serious dimension of world politics.[14] The bridge was completed when the common Article 1 of the two human rights covenants opened for signature in 1966 did what the Universal Declaration failed to do: namely, to anchor the specificity of human rights claims in the fundamental rights of all peoples to self-determination.

But there were other factors at work, as well, that moved generally in the same direction. From the start of the human rights movement there were, situated within the bureaucracies of leading Western states, strong supporters of the idea of applying external pressure on others to uphold human rights standards. Their presence ensured a kind of forward momentum for efforts to strengthen and elaborate an applicable human rights framework, and their influence was particularly great in relation to nascent European institutions and within the United Nations. That is, although realist perspectives tended to dominate the pinnacles of state power, there was a significant partially "subversive" presence within the sinews of government itself that adhered to neo-Wilsonian or idealist views and believed that some sort of global community based on law and morality was both possible and necessary.[15]

The cumulative influence of human rights as legal norms gave the notion of external accountability an increasing credibility, at least in Western Europe, especially after the creation and operation of the Strasbourg human rights mechanisms within the framework of the European Community, which took the radical step of allowing citizens in the participating countries to challenge alleged infringements of human rights in external administrative and judicial arenas.[16]

Secondly, the anti-colonial movement, and later the anti-apartheid campaign, created robust transnational political support for the human rights norm of self-determination, which, although absent from the Universal Declaration, became the foundational basis for human rights in general. The right of self-determination was later elevated to the eminence of being posited in a common Article 1 in both human rights covenants, providing the bridge between economic, social, and cultural rights and political and civil rights. Here, for the first time, historical currents of change associated with anti-colonial nationalism, reinforced by a mixture of geopolitical support (Soviet attitude) and ambivalence (US attitude), gave political backing to the most fundamental of all human rights claims: namely, the right of all peoples to determine the shape of the governance structure at the level of the state and to be free from alien and oppressive rule, at least in the form of colonial administration.

As newly independent countries in Africa and Asia gained access to the United Nations and influenced the recommendations of the General Assembly, important normative backing was given in a series of resolutions to both anti-colonialism and the anti-apartheid campaign directed against South Africa. The US government, leader of the free world, had often to bite its geopolitical tongue, in order to avoid allowing the Soviet Union to stand alone as the great power champion of Third World causes; but, by no means consistently, the United States role in Indochina and its virtually unconditional support for Israel over the years disclose a willingness to subordinate human rights and humanitarian concerns to its strategic priorities. Nevertheless, what made an aspect of the human rights agenda politically potent was the anti-colonial outcome of a convergence between self-determination norms and very powerful, prevailing anti-colonial and anti-racist patterns of nationalism. Furthermore, the geopolitical setting led both superpowers, although asymmetrically and inconsistently, to give their support to such patterns. In the West, as well, there were domestic constituencies in favor of self-determination and anti-racist values that added their political weight to international factors. These latter pressures generally arose from elements in the population of Western constitutional democracies that didn't share the geopolitical analysis or outlook of the policymakers, but were, by contrast, guided by normative conceptions of social and political justice or motivated mainly by ethnic or civilizational solidarity with those being denied fundamental human rights.

Additionally, improving prospects for the implementation of human rights standards and the growing salience of human rights issues can be attributed to the transnationalization of specific civic initiatives directed at these goals. The role of Amnesty International was especially significant in the 1960s and 1970s, with a host of other groups becoming active later on. This unanticipated civic source of agency in relation to human rights lifted the subject matter out of the hands of propagandists and demonstrated the leverage that can be exerted by citizens' groups relying upon the responsible use of information. Of course, rigidly authoritarian countries were the least responsive to such pressures, but many states, especially those linked to the Western alliance, were sensitive about attacks upon their legitimacy, fearing aid cutbacks and a weakening of support.

Even Communist countries were not oblivious to such impartial exposures of severe human rights failures, either because their legitimacy ultimately depended upon being accepted on the international level or because their interest in expanded trade and investment would be furthered by a clean bill of health in relation to human rights. The reliability of the information and the overall integrity of these transnational civil efforts also induced the liberal democracies themselves to take human rights more seriously in their dealings with others. Yet, at best, this responsiveness was partial and selective, being consistently subordinated to geopolitical factors.

The main contention being made here is that this transnational political agency gave to human rights advocacy a political potency, in the domain of implementation, and caused a subversive effect on state–society relations that far exceeded what might have been expected if developments had been truly subject to the discipline of the Westphalian or statist outlook.

At the same time, there is a danger of romanticizing and exaggerating these developments. The main human rights NGOs were very much outgrowths of Western liberal internationalism and looked mainly outward to identify abuses in Communist and Third World countries. In part, this reflected civilizational, as well as partisan and ideologized, orientations. It was expressed by a very selective emphasis by human rights organizations on the abuse of dissenters and political opposition or on the denial of Western-style political liberties.[17] Human rights activism originating in the West ignored almost totally the social, economic, and cultural content of the agreed substantive norms, despite their presence in widely invoked and ratified international instruments.

In other words, human rights progress, while definitely subversive of statist pretensions in certain key respects, still remained generally compatible with the maintenance of existing geopolitical structures of authority and wealth in the world and, as such, exerted only a marginal influence. Authoritarian practices even by states of secondary significance are normally rendered effectively immune from external human rights pressures, whether these emanate from states, the United Nations system, or transnational social forces.[18]

The confused status of human rights in international life is suggested by the treatment of the rights of indigenous peoples. To begin with, until indigenous peoples themselves adopted militant tactics to depict grievances, their distinctive vulnerability and normative demands were totally neglected and, if not forgotten altogether, misunderstood, as was the case in the original human rights instruments. To the extent that the position of indigenous peoples was taken into any specific account, it was in forms that actually embodied antagonistic approaches arising out of paternalistic assumptions.[19]

As a consequence of effective civic activism by indigenous peoples, a generally receptive niche was created within the UN system, and called the Informal Working Group on Indigenous Populations, a name conveying its provisional character and an attitude of political ambivalence on the part of many of the governments that agreed to its establishment. The working group has met annually in Geneva during recent years, for a few weeks each summer, producing an activist transnational network and clarifying the human rights demands of indigenous peoples that had previously been ignored, or worse, by states, international institutions, and even leading NGOs. Whether these symbolic steps of getting on the agenda and influencing the normative architecture will yield impressive, consistent substantive results is doubtful, given the obstacles.

At the very least, however, the dynamics of transnational activism have been indispensable to achieve a clarification of the genuine normative demands of indigenous peoples.[20] As with other human rights struggles, substantive success will depend on mobilizing supportive social forces of sufficient influence, a difficult challenge for indigenous peoples who must combine their wider participation at national, regional, and global levels with battles waged in local, often remote settings where their opponents represent strong vested economic interests, and may involve challenging elaborate development projects with large infusions of capital.

The movement to uphold the basic rights of indigenous peoples has enjoyed enough success over the past two decades to challenge simplistic structural notions of capitalist and modernist primacy. At the same time, the limits of this success help us appreciate the relative strength of these dominant forces that are structuring contemporary world order. As a result, the very survival of indigenous peoples in many specific settings remains in acute jeopardy.

The Added Complication of Globalization

Most thinking about the implementation of human rights remains preoccupied with obstacles at the level of the state. The problems of penetrating the authoritarian state while avoiding the interventionary diplomacy of the colonial era are especially troublesome. The old multilateralism, reinforced by transnational social forces, is evolving into the new multilateralism, in which human rights concerns are of considerable political significance in a series of specific settings. But there are some countervailing tendencies that constrain further development of human rights in the near future, in many circumstances, especially those of an economic and social character. These constraints can be best understood in relation to ideological climate, an altered balance of social forces, and the structural impact of the regionalization and globalization of capital and trade relations.

Ideological climate   The collapse of the Soviet Union, the discrediting of socialism, and the insistence on minimizing state investment and welfare roles contribute to a current policy consensus among elites often usefully identified as "neo-liberalism." In this atmosphere, support for economic and social rights, as specified in the main international law instruments on the subject (including the Right to Development), is virtually nonexistent, although still enjoying nominal or rhetorical support.[21] Addressing the basic needs of the poor is entrusted, essentially, although not completely or evenly, to the operations of the market and the alleged spillover benefits of economic growth, privatization, and increasing investment. Normative claims that insist on immediate and obligatory action by the state to overcome the social distress caused by poverty and joblessness are subordinated to a posture of deference to market forces and to a variety of economic restructuring priorities, most notably deficit reduction and bureaucratic downsizing. This deference is reinforced by the absence of viable alternative orientations toward economic policy.

It should be acknowledged that in a series of Asian countries, sustained economic growth, combined with a reasonably balanced distribution of material benefits to much of their populations, had been effectively achieving the substance of economic and social rights until the financial crisis of mid-1997. As of early 1999 it remains to be seen whether such growth with poverty reduction can be revived. A separate mechanism is not needed to achieve such rights if the dynamics of economic growth result in the material well-being of an increasing proportion of a given society.

Altered balance of social forces   This circumstance of ideological adversity is exacerbated by the decline of organized labor in most countries, giving business and finance-oriented viewpoints greater influence and control over mainstream party politics and in relation to governmental bureaucracies. This decline in the influence of labor arises partly from the same factors that have fashioned the neo-liberal consensus, but partly also from shifts in the nature of work in societies where manufacturing and industry are being superseded by services and tangibles by intangibles. As a result, the industrial/manufacturing core of organized labor is becoming ever more peripheral to the social and economic order.[22] In effect, the role of the state is being reformulated in Europe and North America to minimize its role with respect to the social agenda of society, especially in the countries of the affluent North. For rapidly developing countries in the South the opposite tendencies are evident, with a more modern society expecting a larger role for government in providing a safety net for its citizens – in effect, a leveling down in the North, a leveling up in the South, with varying effects on the role of the state in relation to the realization of economic and social rights.

The discipline of regional and global capital   Perhaps most important of all is the pressure on all governments to avoid burdening economic activity in such a way that competitive pressures reduce market opportunities and performance.[23] The structural character of this pressure is evident in the strong recent tendency of social-democratic political leadership around the world to shift its emphasis deliberately from people-oriented to market-oriented approaches to governmental policy. Even Sweden in a period of Social Democratic Party leadership has been abandoning, by stages, "the Swedish model," which earlier had been a source of pride. The leverage of the private sector is made greater by the transnational mobility of capital, which, through threats of flight, has the effect of exerting downward pressure on domestic tax rates, wages, and business regulation. Throughout the world, this same set of influences seems operative and works against efforts to promote the well-being of the most economically and socially disadvantaged. In this sense, globalization structurally inhibits the protection of economic and social rights in such a way that they are relatively immune, at present, to the new multilateralism, which, to the extent that it addresses these issues, still tends to emphasize civil and political rights.[24] In some of the South and East Asian countries the situation is somewhat inverted, with economic and social rights being a more acceptable agenda priority for activist groups than civil and political rights and more in accord with the performance record of government. To the extent that this latter class of countries is developing very rapidly there are spreading social benefits that include all strata of society, although at rates and with effects that vary from country to country.

There is an emergent tension between the promotion of economic and social rights at the level of the state and the disciplinary impact of global market factors. It poses the difficult question as to whether governments locked into wider competitive frameworks retain the effective discretion to ensure that their own citizens can satisfy basic human needs of an economic and social character.[25] At present, the countries of the North are downsizing in relation to the provision of public goods to their populations, and opposition political parties even of social-democratic persuasion are not challenging such orientations. Regional frameworks could provide, in some settings, a partial solution. The notion of "a social Europe" entails a commitment to reconcile economic factors with the claims of peoples with respect to the full gamut of rights. Whether such a regional approach is viable over time is open to question, as the unevenness of regions in a globalized world economy will sustain the downward pressures on public goods, including the provision of basic needs to the poor.

In other words, globalization, as shaped by a neo-liberal ideology, appears incompatible with the earlier project of the humane or compassionate state and confines the effective role of the new multilateralism, at least for the foreseeable future, to the civil and political domain. An aspect of this pessimistic assessment arises from the dual relationship of neo-liberalism to mobility: the increasing transnational mobility of capital combined with increasing territoriality of labor, creating vulnerability of workers in high-wage countries, reinforcing their hostility to immigrant labor and a special resistance to most categories of transnational economic migration.[26]

Anticipating a Statist Backlash

The emergence of global civil society in the form of multilayered networks of variously aligned transnational forces has so far resulted in an ambiguous response from the old multilateralism, especially that associated with the United Nations system.[27] The UN has remained very much of a statist instrument and, beyond that, operates within limits set by a few dominant or hegemonic states, especially in relation to the peace and security activities of its principal organs. Nevertheless, the organization has opened up spaces that have allowed access of impressive proportions to the new multilateralism of transnational social forces. Reference has already been made to the Informal Working Group on Indigenous Populations, but, perhaps even more significant, has been the participation of transnational social elements in the main UN global conferences on significant policy issues. Starting with the Stockholm Conference on the Human Environment in 1972 and continuing in an upward spiral of influence until the Beijing Conference on Women and Development in 1995.

To be sure, the mode of participation was indirect, by way of counter-conference formats, but the consciousness-raising impact of the conferences, through media attention and the shape of the final documents, was definitely influenced by the efforts of the new multilateralists.

States reacted negatively to the loss of some of their ascendancy in these global conference settings, and have tried to avoid their recurrence. This backlash contrasts with their willing acceptance of a loss of autonomy in relation to the global economy. With respect to globalization, the policy elite tended to be drawn from globalist circles, but in relation to transnational social forces, by and large, the interaction was characteristically an encounter across ideological, class, gender, and ethnic lines. So long as the cold war was at the center of geopolitics, transnational activism was perceived, and even celebrated, as evidence of "freedom" in the West, as contrasted with rigid state controls in the East, and was treated by the East as "a free propaganda good," since the target of activist groups was generally the governments of leading states in the West. But such activism is now perceived by the policy elite more objectively and consensually, and its anti-statist, pro–human rights and environment animus is clearly exposed. In this period of increasing governmental downsizing in relation to the statist organs of the UN and of economic restructuring that involves reduced government spending for social purposes, there is building a more determined, although largely silent, opposition to any kind of subsidization of the new multilateralism, as well as an appreciation that the UN spaces in which these tendencies became most manifest were being effectively, and often antagonistically, appropriated by anti-statist perspectives. If this assessment is generally true, then one would expect the UN system in this period to reassert control over these spaces, making them less available, squeezing the budget supporting the work on indigenous peoples and avoiding sponsorship of consciousness-raising global conferences that serve as mobilization sites for the new multilateralism.

If this statist backlash ensues, then the resilience and resourcefulness of transnational social forces will be put to the test. Can new arenas of interaction be identified and participation financed? Can the use of the Internet generate new types of transnational electronic empowerment to fill part of the vacuum? Can tactics be devised that draw battlelines in symbolically evocative ways? Greenpeace has exhibited great tactical ingenuity throughout its entire period of existence, and several varieties of Green Politics have displayed a comparable political flair at various times, especially during the early green experience in the Federal Republic of Germany.

On the Complicating Relevance of
Culture and Civilization

Suggestions have been prominently made to the effect that the inner normative core of human experience possesses universal validity and is embodied either in "a human rights culture" or in the legal content of international human rights.[28] Such a position claims to locate human rights as norms and claims beyond "the clash of civilizations." The historical circumstances arising out of an ideological climate dominated by neo-liberal perspectives and reinforced by pressures toward competitiveness and fiscal downsizing at corporate and governmental levels encourage universalist perspectives at the policymaking level. There is certainly an attractiveness about reintroducing values into the political arena by way of human rights possessing an equivalent, yet offsetting, universal normative currency. Indeed, the failure to reunite secularism with a seriously applicable moral agenda appears to have generated a dangerous social vacuum that encourages and strengthens various destructive forces: drugs; crime; religious and ethnic extremism; youth suicide, death rock; as well as regressive backlash movements that seek to reimpose on society traditional constraints. Of course, neo-liberalism continues to contend that market-driven politics and secularism are leading to a peaceful world of prosperity and moderation – in effect, the best of all possible worlds. What is actually emerging, however, is a consumerist cult that lacks any inner dynamic of moral responsibility toward those who are excluded or impoverished, including future generations. This challenge has deepened since the end of the cold war due to the collapse of the socialist "other," the related weakening of the labor movement, which provided the main vehicle for promoting social goals in capitalist countries, and the emergence of non-Western civilizational voices.

However, it has turned out to be difficult to promote human rights as an alternative to socialism.[29] For one thing, the market-driven logic is deeply at odds with that portion of human rights protection that is directed toward the satisfaction of individual or group basic needs. For another, the West has used its advocacy of human rights as a way of challenging the behavior of non-Western societies, arousing the suspicion that human rights are, in function, a post-colonial rationale for interventionary diplomacy and the reassertion of Western civilizational superiority. This Western advocacy is further discounted as hypocritical, because of the refusal of the West to apply it self-critically to the failures and ongoing suffering within affluent Western societies. Along similar lines, the moral claims of human rights, as codified, are resisted, because of their Western origins and their purportedly unbalanced emphasis on the rights of the individual without a corresponding concern for well-being of the community; in this regard, the human rights culture, so-called, is being perceived, especially by political Islam, as part of the civilizational decadence of the West, emerging out of a background that included colonial exploitation, racism, and interventionary diplomacy and a foreground of ultra-permissiveness and irreverence, as embodied in Western popular culture, dress codes, and sexual practices.

Against such a background, the civilizational and religious traditions of Asia and elsewhere, it is argued, provide more integral and persuasive moral guidance than can be found in the guidelines for action contained in human rights traditions as applied in the contemporary West. Encouraged by the recent success stories of Asian economic policies, there is a conviction in Asia and elsewhere that a better, non-Western path to prosperity and stability exists than is provided by going the Western consti-tutional way,[30] and, more relevantly, that these non-Western alternative views regarding the place of religion and morality will be effectively destroyed by globalization unless actively resisted, and this includes resistance to a wholesale opting for human rights as inscribed in the main instruments of international law.

And finally, the globally active agents of the new multilateralism in the human rights domain have consistently behaved as if human rights meant only political and civil rights, thereby making it easier to view these transnational initiatives as quasi-conspiratorial extensions of the ideological outlook of globalization-from-above.[31] Such a perception is reinforced because, civilizationally and societally, human suffering in the non-Western world is associated primarily with massive poverty, giving an instinctive priority to such claims as are associated with "the right to development" and economic and social rights as compared to the defense of the liberal agenda of civil and political rights.[32] At the same time, the United States, as the prototypical bearer of human rights in the Western style, is reasonably seen by many non-Western leaders as indif-ferent to homelessness and racism and as the focus of a moral cesspool of sexual depravity, drug use, and crime, hardly a model to be emulated by a society seeking a better future. Under these conditions the tempta-tion is to retreat from universalism to multiculturalism, reinforced by a kind of revived statism detached from any widespread normative com-mitment to democracy.[33]

Part of the resistance to human rights in the non-Western world, espe-cially by oppressive governments, needs itself to be demystified. This kind of reaction will only be effective if it mainly represents a response that emerges from within a country, or at least within a given civilizational constellation. It is important to expose manipulative efforts by repressive elites to avoid even minimal external pressures based on notions of accountability embodied in international law instruments. The governments of China and Indonesia have been particularly notorious in this respect. The true motives of these governments are revealed by their insistence on unconditional sovereign rights, opposing the establishment of external accountability even if based on a regional framework of action, and by a refusal to respect peaceful voices of opposition within their own societies.

Can these temptations to repudiate an international law grounding for human rights be successfully resisted? Can the human rights enterprise, norms and procedures, be sufficiently emancipated from its ambiguous Western antecedents and contemporary mechanism of geopolitics to serve as the basis of human rights in non-Western regions? Does a basis remain, after cultural and civilizational perspectives and differences have been taken into account, to find meta-civilizational support for a human rights culture that is linked to projects to strengthen global civil society and to build cosmopolitan or transnational democracy?[34] Can the opportunistic rejection of human rights be effectively distinguished from genuine and necessary critical scrutiny within all civilizational spaces?

Such questions help to suggest an agenda for the new multilateralism if it is to meet the challenges being posed.

Meeting the Challenge: Positive Perspectives

Globalization is undermining the normative achievements of the old multilateralism in a variety of ways, especially through its tendency to impose the discipline of global and regional capital upon states. Fortunately, other historical forces are working in different and opposite directions, including the emergence of transnational social forces that are animated by a human-centered vision of change and stability. Out of this complex interplay, taking account of dramatic degrees of unevenness in economic, political, social, and cultural circumstance, the struggles for human rights in this era are taking their distinctive shape.

The immediate challenge with respect to human rights is associated with whether the new, bottom-up multilateralism can sustain its momentum in the face of two sets of deteriorating circumstances: the closing off of niches within intergovernmental arenas, especially the United Nations, and the claims of intra-civilizational autonomy in relation to norms and procedures of an allegedly extra-civilizational character that are stigmatized as "Western" or as a Trojan Horse that validates post-colonial intervention by the West. Both these difficulties are linked to globalization, as prior sections have argued. In this final section attention is given to ways forward that are mindful of such obstacles.

Inter-civilizational dialogue   In this period it is of utmost importance to disentangle antagonistic ideological stereotypes – various forms of Orientalism, including its opposite, "Occidentalism" – from support for state–society relations conducive to the realization of human rights comprehensively conceived.[35] The possibility of dialogue presupposes civic space that permits more transnational mutual understanding, which is particularly important in relations between Islam and the West, but also between China and the West.[36]

Because of the hegemonic past and present of the West, it is initially important for the dialogue to move primarily from South to North, from Islam to the West.[37] There are hegemonic features of globalization, including a secular consumerism, that create serious structural difficulties for countries seeking to maintain their non-Western, non-secular identities. Also, the insistence that the community counts, that individuals have duties as well as rights, and that a Universal Declaration of Human Responsibilities could be helpful in creating a greater willingness by non-Western human rights activists to oppose authoritarian cruelties within their own civilizational space.

Economic and social rights   One way to overcome non-Western resistance to calls for inter-civilizational dialogue is to treat economic and social rights as deserving of as much support in specific settings as civil and political rights. Anti-debt coalitions, efforts of the Third World Network, contain projects in which Western human rights initiatives could join forces with activists and their organizations in the South. Regulation of multinational corporations and transnational banking would also enable conditions to exist in which respect for economic and social rights could be improved, and shared transnational, North–South concerns could lead to coalitions of effort and commitment.

Such a dynamic may occur spontaneously. The dramatic, powerful French strikes of December 1995 can be interpreted from various angles, but one factor was opposition to the sorts of budgetary discipline required by Maastricht objectives and, perhaps more broadly, a concern within the French populace in relation to the perceived drift toward supranationalism and its impact on political identity and the character of the French nation. This resistance may be disclosing an emergent radicalism in the West that as a core element will reconceive of human rights by primary reference to economic and social rights, especially if political parties, elections, and representative institutions in these Western societies continue to seem less and less responsive to the range of actual human concerns of large sectors of the citizenry. In one respect, this possible new politics will seek to preserve the nation-state character of governmental outlook in reaction to efforts by business and finance to reconstitute identity in relation to market opportunity.

Ethos of nonviolent politics   The future of the new multilateralism in relation to the promotion of human rights will depend on whether credible political movements can arise to displace existing patterns of leadership. For various reasons, including the degree to which globalization rests upon an ethos of violence, any effective countervailing normative orientation will need to rest its appeal and effectiveness upon nonviolent political orientations. The various democratic transformations of the 1980s encourage the belief that nonviolent mobilization of political energies can effectively challenge a variety of repressive political arrangements. The outcomes in the Philippines, Eastern Europe, the Soviet Union, South Africa, and Israel/Palestine are inspirational, even if the new political realities in these countries are disappointing. Even the various failed democratizing attempts in China, Burma, Nepal, and Thailand are suggestive of the extent to which revolutionary politics in this era are essentially seeking, by nonviolent means, to replace authoritarian and exploitative political systems with a human rights culture.[38]

The new multilateralism, in this sense, will not succeed over time, unless it explicitly and avowedly repudiates the war system as it operates within the framework of the old multilateralism. In this respect, the human rights imperative is a radical one at this stage. Any continued accommodation with mainstream political and cultural violence will increasingly contradict the possibilities of sustaining individual and group conditions of human decency.

Shifting patterns of accountability   There are at least two constructive directions of effort, given the likelihood that intergovernmental initiatives will be stymied: regional and subregional frameworks and citizens' initiatives.[39] The current appeal of regional and subregional frameworks is their potential capacity for reconciling resistance to extra-civilizational pressures with intra-civilizational commitments to the construction of decent human societies, although the dispersion of peoples means that civilizational space is usually far from identical with geographical space. This complicates the whole emphasis on inter-civilizational reality, but in a manner that can be addressed by way of tolerance and respect within territorial space of the various "others."

Also, informal frameworks of accountability could gain increased relevance in the years ahead, focusing attention on transnational patterns that produce human abuses that the old multilateralism prefers to overlook, such as the use of secret banking facilities to hide public funds stolen and appropriated from societies or the encroachments of government and business on the lands and rights of indigenous peoples.

This format for assessing blame was pioneered by Bertrand Russell in a tribunal formed to investigate allegations of US war crimes in Vietnam during the 1960s and has evolved in many settings since then. The Permanent Peoples Tribunal, with its base in Rome, has done notable work for more than two decades, assessing grievances in a series of instances that include the plight of Amazonia, the abusive impact of the Bretton Woods institutions, and the interventionary diplomacy of both superpowers during the cold war in such countries as Afghanistan and Nicaragua. These initiatives undertaken without authorization by states or international institutions have documented those injustices that the guardians of globalization prefer to ignore. Since the media follow, in most instances, the guidelines of these statist and market guardians, it has generally been difficult to attract serious attention for the results of these civic inquiries without statist authorization, even when the outcome carefully documents hitherto unacknowledged infringements of human rights. Whether the new modalities of the Internet will provide such initiatives with more effective ways to gain influence for their activities beyond their local place of occurrence is yet to be established.

Internalization of "universal" norms   The Western origins and orientation of human rights may be a burden in a period of greater civilizational assertiveness, but to some extent non-Western civilizations have their own equivalent or parallel standards of approved conduct that have been shaped through time, including in interaction with the West. In this respect a global socialization process has internalized in all civilizations a resonance to many basic human rights claims, although there are contested zones where contradictory claims are being made and important differences as to language, substance, and relation to the past.

Within this framework the universal and the particular can both find authentic, yet often controversial, expression beneath the overarching rubric of human rights. Just as money or language function both generically and in relation to particularities of time and place, so the same is true for human rights.

Whether these several factors will enable the new multilateralism to grow stronger under current conditions and thereby help human rights to adapt successfully to the rigors of globalization and civilizational resurgence is highly questionable at this point. What seems evident is that such an adaptation will require radical innovations on the part of initiatives identified here as globalization-from-below. If successful, such initiatives could transform the future of world order in beneficial ways; if not, there is likely to be a great deal of disillusionment and mutual recrimination associated with human rights as a dimension of international political life.

7

The Outlook for UN Reform: Necessary but Impossible

The Idea of UN Reform

The generally endorsed project of United Nations reform disappointed even before it failed. It caused disappointment initially in many quarters because the conception of feasible reform was far too narrowly circumscribed. In the public domain, aside from budget trimming and downsizing, UN reform came to be identified almost exclusively with the enlargement of the Security Council. Even this focus was trivialized by the insistence of Western governments that feasible enlargement had to be determined by capacity to contribute, which in turn was understood in largely financial terms and was interpreted so as to qualify only Germany and Japan as potentially acceptable candidates for permanent membership of the Security Council. As we now know, even this minuscule reform has not so far materialized, despite the financial crisis that is now impacting heavily on a whole range of UN activities.

It is the contention of this chapter that the political preconditions for necessary UN reform were not even acknowledged, much less satisfied; and further, that the conception of reform was far too modest to take account of the challenges and opportunities facing the organization. This excessive modesty can be interpreted in *realist* political language by reference to an appreciation of the great potential contributions that the United Nations could make to geopolitical stability and to the strategic interest of its leading members in the containment of conflict and the establishment of order.

It is also possible to go beyond realism by relying on normative, rather than geopolitical or strategic, criteria to shape the agenda of necessary UN reform. Such normative criteria would emphasize democratizing the processes of decision within the United Nations and demilitarizing UN responses to breakdowns of peace and security in the world. In this more radical conception of UN reform, it is evident that, as matters now stand, neither governments of states nor other representatives of market forces are likely to lend support. For these reasons, reform prospects are dependent upon transnational, grass-roots initiatives that coalesce as a movement.

Without such a populist base it is difficult to solve the agency problem of explaining how to get from here to there. At the same time, solving the agency problem conceptually gives little assurance that behavioral patterns will conform. For this reason, it is asserted that UN reform is necessary, but it is also admitted that it is "impossible." It is impossible because it is hard to visualize the growth of a transnational movement of sufficient potency to shake prevailing geopolitical structures and their supportive ideological frames of reference (that is, the realist mind-set).

Despite this "impossibility," a deterministic pessimism is not justified, especially if one reflects upon recent history. Only a fool would have dared anticipate a post–cold war world or a post-apartheid South Africa as recently as the 1980s. The impossible happens. And it happens because dedicated women and men struggle against the odds to make it happen. Such a struggle must precede any serious reformist steps being taken within the UN system.

To support this line of thinking, it may be helpful to consider first why the official reform project was such a failure, even as minimally conceived. Closely related to this failure is the largely unwarranted decline in the reputation of the United Nations as a consequence of the misfit between expectations, missions, and capabilities in the context of recent peace and security activities.

Obstacles to Reform

It was to be expected that all those with a commitment to a more orderly and equitable world community geared up their proposals for reforming the United Nations as the fiftieth anniversary year approached. And the historical setting in the early 1990s appeared to be highly favorable for reform-minded perspectives, including even relevant officials in governmental circles. With the cold war over and the seemingly successful deployment of the United Nations authority in the Gulf War, as well as the high incidence of conflicts that were troublesome without being a challenge to national interests, the scene seemed set for bold moves to strengthen the United Nations both as a means to achieve intergovernmental goals and as a way for transnational social forces to participate more effectively in the shaping of global policy.

But, as we now know, the path to United Nations reform was never cleared of several obstacles that blocked the most modest reformist initiatives. We need to understand why the reformist prospect was always doomed to failure. The official reform agenda was, at best, only cosmetic; besides, leaving existing arrangements in place served entrenched political forces more than opening the sluice gates of reform. Among these inertial elements the following were critical.

Geopolitical closure To reform the United Nations presupposed a wide zone of consensus among the members. This never really existed. The Security Council, in particular, the only prominent item on the reform agenda, was constituted in 1945, a snapshot of the global power structure at the end of World War II. Its anachronistic structure could be adapted to the realities of the 1990s only through voluntary action on the part of the permanent members to relinquish some of their status and authority (that is, the veto). It made no sense to retain both France and Britain as permanent members without adding at least six other states to that category, thereby making the Security Council so unwieldy as to be of virtually no further use as a geopolitical instrument. In light of the refusal of current permanent members to diminish their status and rights, Security Council reform was a nonstarter geopolitically: the North was willing to add Germany and Japan, but not any others, while the South would go along with a further weighting of the top-down hierarchy only if each region in the world had at least one state among the permanent members, and the veto was restricted or eliminated.

Problematic leadership The United States has been the dominant political actor in the United Nations ever since 1945, although it was frequently stymied in its efforts to enlist the Security Council in support of its foreign policy undertakings due to opposition by the Soviet bloc and the Non-Aligned Movement. Since 1989, with the Soviet presence converted into one of overall passivity and the Non-Aligned Movement losing momentum and direction, the dominance of the United States has been essentially unchallenged. Such ascendancy could have been generally benevolent, even visionary, despite lacking the sort of legitimacy that would result from more democratized participation on the part of the non-Western peoples of the world and their representatives. But the United States, itself caught in the backwash of globalization, has failed to provide the momentum for reform. Indeed, it has weirdly combined its dominance of the Organization with a subversive influence designed to minimize UN capacities in many settings, expressed above all by its failure to pay its share of assessed costs for recent UN activities, thereby provoking the worst financial crisis in UN history. This reining in of the Organization has been reinforced by the theme of downsizing, emphasized by the Clinton administration as its main contribution to the fiftieth anniversary debate about reform.

As a result, the leadership provided by the United States government has proved to be negative in two respects: first, it has supported retention of the geopolitical status quo in relation to the outmoded 1945 structures of authority; secondly, it has inhibited bold initiatives ideologically by casting itself in the role of critic, without providing the sort of inspirational motivation that could generate political support for a stronger United Nations. Of course, this failure of ideological leadership reflects a rightwards lurch in US politics that puts any governmental endorsement of internationalism or idealism on hold.

The UN Charter framework   From a reformist perspective, the Charter is a rigid instrument. It can be amended only with the approval of the five permanent members of the Security Council, acting in concert with two-thirds of the General Assembly. Such an amendment procedure means, in effect, that formal changes in the UN authority structure depend on virtual unanimity, including support from those states that are likely to lose influence in the process. Adaptation to changing circumstances can occur opportunistically, either by way of flexible and expansive lines of interpretation or by passivity with respect to implementation. Counting abstentions in the Security Council as "concurring votes" in the sense required by Article 27(3) is an illustration of the former device, whereas the failure to implement Chapter VII on peace enforcement illustrates the latter.

At a more fundamental level, the presuppositions of the Charter as drafted are less and less responsive to the behavioral patterns that control the most significant aspects of political life at a global level. The Charter affirms as sacrosanct the postulate of territorial sovereignty, but the organization of economic life is increasingly transnational and nonterritorially situated. Also, in Article 2(7), by exempting matters "essentially within domestic jurisdiction," the Charter disavows any commitment to address issues that are now posing the greatest threat to the peace and security of people. Additionally, of course, membership and meaningful participation are confined to governments representing states, while many of the activities that shape global reality are manifestly increasingly the work of non-state actors.

The intervention trap   The most urgent demands on the United Nations have been associated with several breakdowns of governmental normalcy at the level of the state. Circumstances of anarchy, chaos, and strife have resulted in widespread human suffering that is reported by way of television in the form of vivid imagery. To do nothing is a confession of impotence and cannot be explained effectively by invoking constitutional restrictions on humanitarian intervention under UN auspices. Yet, to act effectively once conflicts have crossed the threshold of violence is extremely difficult even if capabilities and political will exist. Governments have consistently failed to convert military superiority into political outcomes in the face of nationalist patterns of resistance. Intervention under UN auspices, or even by way of NGO activities, encounters comparable difficulties, as the experience in Bosnia and several sub-Saharan African countries confirms. Alternatives involve preventive and restorative diplomacy, acknowledging the inability to intervene during phases of conflict characterized by recourse and commitment to violent tactics.

Psycho-political globalism   The rise of global media and the proliferation of transnational civil initiatives in many sectors of international life mean that global public opinion is a reality. As such, the initial postulates of patriarchy and hierarchy that continue to pervade UN operations seem unduly antiquated as a foundation for global representation.

Against this generalized background, it is possible to depict the failure of the UN to live up to expectations in the area of peace and security. This failure has been mainly responsible for the collapse of confidence in the United Nations as either a geopolitical or a humanitarian instrument. A brief interpretation of this failure is an essential aspect of any effort to make UN reform a credible project.

Recasting UN Peacekeeping

The UN Charter makes a basic distinction between peacekeeping as specified in Articles 33–8 (Chapter VI) and peace enforcement as set out in Articles 39–51 (Chapter VII), the former being concerned with working out a solution between conflictual parties either by way of their negotiation of a peaceful settlement or through some kind of diplomatic initiative; while the latter relies on decisions of the Security Council to impose a solution on the basis of forcible measures. This way of encouraging settlement of disputes has not been very effective in the history of the United Nations, while enforcement has been relevant only in those exceptional circumstances in which there has been a consensus of leading states to support Security Council decisions and the political will of these and other states to provide the capabilities required for effective action.

Throughout the 50 years of UN existence, this Chapter VII approach has been fully invoked only twice, in Korea (1950–2) and the Gulf War (since 1990), and on both occasions to provide cover for geopolitical undertakings dominated by the United States. During the 1990s, as in Iraq, Bosnia, Somalia, and Haiti, Chapter VII claims of a limited character were posited, but the means to achieve compliance were not provided. Only in Haiti can one speak seriously of enforcement, and there no resistance to the UN effort took hold, and in any event it was basically a unilateral US undertaking.

But what the United Nations has managed to do is to extend the reach of the Charter in a manner compatible with its dominant mission to avoid war and political violence, suggesting a disguised process of "amendment" by way of practice and precedent. In the 1950s Dag Hammarskjöld introduced this enhanced conception of peacekeeping, what came to be called Chapter VI 1/2, to situate its identity midway between dispute settlement and enforcement. The essence of enhanced peacekeeping is the consent of the embroiled parties to the deployment of UN forces as a neutral buffer in circumstances of intractable conflict, accompanied by a commitment of the UN to remain impartial with respect to the respective merits of the adversary positions, as well as a restriction on the use of force by the UN to circumstances of self-defense, and then only in the event of a direct attack on UN personnel. In a sense, such peacekeeping is a holding operation, either freezing the status quo or allowing the underlying dispute to reach a stage where a diplomatic solution can be agreed upon by the parties. It represents an intermediate ground between a recommendatory posture and an enforcement role.

Between 1948 and 1994 there have been 35 UN peacekeeping operations, about half of which are presently in existence, with all but one, that in former Yugoslavia, being located in the Third World. Until the end of the cold war, the peacekeeping effort focused exclusively on separating antagonistic forces in a circumstance of unresolved tensions, as well as monitoring cease-fires once negotiated. With the end of the cold war and increased possibilities for consensus in the Security Council and less disposition by superpowers to engage directly in their own forms of "peacekeeping," the UN was given new assignments, which have exerted major strains on the viability of enhanced peacekeeping and blurred the dividing line between peacekeeping and enforcement both in mandate and in performance. In these assignments, the basis for consent and impartiality has been deliberately eroded, partly because the UN mandate, as in Somalia, Bosnia, Cambodia, Rwanda, and Haiti, was one that either proceeded without the genuine consent of the parties to the conflict or came to be perceived as taking sides in the course of trying to restore government, protect vulnerable elements in the population, and promote a transition to democracy, a dynamic that involved constitutionally opting for a Chapter VII enforcement mandate.

What is worse, this effort since 1989 to augment enhanced peacekeeping and blend it with peace enforcement was not accompanied by a commensurate increase in financial resources and military capabilities placed at the disposal of the United Nations. In effect, the leading states were expanding the responsibilities of the Security Council into domains of the greatest difficulty, while lacking the political will, or even the understanding, to provide the increased or appropriate means required to give this far more ambitious role a reasonable prospect of success.

The tragic experience of the last few years is by now a familiar story, carried to new extremes in Bosnia during May of 1995, when almost 400 UN peacekeepers were seized as hostages by the Bosnian Serbs and used as human shields in the vicinity of probable targets of NATO bombing, leading UN officials to describe Serb operations as possessing a "terrorist" character.[1] In Bosnia the UN peacekeeping effort was designed to provide humanitarian relief for the civilian population, and then at a later time to protect designated safe havens from military attack, but such an undertaking was unsustainable from the outset if seriously challenged by Serbian military forces. Given the inadequate capabilities made available to the UN, it was understandable that there would be a search for greater coercive leverage. Recurrent proposals urging NATO bombing arose out of this situation. But such an attempt by the United Nations to shift from an impartial role to one of enforcement, without the requisite capabilities or political will, almost inevitably generates a "a politics of gesture" (or of resignation) that is exceedingly susceptible to collapse if tested. One dimension of this susceptibility was illustrated by the vulnerability of lightly armed UN troops to capture and humiliation in Bosnia. This circumstance induces extreme UN passivity and demoralization on the part of responsible officials, even when humanitarian commitments are brutally and directly flaunted, as in Bosnia when Serb forces later pressed vicious attacks on UN-designated safe havens.[2]

If a UN-endorsed undertaking is not seriously tested, as was true in Haiti, at least through mid-1996, a peace and security operation can enjoy a measure of apparent success; but note that the locus of initiative generally tends to rest with the most violent and anti-democratic party to the underlying, unresolved conflict.[3] And the external presence, backed up by only a shallow commitment, can lead to pressures that result in withdrawal and policy reversal, as has been vividly illustrated by events during 1993–4 in Somalia, which in turn inhibited even ad hoc emergency initiatives of limited scope to protect the Tutsi in Rwanda from a genocidal onslaught and to discourage the outbreak of comparable violence in neighboring Burundi.

What is evident is that the UN peacekeeping and peace enforcement roles have been irresponsibly discredited and imprudently merged in the period since 1989. By succumbing to a politics of gesture implemented under UN auspices, the UN is being consistently set up to produce a public sense of failure and disappointment. It is given assignments that can easily be converted into missions impossible as a result of resistance tactics organized by parties to a conflict that either have an advantage on the battlefield or else believe that a political outcome under UN authority will work to their disadvantage and thus possess an incentive to restrict sharply the UN role or induce its termination by whatever means.

Events in Bosnia during late May of 1995 are exemplary. As the Belgrade Serbs seemed on the verge of accepting the diplomatic solution being urged by "the contact group" (US, UK, France, Germany, Russia), the Bosnian Serbs stepped up the military pressure, especially around Sarajevo, and improperly repossessed heavy weapons that had earlier been placed by agreement under UN protective custody. This induced NATO, at US urging, to bomb Bosnian Serb targets, which led the Karadzic leadership in Pale to retaliate by increasing military pressure at several points and by seizing UN peacekeepers dispersed around the country and temporarily holding them hostages. The Western response confirms the worst apprehensions about this new cycle of self-destructive peacekeeping, exhibiting a revealing ambivalence as to whether the purpose of increasing the UN military capability in Bosnia in response to this Serb provocation is to arrange for the redeployment of UN personnel in more defensible positions or the prelude to a complete UN withdrawal accompanied by a willingness of Europe and the United States to adopt a fuller posture of support for the Bosnian government as the victim of Serb aggression.

Given these developments, it is hardly surprising that confidence in the UN has fallen to new lows. The Organization has been placed in a position of humiliating impotence amid conflicts of a genocidal character, circumstances where impartiality is inappropriate and consent of a reliable kind unavailable. As such, only the enforcement mode of Chapter VII could provide a sufficient foundation for a UN role. The concern here is not mainly a matter of formal classification, but rather the insufficiency of political will to provide the capabilities needed so as to be reasonably likely to reach a successful outcome, a prospect that needs to be evaluated in each particular situation. But the obstacle here is much less conceptual than it is geopolitical: the realist mind-set of political leaders and their advisors is conditioned by a materialist view of interests that regards human rights factors as peripheral even if presented in acute genocidal form. Thus, if material interests are not seriously engaged, there is little prospect of a response that goes beyond the modest confines of gesture, cheap responses with limited risks. The UN is useful as a vehicle of absolution, as it distances governments as political actors from the prospect and consequences of policy failure; yet it seems to take seriously the moral claims associated with responsibility for the protection of the innocent – namely, the civilian population. The only escape from this vicious circle is to infuse moral responsibility into the political leaders of major states as a condition of their legitimacy, a reorientation of liberal democratic politics that seems indispensable to satisfy the demands of "community" in the global village of the next millennium.

In a sense, the marginalization of the United Nations in the peace and security area was consummated by the process that led to a negotiated end to the fighting in Bosnia by way of the Dayton Agreement. After years of ambivalence, the US government finally decided to throw its full diplomatic weight on the side of peace negotiations and was prepared to impose a solution that effectively ratified much of "the ethnic cleansing" that was at the core of the conflict. What was notable from the perspective of this chapter is the extent to which this turn of events in Bosnia was a combination of superpower initiative and NATO's military prowess. In the process, the role of the United Nations was trivialized; it was cut out of both the negotiations and the central responsibilities for implementing the agreement.

Perhaps, the Bosnian debacle coming to a head during the fiftieth anniversary year will eventually encourage a needed reassessment of the UN role, moving it decisively either to resume the modesty, yet undoubted usefulness, of the earlier generation of Chapter VI 1/2 undertakings or to take on the role of Chapter VI 3/4 by having the capability and political support to move toward enforcement in genocidal circumstances or in situations where consent is abruptly and inappropriately withdrawn by one of the parties in the target country. Such a reform, it must be emphasized, will not come about without new and powerful initiatives from global civil society. These initiatives must alter the political climate sufficiently to challenge the realist consensus that currently shapes geopolitics and the foreign policies of the leading states. It seems to me that shattering this consensus and replacing it with a conception of humane governance is a vital precondition for any plausible approach to UN reform in the peace and security area.[4] How to satisfy this precondition is the focus of the next section.

Restoring Confidence in the United Nations: Seizing the Moment

It may be helpful to reiterate the central thesis of this chapter: the UN engages in a range of useful activities (with greater or lesser success) that far exceeds its central peace and security mandate, but the *overall* reputation of the UN depends almost exclusively, especially in the media and with the citizenry, on how well or badly it does when called upon to act in relation to the global security agenda. To restore confidence in the UN, then, depends on establishing a coherent and successful relationship to *this* agenda or, more problematically, changing perceptions as to what the UN is about. Such an emphasis also underscores the relevance of leading states, especially in their orientation toward what is important enough to justify the risking of lives or the commitment of substantial resources. In the early post–cold war period the US governmental orientation was crucial in explaining both the success and the failure of the UN in the peace and security field.

The argument that has been presented is essentially structural and normative: the UN as an instrument of unequal state power is being shaped, primarily in relation to peace and security activities, by the priorities of an increasingly globalized world economy. Until this preponderant pattern of influence is offset by the unlikely phenomenon of a resurgent labor movement or through the further growth of transnational democracy, the role of the UN, especially on matters of global security, is bound to be severely constrained in contexts where G7 leaders do not perceive their strategic interests at stake.

Intriguingly, where the state is less engaged or supportive – that is, removed from the war/peace agenda – the UN can achieve some impressive results. For instance, the 1994 UN Conference on Population and Development, held in Cairo, seemed at the time to be a great step forward for transnational efforts to face the demographic challenge, especially with respect to the conditions of affliction confronting women in many societies around the world. Reversing a long-held consensus among population experts that insisted that reducing fertility rates was the best means to inhibit population growth, the Cairo conference recommended a stress on improving the education and material circumstances of women, especially young girls, arguing that such an approach was the most effective way to reduce population growth on a global level.

The UN can also contribute impressively, even to peace and security, in those settings where capabilities and mission are more or less congruent. Such has been the case in several peace-building settlements of long-standing or potential conflict in which either the contending parties struck a compromise (as in El Salvador), or one side surrendered (as in Namibia), or a preventive, deterrent deployment was agreed upon (as in Macedonia).[5] In these situations, modest capabilities can suffice if the convergent political will of the parties is maintained; but if consent is withdrawn, these efforts can end up inconclusively or in failure, as has been the case in Afghanistan and to a degree in Cambodia.

In peacekeeping concerns arising from a spectrum of essentially internal conflicts, the eye of the current global storm, the challenge is more formidable, and its extent is often quite unfathomable. Such activity may often depend on the use of force by UN peacekeepers, which traditionally has been the special domain of the state. What seems crucial at this stage is that the UN not seek to intervene in situations of ongoing conflict that it cannot reasonably expect to resolve in a satisfactory fashion within a period of months. In this regard, the UN should be exceedingly wary about becoming committed to any undertaking, even if initiated for purely humanitarian reasons, that depends upon radical political restructuring of the target society, involving either the displacement by force of patterns of governance that have been responsible for generating pathological politics or restoring governmental stability in the context of a failed state.

Under these circumstances, the UN should instead restrict its role to relief work (as in the early stages of its Somalia involvement or in relation to Bosnia), make this restriction on its mission as clear as possible in public discourse, and avoid having its mission linked to partisan external actors, as when the UN became dependent on NATO in Bosnia.[6] One of the strengths of the International Committee of the Red Cross over the years has been its ability to delimit its role by strict, consistent adherence to humanitarian goals in manageable terms that do not often generate disappointment or criticism. Unlike the UN, the involvement of the Red Cross does not raise unrealistic or ambiguous expectations.[7] An alternative and a complement to dumping missions impossible on the UN Security Council would be to enhance the relief capabilities of humanitarian NGOs in these low-profile geopolitical settings of failed states or extreme civil strife, thereby avoiding entangling the UN in destructive conflicts that it is unable to resolve. These non-state actors are generally more able to separate their humanitarian activities from a partisan involvement in the underlying conflict; but even NGOs cannot be expected to be impartial in the face of genocidal behavior, nor should they be. The predicament can be accordingly truly tragic: there exists insufficient strategic motivation to induce effective intervention to prevent genocide, and it is morally and practically impossible to adhere to a purely humanitarian approach that makes no distinction between victims and perpetrators without becoming tainted by the genocide.

Where rival territorial factions or parties have reached a point of exhaustion, the UN can often play a constructive role even in the present negative climate, especially by encouraging a negotiated return to normalcy, as it has done in such countries as Cambodia and El Salvador. The UN can usefully provide the auspices for this process, basing its role on the consent of the parties. As events in Cambodia during the early 1990s demonstrated, consent can be shaky and be subject to withdrawal even when formally present at the outset of a peacemaking process, thereby undermining the UN role in a dangerous fashion. As discussed earlier, this prospect of augmenting first-generation UN peacekeeping, in the spirit of Hammarskjöld's original emphases, should remain a source of guidance, counseling action and restraint as appropriate; but it is also necessary to become more sensitive to the new circumstances of world order, especially with its absence of political will and logistical capabilities to stay involved in unresolved conflict in the absence of a distinct strategic motivation by leading states, and particularly the United States.

A more ambitious approach to UN reform would emphasize the need for a more autonomous UN, an Organization more capable of responding in peace and security situations without having to solicit the heavy involvement of its leading members on an ad hoc basis. Essentially, greater autonomy for the UN would require a more secure, independent financial base, with awareness that the financial troubles of the UN are not about money, but about political influence. Keeping the UN on a short financial leash has assured dominant members additional leverage in relation to key activities. The US government has exploited this position in recent years. But it should be evident that hovering at the edge of bankruptcy is not consistent with the goal of an effective and respected UN. More UN autonomy would also require, over time, the development of an independent, specially trained UN peace force that would seek to intrude itself in pathological conflict situations and exert leverage on behalf of a variety of humanitarian missions, including safeguarding multiethnic tolerance as the agreed universal grounding of legitimate governance.[8]

With the fiftieth anniversary year of the UN behind us, it is a natural time to take stock of how the Organization might better serve the needs of the peoples of the world, given changes in the patterns of conflict and considering the extent to which ascendant states are acting as agents of global market forces rather than of their own territorial constituencies. Unless due account is taken of this wider structural framework, efforts to build stronger public support for the UN are bound to fall short, particularly in the face of continuing, widespread pathological anarchism assuming distressing new forms in a variety of states, predominantly situated in sub-Saharan Africa.

Perhaps, over time, the accumulation of human suffering will produce a demand by enough of the public, as well as generate sufficient discomfort among political leaders and even within the boardrooms of transnational banks and corporations, to revive a *realist* consensus in support of an effective, autonomous United Nations. Expressed differently, for such patterns of vital support to emerge would presuppose that an effective, respected UN had become a strategic interest for the shaping political forces of this era. At present, a mood of disillusionment prevails, but it may turn out to be as transitory as the atmosphere of euphoria about the future of the UN that was prevalent in the weeks after the 1991 cease-fire in the Gulf War. In any event, the public perception of an effective UN will remain tied, for the foreseeable future, to how well the Organization does in relation to peace and security; but this should not stop more sophisticated observers from appreciating in a more nuanced fashion the many other contributions being made by the UN across the extraordinary range of its activities.

One strong testimonial to the continuing worth of the Organization is the near universality of its reach as measured by the membership of states currently representing more than 99 percent of humanity. Unlike the League of Nations, which was plagued from its inception by the nonparticipation and withdrawal of important states within the Euro-American geopolitical core and by the virtual exclusion of the entire non-Western world as a result of the colonial system, membership in the UN has come to be regarded as an almost indispensable element of statehood and statecraft for virtually every government in the world, and even those states that are repeatedly censured or have become the target of forcible measures by UN mandate have not moved to quit the Organization.

As yet, governments have not interpreted this imperative to join and participate in the United Nations as conferring upon the work of the Organization a strategic significance in relation to the peace and security agenda. This refusal has become evident in relation to the containment of disorder caused by black hole properties that tear apart weak states. Two mutually reinforcing approaches to enhance the stature of the UN seem indispensable to achieve reform, although neither is likely to materialize in the near future: first, an increased pressure from transnational global forces dedicated to globalization-from-below and the building of cosmopolitan democracy;[9] and second, a reconceptualization of geopolitics, here understood as the calculus of strategic interests by leading states, to take account of the vulnerability of world order in its current phase to the breakdown of weak states, a widespread dynamic referred to here by the rubric of pathological anarchism. This combination of developments could rebuild support for the United Nations in a form that would eventually increase its effectiveness in the political life of the planet over the course of its second half-century of existence.

Such a conceptualization of "reform" in the setting of the United Nations presupposes the possibility of two intersecting vectors of effort: first of all, a non-realist movement of transnational character driven by humanistic values and a shared commitment to democratization in all arenas of power and authority; and secondly, a shift in geopolitical calculations so as to upgrade the status of the United Nations as a practical instrument for the pursuit of statist and market interests. Is such a convergence possible? It seems so. Is it likely? It seems not, at least at present. Should such an eventuality be advocated? Assuredly, since it is one path to a future that includes a strong United Nations oriented toward the mitigation of human suffering.

But it is not the only path that leads in such a direction. Another more radical possibility is by way of a displacement of political realism as the basis for governance at all levels of social organization. Such a displacement could take many forms, but perhaps the most appealing prospect from the vantage point of the present is some combination of Gandhiism and what has come recently to be called "the culture of human rights." Such an aspirational future seems like a pipe dream at present; but, as observed earlier, only a decade ago so did a post–cold war world and a post-apartheid South Africa. How could such developments have occurred without the presence of concealed, yet latent and formidable, social forces committed to images of drastic reform that were condescendingly dismissed in realist circles as "utopian" and "irrelevant"? Presumably, such concealed opportunities for transformative politics exist in relation to the future of the United Nations and are worth commitment and struggle to actualize.

Part III
New Directions

8

Resisting "Globalization-from-Above" through "Globalization-from-Below"

A Normative Assessment of Globalization

Globalization, with all its uncertainties and inadequacies as a term, does usefully call attention to a series of developments associated with the ongoing dynamic of economic restructuring at the global level. The negative essence of this dynamic, as unfolding within the present historical time frame, is to impose on governments the discipline of global capital in a manner that promotes economistic policymaking in national arenas of decision, subjugating the outlook of governments, political parties, leaders, and elites and often accentuating distress to vulnerable and disadvantaged regions and peoples.

Among the consequences is a one-sided depoliticizing of the state as neo-liberalism becomes "the only game in town," according to widely accepted perceptions that are dutifully disseminated by the mainstream media to all corners of the planet. Such a neo-liberal mind-set is deeply opposed to social public sector expenditures devoted to welfare, job creation, environmental protection, health care, education, and even the alleviation of poverty. To a great extent, these expenditures are entrenched and difficult to diminish directly because of legal obstacles and citizen backlash, as well as varying degrees of electoral accountability in constitutional democracies. Nevertheless, the political tide is definitely running in the neo-liberal direction and will continue to do so as long as the public can be induced to ingest the pill of social austerity without reacting too vigorously. To date, the mainstream has been generally pacified, especially as represented by principal political parties, and what reaction has occurred has too often been expressed by a surge of support for nativist, right-wing extremism that indicts global capital and blames immigrants for high unemployment and stagnant wages.

This set of circumstances, if not properly mitigated, presages a generally grim future for human society, including a tendency to make alternative orientations towards economic policy appear irrelevant; to the extent believed, this induces a climate of resignation and despair. To the extent that normative goals continue to be affirmed within political arenas, as is the case to varifying degrees with human rights and environmental protection, their substantive claims on resources are treated either as an unfortunate, if necessary, burden on the grand objectives of growth and competitiveness or as a humanitarian luxury that is becoming less affordable and acceptable in an integrated market-driven world economy.

Indeed, one of the obvious spillover effects of the mind-set induced by globalization is to exert strong downward pressure on public goods expenditures, especially those with an external or global dimension. The financial strains being experienced by the United Nations, despite the savings associated with the absence of strategic rivalry of the sort that fueled the cold war arms race, is emblematic of declining political support for global public goods and runs counter to the widespread realization that the growing complexity of international life requires increasing global capabilities for coordination and governance, at minimum for the sake of efficiency.[1]

In the context of international trade, both domestic labor and minority groups in rich countries of the North mount pressure to attach human rights and environmental conditionalities to trade considerations, whereas business and financial elites resist such advocacy (unless they happen to be operating outside the global marketplace and hence have an anachronistic territorial, statist outlook on sales and profits) as it diminishes their "out-sourcing" opportunities to take advantage of dramatically lower labor costs and weaker regulatory standards in most of the South.

Economic globalization has also had some major positive benefits, including a partial leveling-up impact on North–South relations and a rising standard of living for several hundred million people in Asia, which has included rescuing many millions from poverty. Indeed, according to recent UNDP figures the proportion of the poor globally, but not their absolute number, has been declining during the past several years. There are some indications that after countries reach a certain level of development, especially in response to the demands of an expanding urban middle class, pressures mount to improve work-place and environmental conditions. Such governments also become more confident actors on the global stage, challenging inequities and biases of geopolitical structures; Malaysia typifies such a pattern. There is nothing inherently wrong with encouraging economies of scale and the pursuit of comparative advantage so long as the social, environmental, political, and cultural effects are mainly beneficial. What is objectionable is to indulge a kind of market mysticism that accords policy hegemony to the promotion of economic growth, disregarding adverse social effects and shaping economic policy on the basis of ideological certitudes that are not attentive to the realities of human suffering.

Globalization is also historically influenced by several contingent factors that intensify these adverse human effects – that is, the social costs of the process. First of all, in the current period globalization is proceeding in an ideological atmosphere in which neo-liberal thinking and priorities go virtually unchallenged, especially in the leading market economies; the collapse of the social "other" has encouraged capitalism to pursue its market logic with a relentlessness that has not been evident since the first decades of the industrial revolution. Second, this neo-liberal climate of opinion is reinforced by an anti-government societal mood that is composed of many elements, including a consumerist reluctance to pay taxes, an alleged failure by government to be successful when promoting social objectives, a "third wave" set of decentralizing technological moves that emphasize the transformative civilizational role of computers and electronic information, and a declining capacity of political parties to provide their own citizenry with forward-looking policy proposals. Third, the policy orientation of government has also grown steadily more business-focused, reflecting the decline of organized labor as a social force, resulting in a serious erosion of the perceived threat of revolutionary opposition from what Immanuel Wallerstein usefully identifies as "the dangerous classes."[2] In addition, the mobility of capital is increasing in a world economy that is shaped much more by financial flows and the acquisition of intellectual property rights than it is by manufacturing and trade in tangible goods and services. Fourth, the fiscal imperatives of debt and deficit reduction in the interests of transnational monetary stability reinforce other aspects of globalization. Fifth, this unfolding of globalization as a historical process is occurring within an international order that exhibits gross inequalities of every variety, thereby concentrating the benefits of growth upon already advantaged sectors within and among societies and worsening the relative and absolute condition of those already most disadvantaged. The experience of sub-Saharan Africa is strongly confirmatory of this generalization.[3]

Thus it is that globalization in *this* historical setting poses a particular form of normative challenge that is distinctive and different from what it would be in other globalizing circumstances. The challenge being posed is directed, above all, at the survival of, and maybe the very possibility of sustaining, the compassionate state, as typified by the humane achievements of the Scandinavian countries up through the 1980s and by the optimistic gradualism of social-democratic approaches to politics.[4] The impacts attributed to globalization have been strongly reinforced by the most influential readings given to the ending of the cold war, discrediting not only utopian socialism, but any self-conscious societal project aimed at the betterment of living conditions for the poor or regarding the minimizing of social disparities as generally desirable.

These ideological and operational aspects of globalization are associated with the way in which transnational market forces dominate the policy scene, including the significant co-optation of state power. This pattern of development is identified here as "globalization-from-above," a set of forces and legitimating ideas that is in many respects located beyond the effective reach of territorial authority and that has enlisted most governments as tacit partners. But globalization, so conceived, has generated criticism and resistance, both of a local, grass-roots variety, based on the concreteness of the specifics of time and place – for example, the siting of a dam or a nuclear power plant or the destruction of a forest – and on a transnational basis, involving the linking of knowledge and political action in hundreds of civil initiatives. It is this latter aggregate of phenomena that is described here under the rubric of "globalization-from-below."[5]

Given this understanding, it is useful to ask the question, What is the normative potential of globalization-from-below? The idea of normative potential is to conceptualize widely shared world order values: minimizing violence, maximizing economic well-being, realizing social and political justice, and upholding environmental quality.[6] These values often interact inconsistently, but they are normatively coherent insofar as they depict the main dimensions of a widely shared consensus as to the promotion of benevolent forms of world order and seem at odds in crucial respects with part of the orientation and some of the main impacts of globalization-from-above in its current historical phase. In all probability, globalization-from-above would have different, and generally more positive, normative impacts if the prevailing ideological climate were conditioned by social democracy rather than by neo-liberalism or if the adaptation of the state were subject to stronger countervailing societal or transnational pressures of a character that accorded more fully with world order values. This historical setting of globalization exhibits various tendencies of unequal significance, the identification of which helps us assess whether globalization-from-below is capable of neutralizing some of the detrimental impacts of globalization-from-above. A further caveat is in order. The dichotomizing distinction between above and below is only a first approximation to the main social formations attributable to globalization. Closer scrutiny suggests numerous cross-cutting, diagonal alignments that bring grass-roots forces into various positive and negative relationships with governmental and neo-liberal policies. Coalition possibilities vary also in relation to issue area. For instance, transnational social initiatives with respect to economic and social rights may be affirmed by some governments, while comparable initiatives directed at environmental protection or disarmament would appeal to other governments.

The New Politics of Resistance in an Era of Globalization

Political oppositional forms in relation to globalization-from-above have been shaped by several specific conditions. First, there is the virtual futility of concentrating upon conventional electoral politics, given the extent to which principal political parties in constitutional democracies have subscribed to a program and orientation that accept the essential features of the discipline of global capital. This development may not persist if social forces can be mobilized in such a way as to press social-democratic leaderships effectively to resume their commitment to the establishment of a compassionate state and if such an outlook proves to be generally viable in the context of governing. Success, except under special circumstances, would imply that globalization-from-above was not structurally powerful enough to prevent defections at the unit level of the state. Of course, variations of constraining influence arise from many factors, including the ideological stance of the leadership, efficiency in handling the social agenda, disparities in wealth and income, and the overall growth rates of the national, regional, and global economies. The main conclusion stands, however. Resistance to economic globalization is not likely to be effective if it relies on matters of political economy.

Second, criticism of economic globalization at the level of societal politics is unlikely to have a major impact on public and elite opinion until a credible alternative economic approach is fashioned intellectually and such an alternative approach has enough mobilizing effect on people that a new perception of the "dangerous classes" – which this time is not likely to be the industrial working class – enters discourse, again making economic and political elites nervous enough about their managerial ability to contain opposition to begin seriously entertaining more progressive policy options. In such an altered atmosphere it is easy to imagine the negotiation of social contracts that restore balance to the interests of people and those of markets.

Third, aside from the reemergence of dangerous classes, there are prospects that ecological constraints of various sorts will induce the market to send a variety of signals calling for a negotiated transition to managed economic growth in the interest of sustainability. Under these circumstances, with limits on growth required for both environmental reasons and middle-term business profitability, it may be possible at some now unforeseen point in the future to reach a series of agreements on a regional basis, and perhaps even globally, that amount to a global social contract. The objective of such an instrument, which would not need to be formally agreed upon, would be to balance anxieties about the carrying capacity of the earth against a range of social demands about securing the basic needs of individuals and communities, quite possibly on a regional level.

Fourth, globalization-from-above is definitely encouraging a resurgence of support for right-wing extremism, a varied and evolving array of political movements that may scare governments dominated by moderate outlooks into rethinking their degree of acquiescence to the discipline of global capital. Electoral results in several European countries, including Austria and France, reveal both growing support for the political right and a turn to the far right by citizens faced with the fiscal symptoms of economic globalization, including cutbacks in social services, high interest rates, capital outflows, and instability in employment and prospects. Will national political parties and governments be able to recover their legitimacy and authority by responding effectively to this challenge without successfully modifying the global setting and its current impact on the policymaking process?

Fifth, will labor militancy become somewhat more effective and socially visible as it shifts its focus from industrial age priorities of wages and work-place conditions to such emerging concerns as downsizing, outsourcing, and job security? There are also possibilities of engaging wider constituencies than organized labor in this struggle: individuals and groups that are feeling some of the negative effects of globalizing tendencies. Jacques Chirac seemed sufficiently shaken by the December 1995 large-scale work stoppages and demonstrations to partially reverse ideological course, at least rhetorically, and call for the creation of "a social Europe," which was a retreat from a basic tenet of neo-liberalism and thus provided a psychological victory for the perspectives favoring globalization-from-below. Subsequent demonstrations and strikes in

France appear to be generalized societal, especially urban, reactions against the austerity budget being implemented by the government so as to qualify the country for participation in plans to establish currency and monetary union within the framework of the European Union. But rhetorical victories do not necessarily produce adjustments in policy, particularly if the structures that underpin the neo-liberal approach are strong and elusive, as is the case with the world economy. In retrospect, Chirac's supposed conversion to the cause of a social Europe seems like little more than a tactical maneuver designed to gain more operating room, comparable perhaps to George Bush, the arch realist, momentarily extolling the virtues of the United Nations during the Gulf crisis and proclaiming a new world order. After the crisis passed, so did Bush's opportunistic embrace of a more law-oriented system of security for international society.

Another indicative development with respect to labor is a renewed recourse to strikes as a means for working people to resist globalization. Organized labor, despite economic growth in the North, has not been able to share in the material benefits of a larger economic pie, because of the impinging effects of competitiveness and fiscal austerity, and in numerous economic sectors it has been losing jobs and facing a continuous threat of industrial relocation. The General Motors strike of October 1996 in Canada may be a harbinger of both a new wave of labor militancy and a new agenda of grievances. The strike focused on precisely these issues, involving a direct challenge to the approach of the managers of economic globalization. It is symbolically, as well as intrinsically, important, suggesting a new direction of emphasis in the labor movement that has all sorts of potential for transnational cooperative activities across societies whose workers have benefited from globalization, but whose working conditions are miserable in a variety of respects.

Sixth, and informing the whole process of globalization, whether from above or below, is the weakening of control by the state over identity politics, with a variety of positive and negative consequences. Transnational networks of affiliation in relation to gender, race, and class have become more tenable, although, confusingly, they coexist with an ultra-nationalist backlash politics that seeks to reappropriate the state for the benefit of traditional ethnic identities. In important respects, backlash politics represents an inversion of globalization-from-below – that is, a repudiation of globalization-from-above by a reliance on the protectionist capabilities of the state, a tactic that has generally been an economic failure, most spectacularly in relation to the experience of the Soviet bloc countries in the latter stages of the cold war. By contrast, China, with its opening to the forces of globalization-from-above, while suppressing those associated with globalization-from-below, has enjoyed spectacular economic success, although at high human costs. The main point, however, is that the democratic spaces available to resist globalization-from-above tend to be mainly situated at either local levels of engagement or transnationally. One very invisible siting has been in relation to global conferences under the auspices of the United Nations on a variety of policy issues, including environment, development, human rights, the role of women, the social responsibilities of government, population pressures, and problems of urban life and habitat. Most impressive have been the creative tactics used by transnational participating groups, denied formal access because of their lack of statist credentials, yet exerting a considerable impact on the agenda and substantive outcomes of intergovernmental activities and at the same time strengthening transnational links. Starting with the Rio Conference on the Environment and Development in 1992, through the 1993 Vienna Conference on Human Rights and Development, the 1994 Cairo Conference on Population and Development, the 1995 Social Summit in Copenhagen, and the Beijing Conference on Women and Development, to the 1996 Istanbul Conference on Habitat and Development, there has been a flow of gatherings that acknowledged to varying degrees the emergent role of globalization-from-below. These events were early experiments in a new sort of participatory politics that had little connection with the traditional practices of politics within states and could be regarded as fledgling attempts to constitute "global democracy."

Such developments, representing a definite effort to engage directly both statist and market forces, produced their own kind of backlash politics. At first, at Rio and Vienna, the effort was a co-optive one, acknowledging the participation of globalization-from-below as legitimate and significant, yet controlling outcomes. But later on, at Cairo, Copenhagen, and Beijing, the more radical potentialities of these democratizing forces were perceived as adversaries of the neo-liberal conception of political economy, and the format of a global conference open to both types of globalization began to be perceived as risky, possibly an early sighting of the next wave of revolutionary challenge, the rebirth of dangerous classes in the sense earlier reserved for the labor movement.

If this assessment of action and reaction is generally accurate, it suggests the probability of several adjustments. To begin with, there may emerge a reluctance to finance and organize global conferences under the banner of the United Nations that address nontechnical matters of human concern. There will be a search for new formats by forces associated with globalization-from-below, possibly increasing the oppositional character of participation, creating a hostile presence at meetings of the Group of Seven or at the annual meetings of the Board of Governors of the IMF or World Bank, possibly organizing tribunals of the people to consider allegations against globalization-from-above. In effect, if the challenge of globalization-from-below is to become dangerous enough to tempt those representing globalization-from-above to seek accommodation, new tactics will have to be developed. One type of activity that is easier to organize concentrates energies of resistance at the regional levels of encounter, especially in Europe and Asia–Pacific, at intergovernmental gatherings devoted to expanding relative and absolute growth for the region vis-à-vis the global economy. The Third World Network, based in Penang, has been very effective in educating the cadres of resistance to globalization-from-above about adverse effects and encouraging various types of opposition. Otherwise, resistance to globalization-from-above and the ascendancy of market forces is likely to be ignored.

Seventh, it has become necessary to formulate a programmatic response to this pattern of action and reaction between political tendencies seeking to embody the logic of the market in structures of global economic governance, such as the World Trade Organization and the Bretton Woods institutions, and the transnational political forces seeking to realize the vision of cosmopolitan democracy.[7] More directly, militant tactics may also be selectively employed to supplement the regulatory efforts, feeble at best, of national governments. Such a dynamic was initiated successfully by Greenpeace a few years ago to reverse a decision by Shell Oil, approved by the British government, to sink a large oil rig named *Brent Spar* in the North Sea. The issue here was one of environmental protection, but the tactic of consumer leverage is potentially deployable in relation to any issue that finds its way onto the transnational social agenda. What induced the Shell turnaround – although it never conceded the possible environmental dangers of its planned disposal of the oil rig – was the focus of the boycott on Shell service stations, especially those located in Germany. Indeed, the impact of this initiative was so great that both the *Wall Street Journal* and the *Financial Times* editorialized against Greenpeace, complaining that it had become "an environmental superpower."

At this stage, the politics of resistance in this emergent era of globalization are in formation. Because of the global scope, combined with the unevenness of economic and political conditions, the tactics and priorities will be diverse, adapted to the local, national, and regional circumstances. Just as globalization-from-above tends towards homogeneity and unity, so globalization-from-below tends towards heterogeneity and diversity, even tension and contradiction. This contrast highlights the fundamental difference between top-down hierarchical politics and bottom-up participatory politics. It is not a zero-sum rivalry, but rather one in which the transnational democratic goals are designed to reconcile global market operations with the well-being of peoples and with the carrying capacity of the earth. Whether such a reconciliation is possible is likely to be the most salient political challenge at the dawn of a new millennium.

9

Global Civil Society: Perspectives, Initiatives, Movements

A Note on Terminology

The emphasis of this chapter is upon social forces that respond to the patterns of behavior associated with the phenomena of economic globalization. As a consequence, it seems preferable on balance to frame such activity by reference to "global civil society" rather than to "transnational civil society." Even so, the word *society* is definitely problematic at this stage of global social and political evolution, due to the absence of boundaries and the weakness of social bonds transcending nation, race, and gender. Such a difficulty exists whether the reference is to "transnational civil society" or to "global civil society." But the transnational referent tends to root the identity of the actors in the subsoil of national consciousness to an extent that neglects the degree to which the orientation is not one of crossing borders, but of inhabiting and constructing a polity appropriate to the global village. Such a nascent global polity is already partly extant, yet remains mostly emergent.[1]

A similar issue arises with respect to the terminology useful in aggregating the actors. It seems convenient to retain the term "nongovernmental organizations" (NGOs) to designate those actors associated with global civil society, because it is accurate and convenient, being so widely used and thus easily recognizable. But it is also somewhat misleading in relation to the fundamental hypothesis of a diminishing ordering capability by the sovereign state and states system. To contrast the actors and action of global civil society with the governments of states, as is done by calling them NGOs, is to confer a derivative status and to imply the persistence of a superordinate Westphalian world of sovereign states as the only effective constituents of contemporary world order.

Until recently this hierarchical dualism was justifiable, because the pre-eminence of the state was an empirical reality, reinforced by the absence of any other significant international actors capable of autonomous action.

To overcome this difficulty of relying upon this somewhat anarchistic statist rhetoric, James Rosenau has proposed an alternative terminology to that of NGOs, calling such entities "sovereignty free actors."[2] Besides being obscure, such a substitute terminology is still operating in a Westphalian shadowland in which actor identities are exclusively derived from sovereign actors – namely, states. A comparable problem exists if the reference is to "transnational social forces," although the sense of "transnational" is more flexible and autonomous than "sovereignty free." Another possibility was proposed some years ago by Marc Nerfin,[3] in the form of a framework that recognized the social reality of "the third system" (the first sector being that of states, the second of market forces), from which issued forth civil initiatives of motivated citizens supportive of the global public good.

There is by now a wide and growing literature on "global civil society," especially as related to environmental politics on a global level.[4] For the purposes of this chapter "global civil society" refers to the field of action and thought occupied by individual and collective citizen initiatives of a voluntary, nonprofit character, both within states and transnationally. These initiatives proceed from a global orientation and are responses, in part at least, to certain globalizing tendencies that are perceived to be partially or totally adverse. At present, most of the global provocation is associated directly or indirectly with market forces and the discipline of regional and global capital. As will be made clear, such a critical stance toward economic globalization does not entail an overall repudiation of these developments, but it does seek to regulate adverse effects and to correct social injustices.

To focus inquiry further, I also propose to rely upon a distinction that I have used previously: drawing a basic dividing line between global market forces identified as "globalization-from-above" and a set of oppo-sitional responses in the third system of social activism that is identified as "globalization-from-below."[5] This distinction may seem unduly polar-izing and hierarchical, apparently constructing a dualistic world of good and evil. My intention is neither hierarchical nor moralistic, and I have no illusion that the social forces emanating from the third system are inherently benevolent, while those from the first and second systems are necessarily malevolent. Far from it. One of my arguments here is that there are dangerous chauvinistic and extremist societal energies being released by one series of responses to globalization-from-above, which are threatening the achievements of the modern secular world that have been based on the normative side of the evolution of an anarchic society of states in the cumulative direction of humane governance.[6] To situate the argument, it is important to acknowledge that there are strong positive consequences and potentialities arising from the various aspects of globalization-from-above. At the same time, the historic role of globalization-from-below is to challenge and transform the negative features of globalization-from-above, both by providing alternative ideological and political space to that currently occupied by market-oriented and statist outlooks and by offering resistance to the excesses and distortions that can be properly attributed to globalization in its current phase. That is, globalization-from-below is not dogmatically opposed to globalization-from-above, but addresses itself to the avoidance of adverse effects and to providing an overall counterweight to the essentially unchecked influence currently exerted by business and finance on the process of decision at the level of the state and beyond.

Deforming Historical Circumstances

The distinctive challenges posed by globalization-from-above have been accentuated by certain defining historical circumstances. Above all, the ending of the cold war generated an ideological atmosphere in the North supportive of an abandonment of Keynesian approaches to economic policy and their replacement by a strong version of neo-liberal reliance on private sector autonomy and an economistic approach to social policy, thereby eroding the social compromises between labor and business by way of achieving fiscal austerity, efficient allocation of resources, privatization, and international competitiveness. There were other pressures to move in these directions, including a pendulum swing in societal attitudes against "the welfare state" in many states, a generalized distrust of government and public sector approaches to problem solving, the steadily declining political leverage of organized labor, the waning of industrialism and the waxing of electronics and informatics, an overall disenchantment with ameliorative rhetoric and proposals, and, above all, pressures to neutralize the alleged competitive advantages of countries in the South, especially those in the Asia–Pacific region.

These alleged competitive advantages are associated with the political and economic unevenness of states, and refer especially to cheap skilled labor, minimal regulation, and high profit margins, which have been supposedly draining jobs and capital away from the North. These differentials have ethically ambiguous consequences, reinforcing neo-liberal rationalizations for harsher economic policy and contributing to chauvinistic backlash politics in the North, while liberating many of the most populous countries in the South from centuries of acute poverty and massive human suffering.

In effect, the material and technological foundation of globalization, based on the possibilities for profitable expansion of business operations without regard to state boundaries, did not necessarily have to be linked to an ideological abandonment of the social agenda and downsizing pressures on public goods, including a disturbing decline in support for mechanisms to protect the global commons and the global public good. Neo-liberal approaches and ideological justifications have been latent in market economies ever since the birth of capitalism during the industrial revolution, but, somewhat surprisingly, the nastiest features of early capitalism were moderated to varying degrees in the nineteenth and twentieth centuries in response to the rise of "the dangerous classes," the labor movement, the ordeal of business cycles culminating in the Great Depression, and the adjustments promoted by different versions of "social democracy" and what came to be known in the United States as "liberalism."

Indeed, the recent change in ideological atmosphere can be rapidly understood by the delegitimation of liberalism in the United States since the 1980s, making even the most socially sensitive leaders in the Democratic Party unwilling any longer to use or accept liberalism as a label – what came to be derisively called "the L word." What has emerged in this first stage of globalization after the end of the cold war is a neo-liberal consensus among political elites in the world, powerfully disseminated by business-oriented and consumerist global media, a power shift that helps explain the economistic orientation of most governments.[7] In the North, this consensus tends to be justified by reference to the discipline of global capital, or simply by reference to "competitiveness," the struggle for market shares, and the virtues of free trade. Such an ideological setting is often merged with globalization, to make the one indistinguishable from the other.

The evolving perspective of social forces associated with globalization-from-below is that it remains possible and essential to promote the social agenda while retaining most of the benefits of globalization-from-above.[8] In effect, globalization can be enacted in a variety of governance and fiscal scenarios, including some that are more people-oriented and supportive of global public goods and the goals of the social agenda. The ideological infrastructure of globalization is, rather, structural, and its reformulation is at the core of the convergent perspectives implied by the emergence of global civil society as the bearer of alternative visions of a more sustainable and compassionate future world order.[9] Often this normative convergence is concealed beneath the more particularized banners of human rights, environmental protection, feminism, and social justice that have been unfurled within global civil society by issue-oriented social movements that have been transnationally active during the last several decades.

It is also important to acknowledge the limited undertaking of globalization-from-below. It is not able to challenge globalization as such, only to alter the guiding ideas that are shaping its enactment. Globalization is too widely accepted and embedded to be reversible in its essential integrative impact. Recent global trends establish the unchallengeable dominance of markets and their integration. In Jeffrey Sachs's words, "capitalism has now spread to nearly 90% of the world's population, since nearly all parts of the world are now linked through open trade, convertible currencies, flows of foreign investment, and political commitments to private ownership as the engine of economic growth."[10] Sachs points out that only 20 years earlier such conditions were those of only 20 percent of the world's population, the rest of humanity being subject either to command socialist economies or to clumsy Third World efforts to combine capitalism and socialism. Such a shift in so short a time, of course, inevitably produces a fundamental reshaping of the ideas and practices constitutive of world order.

It is this process of economic restructuring according to the logic of markets that establishes the context for globalization-from-below. The strategic question is, How can these forces effectively challenge the uneven adverse effects of globalization-from-above as it is currently evolving? These adverse consequences include insufficient attention to environmental protection and resource conservation, failures to offset severe vulnerabilities of social segments, countries, and regions that are not currently able to gain sufficient access to the market, and a generalized lack of support for the social agenda and global public goods, including the United Nations, especially in its efforts to coordinate and promote moves to overcome world poverty and to close the gaps that separate rich from poor.

Responding to Economic Globalization

There have been various failed responses to economic globalization, conceived of as the capitalist portion of the world economy. Without entering into an assessment of these failures, it is worth noticing that both

Soviet-style socialism and Maoism, especially during the period of the Cultural Revolution, were dramatic efforts to oppose economic globalization that ended in disaster. By contrast, despite the difficulties, the subsequent embrace of the market by China under the rubric of "modernization" in the form of the capitalist path have been spectacularly successful. The same is true for many Third World countries that forged a middle path between socialism and capitalism that made the state a major player in the economy, particularly with respect to public utilities and energy; for most of these countries, as well, the change from a defensive hostility to the world market to a position of unconditional receptivity has been generally treated as a blessing.

The learning experience at the level of the state has been one of submission to the discipline of global capital as it pertains to the specific conditions of each country. Fashionable ideas of "delinking" and "self-reliance" are in a shambles, perhaps most easily appreciated by the inability of North Korea to feed its population, while its capitalist sibling in South Korea is scaling the peaks of affluence. In effect, the geopolitical managers of the world economy use such policies as a punishment for supposedly deviant states, seeking to legitimize the exclusion under the rubric of "sanctions," a policy often widely criticized in this period because of its cruel effects on the civilian population of the target society. Even Castro's Cuba, for so long an impressive holdout, is relying on standard capitalist approaches to attract foreign investment and open its economy to market forces. Fukuyama's notorious theme of the end of history is partially correct, at least for now, if understood as limited in its application to economic aspects of policy and not extended to political life.[11]

Another kind of response to economic globalization has been negative. This takes the form of backlash politics that looks either to some pre-modern traditional framework as viable and virtuous (as with religious extremists of varying identity or indigenous peoples) or to ultra-territorialists that seek to keep capital at home and exclude foreigners to the extent possible. These responses, aside from those of indigenous peoples, have a rightist flavor, because of their emphasis on the sacred religious or nationalist community of the saved that is at war with an evil "other," either secularist or outsider. To the extent that such movements have gained control of the state, as in Iran since the Islamic Revolution, or have even threatened to do so, as in Algeria since 1992, the results have been dismal: economic deterioration, political repression, and widespread civil strife. Specific causes of these backlash phenomena are connected to the failures of globalization and its related secularist outlook, but the correctives proposed have yet to exhibit a capacity to generate an alternative that is either capable of successful economic performance or able to win genuine democratic consent from relevant political communities.

Related to this predominance of market forces are a series of attempts by civil society to avoid the adverse effects of economic globalization. The most effective of these responses have been issue-oriented, often involving local campaigns against a specific project. One notable attempt to enter the domain of transformative politics more generally was made by the green parties in Europe during the 1980s. This green movement often exhibited tactical brilliance in its moves to expose the deficiencies of globalizing trends, especially their dangers to the environment. Its political success was less its ability to mobilize large numbers in support of its causes and programs as the extent to which its challenge influenced the whole center of the political spectrum to put the environmental challenge high on its policy agenda. But the green movement's attempt to generalize its identity so as to provide an alternative leadership for the entire society across the full range of governance or to transnationalize its activities to promote global reform met with frustration and internal controversy that fractured green unity, most vividly in Germany, but elsewhere as well. Those who argued for a new radicalism beyond established political parties within a green framework were dismissed as utopian dreamers, while those who opted for influence within the existing framework were often scorned as victims of co-optation or derided as opportunists. The green movement and its political parties have persisted in the 1990s, but as a voice on the margins, with neither a credible alternative world view to that provided by globalization nor a sufficiently loyal constituency to pose a threat to the mainstream.

Localism has been another type of response, directed at the siting of a nuclear power reactor or a dam, mobilizing residents of the area facing displacement and loss of their traditional livelihood and sometimes involving others from the society and beyond who identify with the poor or nature. These struggles have had some notable successes.[12] But these are reactions to symptomatic disorders associated with globalization and do little more than influence entrepreneurial forces to be more prudent or to make more of a public relations effort.

More relevant have been attempts by elements of global civil society to protect the global commons against the more predatory dimensions of globalization. Here Greenpeace has a distinguished record of activist successes, exhibiting an imaginative and courageous willingness to challenge entrenched military and commercial forces by direct action that has had an impact: helping to discourage whaling, protesting against the effort of Shell Oil to dispose of the oil rig *Brent Spar* in the North Sea, supporting a 50-year moratorium on mineral development in Antarctica, and, most memorably, resisting for many years nuclear testing in the Pacific. Rachel Carson's lyrical environmentalism and Jacques Cousteau's extraordinarily intense dedication to saving the oceans show the extent to which even single, gifted individuals can exert powerful counter-tendencies to the most destructive sides of an insufficiently regulated market. But these efforts, although plugging some of the holes in the dikes, are not based on either a coherent critique or an alternative ideology, and thus operate only at the level of the symptom, while neglecting the disorders embedded in the dynamics of globalization.

Some other efforts to awaken responses have arisen from global civil society on the basis of a more generalized assessment. One of the earliest such initiatives was that promoted by the Club of Rome, a transnational association of individuals prominent in business, science, and society that led to the famous study *The Limits to Growth*.[13] The argument, tied closely to a sophisticated computer program that was measuring trends in population growth, pollution, resource scarcity, and food supply, concluded that industrialism as practiced was not sustainable, but was tending toward imminent catastrophe. Around the same time a group of distinguished scientists from various countries working with the British journal *The Ecologist*, issued its own warning call under the title *Blueprint for Survival*.[14] These alarms provoked a debate and led to some adjustments, but the resilience of the world capitalist system was such that no fundamental changes occurred, and the warnings issued as signals soon faded into the cultural noise. Neither a sense of an alternative nor a movement of protest and opposition took hold.

The World Order Models Project is illustrative of a somewhat more remote effort to challenge the existing order and find alternatives, through the medium of diagnosis and prescription by a transnational group of independent academicians. The efforts of this group have been confined to the margins of academic reflection on world conditions. Also, until recently, the policy focus and animating preoccupation was war, which then broadened to include environmental danger. Although WOMP produced overall assessments, its background and participants made it less sensitive to the distinctive challenges and contributions of economic globalization.[15] As such, its emphasis on war and the war-making sovereign state did not come to terms with either the durability of the state or the need to avoid its *instrumentalization* by global market forces. The principal world order danger is no longer the absolute security claims of the sovereign state, but rather the inability of the state to protect its own citizenry, especially those who are most vulnerable, in relation to the workings of the world economy.

A better-connected effort to address overall global issues was attempted by the Commission on Global Governance, as expressed in its main report, *Our Global Neighborhood.*[16] This initiative, claiming authority and credibility on the basis of the eminence of its membership drawn from the leading ranks of society and stressing past or present government service at leadership or ministerial levels, seemed too farsighted for existing power structures and too timid to engage the imagination of the more activist and militant actors in civil society. The Commission report failed to arouse any widespread or sustained interest, despite the comprehensiveness and thoughtfulness of its proposals. As an intellectual tool it is also disappointing, failing to clarify the challenge of globalization and the troublesome character of Bretton Woods approaches to world economic policy. As a result, its efforts to anchor an argument for global reform in an argument for "global governance" seemed more likely to consolidate globalization-from-above than to promote a creative equilibrium relying on the balancing contribution of globalization-from-below. In part, this Commission was unlucky, beginning its efforts in the aftermath of the Gulf War, when attention and hopes were centered on the future of the United Nations, and finishing its work at a time when the world Organization was widely, if somewhat unfairly, discredited as a result of the outcomes in Somalia, Bosnia, and Rwanda. But this was not the fundamental problem, which was more a failure of nerve to address the adverse consequences of globalization, a focus that would have put the Commission on a collision course with adherents of the neo-liberal economistic world picture. Given the claims of "eminence" and "independent funding" that characterize such a commission, it is not to be expected that it would be willing or able to address the structural and ideological deficiencies attributable to the prevailing world order framework. This means that its best efforts confirm pessimism about finding an alternative world picture to that provided by the neo-liberal prism on globalization.

What is being argued, then, is that the challenges posed by economic globalization have not as yet engendered a sufficient response in two connected respects: first, the absence of an ideological posture that is comparably coherent to that underlying various renditions of neo-liberalism and that could provide the social forces associated with globalization-from-below with a common theoretical framework, political language, and program; secondly, a clear expression of a critique of globalization-from-above that cuts deeply enough to address the most basic normative challenges associated with poverty, social marginalization, and environmental decay, while accepting the emancipatory contributions being made, as well as the unchallengeable persistence of state and market; the political goals of globalization-from-below are thus at once *both* drastic and reformist.

It is essential to realize that the world order outcome arising from the impact of economic globalization is far from settled and in no sense predetermined. The forces of globalization-from-above have taken control of globalization and are pushing it in an economistic direction that considerably instrumentalizes the state on behalf of a set of attitudes and policies: privatization, free trade, fiscal austerity, and competitiveness. But there are other options: "sustainable development," "global welfare," "cybernetic libertarianism." The eventual shape of globalization will reflect the play of these diverse perspectives and priorities. The perspectives and priorities of globalization-from-above are being challenged in various ways, but mainly piecemeal. The effort of the final section is to encourage a mobilization of the now disparate forces of globalization-from-below in the direction of greater solidity and political weight. It is my conviction that such mobilization is most likely to occur beneath the banner of democracy, but democracy reformulated in relation to the basic aspirations of peoples everywhere to participate in the processes that shape their lives.

The purpose of the next section is mainly to clarify what is meant by "democracy" in relation to the analysis of globalization.

Toward Coherence: The Theory and Practice of Normative Democracy

To introduce the idea of "normative democracy" is to offer a proposal for a unifying ideology capable of mobilizing and unifying the disparate social forces that constitute global civil society and of providing the political energy that is associated with globalization-from-below. The specification of normative democracy is influenced strongly by David Held's work on democratic theory and practice, particularly his conception of "cosmopolitan democracy"; but it offers a slightly different terminology, so as to emphasize the agency role of global civil society with its range of engagements that go from the local and grass roots to the most encompassing arenas of decision.[17] Normative democracy also draws upon and will invoke Walden Bello's call for "substantive democracy," set forth as a more progressive movement alternative to the more limited embrace of "constitutional democracy."[18] I prefer *normative* to *substantive* democracy because it highlights ethical and legal norms, thereby reconnecting politics with moral purpose and values, which calls attention to the moral emptiness of neo-liberalism, consumerism, and most forms of secularism. There is also a practical reason: to weaken the political appeal of resurgent organized religion while at the same time acknowledging the relevance of moral purpose and spiritual concerns to the renewal of progressive politics.

Contra widespread claims in the West, there is no empirical basis for the argument that economic performance is necessarily tied to constitutional democracy and human rights. Several countries in the Asia–Pacific region, most significantly China, have combined an outstanding macro-economic record with harsh authoritarian rule. Globalization-from-above is not an assured vehicle for the achievement of Western-style constitutional democracy, including the protection of individual and group rights. But democracy, as such, is of the essence of a meaningful form of political action on the part of global civil society, especially to the extent that such action, even when revolutionary, refrains from and repudiates violent means. In this regard, there is an emergent, as yet implicit, convergence of ends and means on the part of several distinct tendencies in civil society: issue-oriented movements, nonviolent democracy movements, governments that minimize their links to geopolitical structures. This convergence presents several intriguing opportunities for coalition building and greater ideological coherence in the outlook associated with globalization-from-below. Against this background, normative democracy seems like an attractive umbrella for theorizing, not dogmatically, but to exhibit affinities.

Normative democracy adopts comprehensive views of fundamental ideas associated with the secular modern state: security is conceived as extending to environmental protection and to the defense of economic viability;[19] human rights are conceived as extending to social and economic rights, as well as to such collective rights as the right to development, the right to peace, the right of self-determination; democracy is conceived as extending beyond constitutional and free, periodic elections, to include an array of other assurances that governance is oriented toward human well-being and ecological sustainability, and that citizens have access to arenas of decision making.

The elements of normative democracy can be enumerated, but their content and behavioral applications will require much amplification in varied specific settings. This enumeration reflects the dominant orientations and outlook of the political actors that make up the constructivist category of "globalization-from-below." It is thus not an enumeration that is a wish list, but intends to be descriptive and explanatory of an embedded consensus. The elements of this consensus are as follows:

1   *Consent of citizenry*   This requires some periodic indication that the permanent population of the relevant community is represented by the institutions of governance and confers legitimacy through the expression of consent. Elections are the established modalities for territorial communities to confer legitimacy on government, but referenda and rights of petition and recall may be more appropriate for other types of political community, especially those of regional or global scope, while direct democracy may be most meaningful for local political activity; the idea is to be flexible and adaptive.

2   *Rule of law*   This requires that all modes of governance are subject to the discipline of law as a way of imposing effective limits on authority and of assuring some form of checks and balances as between legislative, executive, judicial, and administrative processes; also, that sensitivity exists to the normative claims of civil initiatives associated with codes of conduct, conference declarations, societal institutions (for instance, Permanent Peoples Tribunal in Rome).

3   *Human rights*   This requires taking account of differing cultural, economic, and political settings and priorities, the establishment of a mechanism for the impartial and effective implementation of human rights deriving from global, regional, state, and transnational civil sources of authority; human rights are being comprehensively conceived as encompassing economic, social, and cultural rights, as well as civil and political rights, with a concern for both individual and collective conceptions of rights, and emphasizing tolerance toward the various dimensions of difference and fundamental community sentiments.

4   *Participation*   This calls for effective and meaningful modes of participation in the political life of the society, centered upon the processes of government, but extending to all forms of social governance, including work place and home; participation may be direct or indirect – that is, representational – but it enables the expression of views and influence upon the processes of decision on the basis of an ideal of equality of access; creativity is needed to find methods other than elections by which to ensure progress toward significant participation.

5   *Accountability*   This requires suitable mechanisms for challenging the exercise of authority by those occupying official positions at the level of the state, but also with respect to the functioning of the market and of international institutions; the ideal of an inter-

national criminal court is one mechanism for assuring accountability by those in powerful positions that have been traditionally
treated as exempt from the rule of law.

6 *Public goods* This calls for a restored social agenda that corrects
the growing imbalance, varying in seriousness from country to
country, between private and public goods in relation to the
persistence of poverty amid affluence, pertaining to health, education, housing, and basic human needs, but also in relation to
support for environmental protection, regulation of economic
globalization, innovative cultural activity, infrastructural development for governance at the local, regional, and global levels.
In these regards, a gradual depoliticalization of funding, either
by reliance on a use or transaction tax imposed on financial
flows, global air travel, or some form of reliable and equitable
means to fund public goods of local, national, regional, and global
scope.

7 *Transparency* This calls for an openness with respect to knowledge and information that builds trust between institutions of governance and the citizenry at various levels of social interaction –
in effect, establishing the right to know as an aspect of constitutionalism, including a strong bias against public sector secrecy and
covert operations, and criminalizing government lies of the sort
recently revealed, where for years, to protect air force spy missions,
the CIA lied about alleged "UFO sightings"; internationally, transparency is particularly important in relation to military expenditures and arms transfers.

8 *Non-violence* The underpinning of globalization-from-below
and the promotion of substantive democracy is a conditional
commitment to nonviolent politics and conflict resolution. Such
a commitment does not nullify rights of self-defense as protected
in international law, strictly and narrowly construed; nor does
it necessarily invalidate limited recourse to violence by oppressed
peoples; such an ethos of nonviolence clearly imposes on governments an obligation to renounce weaponry of mass destruction
and to pursue diligently the negotiation of phased disarmament
arrangements, but also to make maximum commitments to
demilitarizing approaches to peace and security applicable to all
forms of social interaction, including peace and security at the
level of city and neighborhood; such a commitment suggests
the principled rejection of capital punishment as an option of
government.

Globalization-from-Below and the State: A Decisive Battle

It seems – although I shall not enter into detailed discussion – that different versions of neo-liberal ideology have exerted a defining influence upon the orientation of political elites governing sovereign states. Of course, there are many variations reflecting conditions and personalities in each particular state and region, but the generalization holds without important exception.[20] Even China, despite adherence to the ideology of state socialism, has implemented by state decree, with impressive results, a market-oriented approach to economic policy. The state can remain authoritarian in relation to its citizenry without necessarily jeopardizing its economic performance, so long as it adheres, more or less, to the discipline of global capital, thereby achieving competitiveness by reference to costs of production, savings, and attraction of capital. In these respects, neo-liberalism as a *global* ideology is purely economistic in character and does not imply a commitment to democratic governance in even the minimal sense of periodic fair elections.

Globalization-from-below, in addition to entailing a multitude of local struggles, is also a vehicle for the transnational promotion of substantive democracy as a counterweight to neo-liberalism. It provides an alternative, or a series of convergent alternatives, that has not yet been posited as a coherent body of theory and practice, but remains the inarticulate common ground of emergent global civil society. Substantive democracy, unlike backlash politics that closes off borders and identities, seeks a politics of reconciliation that maintains much of the openness and dynamism associated with globalization-from-above, while countering its pressures to privatize and marketize the production of public goods. In effect, the quest of substantive democracy is to establish a social equilibrium that takes full account of the realities of globalization in its various aspects. Such a process cannot succeed on a country-by-country basis, as the rollback of welfare in Scandinavia suggests, but must proceed within regional and global settings. The state remains the instrument of policy and decision making most affecting the lives of peoples and the primary link to regional and global institutions. The state has been instrumentalized to a considerable degree by the ideology and influences associated with globalization-from-above, resulting in declining support for public goods in an atmosphere of strong sustained economic growth and in polarization of outcomes, with incredible wealth for the winners and acute suffering for the losers. An immediate goal of those disparate social forces that constitute globalization-from-below is to reinstrumentalize the state to the extent that it redefines its role as mediating between the logic of capital and the priorities of its peoples, including their short-term and longer-term goals.

Evidence of this reinstrumentalization of the state is present in relation to global conferences on broad policy issues that were organized under UN auspices and made an impact on public consciousness and behavioral standards in the 1990s. These UN conferences increasingly attracted an array of social forces associated with global civil society and gave rise to a variety of coalitions and oppositions between state, market, and militant citizens organized to promote substantive goals (for example, human rights, environmental protection, economic equity and development). These UN conferences became arenas of political participation that operated outside the confines of state control and were regarded as threatening by the established order based on a core coalition between market forces and geopolitical leaders. One result is to withdraw support for such UN activities, pushing the organization to the sidelines on global policy issues, as part of a process of recovering control over its agenda and orientation. Such a reaction represents a setback for globalization-from-below, but it also shows that the social forces that are associated with the promotion of normative democracy can be formidable adversaries.

Such a process of reinstrumentalization could also influence the future role and identity of regional and global mechanisms of governance, especially as regards increasing the regulatory mandate directed toward market forces and the normative mandate with respect to the protection of the global commons, the promotion of demilitarization, and the overall support for public goods.

Conclusion

In this chapter it is argued that the positive prospects for global civil society depend very much on two interrelated developments: achieving consensus on "normative democracy" as the foundation of coherent theory and practice and waging a struggle for the outlook and orientation of institutions of governance with respect to the framing of globalization. The state remains the critical focus of this latter struggle, although it is not, even now, a matter of intrinsic opposition between the state as instrument of globalization-from-above and social movements as instrument of globalization-from-below. In many specific settings, coalitions between states and social movements are emerging, as is evident in relation to many questions of environment, development, and human rights. It may even come to pass that transnational corporations and banks adopt a longer-term view of their own interests and move to alter the policy content of globalization-from-above to soften the contrast with the preferences of globalization-from-below. It is helpful to remember that such an unanticipated convergence of previously opposed social forces led to the sort of consensus that produced "social democracy" and "the welfare state" over the course of the nineteenth and twentieth centuries. There is no evident reason to preclude such convergences on regional and global levels as a way of resolving some of the tensions being caused by the manner in which globalization is *currently* being enacted.

10

Recasting Citizenship

Framing the Argument

The dominant modern idea of citizenship was definitely linked closely to the emergence of individuals endowed with entitlements or rights in relation to the governments of territorial sovereign states. Thus the history of citizenship could be traced from the entitlement associated with freedom *from* abuses of governmental authority, especially arbitrary exertions of coercion, to freedoms *to* – that is, freedoms of a more affirmative character to participate directly or indirectly in the governing process – and, finally, to a series of entitlements associated with social democracy or the welfare state.[1]

Secular varieties of nationalism were not an invariable backdrop, but nationalism of some sort was the most characteristic political framework in which modern forms of citizenship flourished. In such conditions the state was the focal point of a juridically conceived nationalism – that is, a geographically bounded ideal of political community. This contrasts with an ethnically or religiously conceived nationalism whose borders are rarely coterminus with those of a sovereign state. Thus, secular nationalism emphasizes the inclusiveness of carefully delimited and widely recognized international boundaries that specify, with dogmatic clarity, the distinction between the political community that is inside and the international anarchy that is outside.[2] Such a dichotomizing of political reality underscores the importance of full membership in a political community, as opposed to the vulnerability of "the stateless person." Citizenship in one of its dimensions is a means of ensuring the full rights of membership, including engaging both the protective responsibilities of the state under international law and the duty of loyalty by the individual to a particular state.[3]

Despite the external juridical equality of citizens/nationals of states themselves, internal discriminatory practices within states have made the struggle for equal participation by all citizens a momentous, unfinished struggle, raising a myriad of subsidiary questions about gender, race, class, religion, and region. Nevertheless, citizenship has often served as a focal point for individual rights and benefits, the latter especially with respect to social and economic concerns. This highlighting of citizenship is an enduring tribute to the seminal importance of the French Revolution in defining the relationship between the individual and the government at the level of the sovereign state. More widely conceived, it was a direct outcome of the struggles in Europe against absolutist claims made on behalf of royal and divine authority, a process that in various ways can be traced back at least as far as the Magna Carta. What emerged from this historical process was an assurance of formal equality under the law, independent of specific class, ethnic, and religious identities, which was no mean achievement viewed against the backdrop of the feudal hierarchies that preceded modernity.

It is against this background that the impact of an increasingly globalized world economy on citizenship must be understood. The essential argument is that economic globalization is weakening territorial ties between people and the state in a variety of ways that are shifting the locus of political identities, especially of elites, in such a manner as to diminish the relevance of international frontiers, thereby eroding, if not altogether undermining, the foundations of traditional citizenship. But the consequences are divergent and even contradictory. Some individuals adversely affected by globalization are more territorial and chauvinistic than ever. In keeping with the postmodern mood, it has become fashionable in certain circles to talk grandly these days of being "a global citizen," "a citizen of Europe," "a citizen pilgrim," "a netizen," and the like. Such de-territorializing of citizenship seems presently, and for the foreseeable future, to reflect exceedingly "thin" sentiments (either superficial and utopian or real, as with ardent Internet surfers, but engaging only a tiny fragment of society) as compared to the still "thick" affinities that bind the overwhelming majority of generally patriotic citizens to their state and its flag. These are ties of loyalty unto death, if such an ultimate sacrifice is perceived as necessary for the defense of the realm. The sovereign state in its heyday was the recipient of thick feelings of loyalty.[4]

It needs to be appreciated more than is generally the case that this discourse on citizenship and its changing character remains an essentially

Western experience that has not taken existential hold in non-Western societies nearly to the extent as have such other quintessential Western conceptions as territorial sovereignty, international diplomacy, the rule of law, and even human rights. Further, in the context of progressive forms of resistance to the abusive aspects of economic globalization, there has been a strong tendency for individuals to bond across boundaries, which weakens in other respects traditional territorially based citizenship and its core reality of a symbiotic relationship to the state. By contrast, it is the generally regressive forms of resistance to globalization that have been reviving exclusivist notions of national identity via the revival of chauvinism, patrioteering, and anti-immigrant postures, thereby eroding notions of tolerance that had come to animate the idea of being a citizen and even more so the liberal ideal, of being an active citizen in a modern secular state. This secular emphasis is especially true for those exemplar states that were until recently making steady progress in combining prosperity and deepening constitutionalism in the setting of a multiethnic, plural religious population. As a result, economic globalization and its diverse impacts seem likely to produce a decline in the quality and significance of citizenship unless the idea of political membership and existential identity can be effectively transferred to the global village realities of community and participation in a post-statist or postmodern world. If such a process is to succeed, it must proceed in a manner that is able to engage non-Western as well as Western social and political forces, one that is psychologically meaningful for large numbers of people at all levels of society.

In an important book written shortly before he became Secretary of Labor in the first Clinton administration, Robert Reich argued for a major public commitment of resources devoted to reeducation and retraining, to enable the vast majority of Americans currently being denied the benefits of economic globalization to participate more positively in the future. Arguing from a sense that "an American economy is becoming meaningless," given the de-territorializing realities of economic globalization, Reich suggests that "[t]he real economic challenge facing the United States in the years ahead – the same as that facing every other nation – is to increase the potential value of skills and capacities and by improving their means of linking their skills and capacities to the world market."[5] Reich believes that this challenge is first and foremost a test of community solidarity within geographic boundaries. According to Reich, a constructive response "will depend on whether there is still enough concern about American society to elicit sacrifice from all of us – especially from the most advantaged and successful of us – to help the majority regain the ground it has lost and fully participate in the new global economy." And he affirms that "[t]he same question of responsibility confronts every other nation whose economic borders are vanishing."[6]

Unfortunately, the ideological climate of the 1990s is not at all receptive to Reich's line of thinking, especially in the United States, but to some degree also in Europe. The dominant outlook in the West, with its embrace of unvarnished versions of neo-liberalism, is exerting downward pressure on government expenditures for public goods (other than defense), including education, with responsibility increasingly being left to the generally untender mercies of the private sector.[7] Furthermore, the possibility of taxing the rich to facilitate the entry of more of the disadvantaged of one's own country onto the world stage goes contrary to the ascendancy of self-aggrandizing market logic of shifting capital to where the costs of production are lowest, a downsizing of the social agenda, as well as the emergent borderless self-image of these global operators as being "global citizens," and thus being quite unreceptive to the argument that it is beneficial to invest more heavily in the disadvantaged of one's own country than elsewhere.[8] Perhaps more revealingly, at no point in the history of the West did privileged sectors of society act voluntarily to improve the condition of disadvantaged fellow citizens unless put under effective pressure in the form of a serious challenge to preeminence mounted by those whom Immanuel Wallerstein has usefully labeled as "the dangerous classes."[9] Whether the pressures of globalization are in the process of reconstituting dangerous classes among the losers in various countries and regions is beginning to be an interesting question in the late 1990s.[10] Such a process has been difficult to discern because of the absence of an ideological alternative, making resistance to globalization assume an ad hoc and exceedingly local character that may be concealing systemic implications.

These generalizations about the withdrawal of the state from the social domain of policy appear to apply with far less force to the countries of East Asia, where the governments are more paternalistically oriented toward their societies and more interventionist on economic policy, but, somewhat paradoxically, are least inclined to endow citizens, as individuals, with rights as these have become entrenched in the West.[11] Revealingly, it is these states, with their Confucian heritage, that now appear to be providing the best educational preparation, along the lines proposed by Reich, enabling a larger proportion of their societies to contribute to and benefit from economic globalization.[12] Significantly, it is precisely these societies which have until very recently been enjoying the most spectacularly successful records of participation in the world economy. Despite certain democratizing moves, impressive grass-roots activism, and some expansion in the political space available for individual initiative, the members of these societies continue to resemble subjects more than citizens when it comes to their relationship to the governing process. Their identities seem to be forged these days mainly by the ambiguous assertion of civilizational identities in the form of Asian values and the like, which is surely suspect to the extent that it is opportunistically invoked to shield oppressive regimes from domestic discontent.

It is too soon to depict the impact of the financial and currency crises of 1997–8 on the Asian model of capitalism and on Asian political identity. To the extent that Asian governments swallow a heavy dosage of neo-liberal fiscal medicine as the price for an IMF bail-out, the American model of state/society will gain further global ascendancy.

Reich's attempt to promote what he calls "positive economic nationalism" on behalf of America tries to combine the logic of territorial loyalty with the logic of market opportunity.[13] It flies in the face of another feature of Western political culture since the Enlightenment, especially in its American embodiment, which is the celebration of the individual and an ethos of individualism. Thus Reich's plea is unlikely to achieve more than cosmetic results unless a politics of resistance takes shape in a form that threatens the stability of the domestic political order, as arguably has been the effect of the French strikes over the past few years, yielding by now a stream of concessions on grievances that were at odds with neo-liberal precepts and inconsistent with the French government's own embrace of fiscal austerity, which partly reflects its effort to remain on the fast lane of European economic integration. But the stagnancy of the French economy in the last several years raises serious questions as to whether an economy of even France's size can modify the social costs of globalization without serious losses of market share.

The discipline of global capital seems far too strong to be resisted by ethical appeals mounted on behalf of territorial constituencies, unless these are powerfully reinforced by political movements that share the curative vision that Reich advocates. In this regard, the decline of citizenship as a meaningful foundation for the assertion of claims on resources suffers from a lack of ideological legitimacy, of political clout, and in the West of cultural reinforcement. Whether the opposition to globalization will coalesce effectively remains to be seen and may depend on both the experience of serious economic crises and a creative leadership that provides an alternative approach to economic policy.[14] The resistance is definitely growing, flexing its muscles, and the depth and will of the neo-liberal consensus are being tested for the first time since the end of the cold war in a variety of settings.

This thesis on the decline of citizenship will be analyzed by reference to a series of different factors: (1) the changing role of the state; (2) the rise of civilizational, religious, and ethnic identities; (3) new forms of backlash politics; (4) the assertion of non-Western perspectives; (5) trends toward post-heroic geopolitics; (6) the rise of transnational social forces. A final section of the chapter will examine the future of citizenship in an era of economic globalization with an eye toward reversing adverse effects, arguing that decline seems probable but not inevitable.

The Decline of Citizenship: Some Dimensions of Adjustment

The changing role of the state   The modern state, with its overriding sense of spatial enclosure, has privileged the people living within its boundaries, endowing them with a primary identity associated with the most powerful and durable ideology ever devised, that of nationalism. As is well known, ruled and ruler in the West struggled over the centuries to achieve a dynamic equilibrium, which was formulated with primary reference to the rights and duties of the citizen, a status that was to be sharply distinguished from the earlier royalist notion of the individual as a subject. The advent of political democracy sharpened this distinction, emphasizing the legitimating role of citizens in the selection of leaders through the medium of periodic, free elections and the selection of accountable representatives, as well as a constraining constitutional framework that imposed limits on government and ensured rights. As Marxist and other lines of critique established, governments, despite democratic pretensions and electoral rituals, were often governed largely on behalf of dominant interest groups. Nevertheless, their orientation was territorial in its essential functioning. And citizens, with varying degrees of commitment and alienation, conceived of their future exclusively within the framework of the state. Even workers of socialist persuasion with little to lose but their chains proved to be poor converts to transnational identities premised on the imperatives of class solidarity. In wartime during this century, nationalist identities and patriotic appeals easily overwhelmed calls for socialist solidarity with comrades on the other side of international frontiers.[15]

But the effects of globalization, while uneven, have been reorienting the state and the outlook of dominant elites, giving their perspectives an increasingly nonterritorial character, which is definitely weakening the sense of national identification. This generalization applies with particular force to the individualistic West since the end of the cold war. It applies most strongly of all to those states that have never developed a paternalistic relationship toward their citizenry – that is, where the memories of kings and bishops are dimmest, or nonexistent. More concretely, governments are adapting their role and function to globalization by accepting as priorities expanded trade, favorable budgetary balances, sound fiscal and macroeconomic policy, and maximum opportunities for capital mobility. The mentality of the ruling classes is de-territorialized to the extent that even "security" is defined more by reference to the global economy than in relation to the defense of territorial integrity.[16] The Gulf War exhibited these priorities, as well as new patterns of collective action in support of shared interests. By contrast, the largely civil tensions of the former Soviet Union and Yugoslavia and the torments of sub-Saharan Africa have been treated as strategically trivial – that is, neither capable of inspiring significant collective action nor perceived by governments as worth fighting or dying for.

What happens to citizenship, given these circumstances? First of all, the influence of globalization tends to minimize political differences *within* states among contending political parties, thereby trivializing electoral rituals. The options offered to the citizen are becoming far less meaningful, especially for that bottom 80 percent of the citizenry that appears to be losing out as a consequence of economic globalization. Passivity, despair, and alienation result, with the privileged 20 percent feeling more and more detached from the misfortunes of their fellow citizens except to the extent that backlash phenomena serve as a reminder that territorial passions can, if aroused, still exert considerable influence. Bonds of solidarity among the citizenry, never too strong in the face of antagonistic interests and against the grain of individualism, have been fraying badly as of late.

The disadvantaged citizenry fragments into the following main components: first and foremost, an inert, confused mass public; secondly, an angry, misled tribalist minority giving renewed vitality to right-wing fringe politics; and thirdly, a visionary, activist minority that organizes itself locally and transnationally (but not nationally and not yet politically), giving rise to an alternative globalization, an emergent project to construct a global civil society premised on an ethos of cosmopolitan democracy.[17] This project to reconstitute democracy is animated by a greater sensitivity to disparate identities associated with gender, race, and metaphysical standpoint, giving rise to various feminisms, diverse types of ecological consciousness, and many efforts to recover spiritual traditions, including those belonging to native peoples. Citizenship, as preoccupied with membership and participation in the secular, territorial state, seems very marginal to these normative endeavors that are undoubtedly, in part, psychopolitical adjustments to the de-territorializing of the state.

The rise of civilizational, religious, and ethnic identities   Closely connected with the partial displacement of the state as a source of political identity, as well as an indirect response to the homogenizing dimensions of global village life, is the reemergence of several alternative sources of identity, especially those connected with civilizational, religious, and ethnic perspectives. This feature of the end of the millennium is unmistakable, whether one thinks of the extraordinary global resonance evoked by Samuel Huntington's thesis that a clash of civilizations was imminent, as well as by the emergence of powerful linkages between religion and politics, and by the rise of ethnic separatist movements. Each of these tendencies drains energy away from the kind of political identity that citizenship in a secular state aspires to achieve, which, above all else, is associated with the separation of church and state and the consequence that loyalty is connected with juridical nationality derived from the status of being a citizen.

The causal connections of these developments with economic globalization are difficult, if not impossible, to establish, since all such cultural moves connected with something as fundamental as political identity are overdetermined, meaning that several convergent explanations are intertwined. Beyond that, each society has its own story, its own ways of responding to a mix of external and internal social forces active at a particular historical time. Nevertheless, the intensity, specificity, and widespread nature of the magnetism of these non-secular poles of identity seem definitely connected with meeting the combined challenges of globalization and modernization without succumbing to Westernization. Take Malaysia or Singapore as instances of countries that are successful in their efforts to benefit economically by participating in the world economy, yet are governed by political leaders who are seeking to stress cultural specificity as a self-conscious mode of resistance directed at the alleged menace of Westernization. In these instances it is government leaders who are encouraging a societal emphasis on civilizational, ethnic, and religious identities, finding indigenous cultural foundations for inter-ethnic tolerance rather than relying mainly on the rule of law and secular constitutionalism to instill respect for difference. What is striking here is that there is far less opportunity for the emergence of a strong sense of being a citizen, especially given the cultural effort to repudiate the individualism of the West and the claim of an alternative ethos, often articulated as "Asian values," based on the salience of sentiments of community.[18] In the West the context is different, as globalization is not experienced as culturally alien or as victimization arising from a hegemonic project that imposed heavy costs in the past. So the adjustment of identity for Westerners is either in the Huntington mode of an integrative shift to a civilizational locus that is embattled and defensive in relation to non-Western civilizations or in disintegrative multicultural moves, as has been a major feature of cultural postmodernism. Both these patterns of adjustment transform the normal domain of the citizen into a subordinate category of identity.

In effect, the rootlessness associated with globalization generates a series of dialectical responses that represent efforts to ground identity; but, given the strength of the discipline of global capital in reorienting and appropriating the outlook of the state, these efforts marginalize the role and function of the citizen. Thus, it is not so much the state that responds defensively to the adverse territorial impacts of globalization as the state itself that is most often under the primary control of globalizing elites and responsive to their claims.

Backlash politics   When the French truckers' strike of November 1996 achieved success, the market-oriented media commented that this was a new type of labor militancy. It was not a strike against corporate managers or against the French state: it was a strike against the world economy. And so it seemed, although this focus was not explicitly mentioned in the articulation of demands by the workers. Moreover, despite being completely disruptive in relation to the overall activities of society, it was an act of resistance supported by an estimated 80 percent of the French populace, which is suggestive of the extent to which, under certain circumstances, the backlash against globalization is moving from the margins into the mainstream as a new political phenomenon.

But backlash politics associated with opposition to globalization has generally functioned in the West as a source of reinvigoration for right-wing populism. In this regard, opportunistic politicians have tended to build on grass-roots discontent by contending that jobs were being lost to overseas markets where labor conditions were horrible and that immigrants were driving down domestic wages and exerting pressure on public services, all to the detriment of the ordinary worker and his or her family. Such backlash politics has become a structural feature of this period, present in virtually every advanced industrial society. It fosters chauvinistic and xenophobic types of nationalism that are essentially intolerant of difference, and hence radically inconsistent with the sort of juridical nationalism that is the ideological taproot of the modern secular state, including its stress on the citizen as an individual member, purged for political purposes of secondary identities and pledged to reconcile private concerns with the promotion of the public good for the whole of society.

There is also beginning to emerge a violent backlash in some Third World contexts against the domestic policies of a governmental turn to neo-liberalism, especially if promises made by politicians fall short. Several Latin American countries, for instance, are experiencing a new round of revolutionary violence, but this time as a reaction to the failures of globalization to address the misery of the poor and marginal.

The rise of non-Western perspectives The relevant point here is the extent to which world order is currently being reconstituted, at least provisionally, by the interplay of inter-civilizational forces.[19] As argued earlier, this development represents a deliberate attempt to disengage modernization as a significantly positive dynamic from Westernization as a largely negative dynamic, the latter being seen as bringing to bear deficient values and carrying forward the hegemonic project of the West in a postcolonial era.[20] Such developments constrain the space and role of the citizen, at least as conceived in the modernist sense of acting within the territorial state in dynamic interaction with the government and as presumed in times of emergency to be loyal to the official policies of the country.[21]

The further point here is that to the extent that the ethos of world order is becoming inter-civilizational in dialogue and practices, the saliency of individualism and citizenship is being lost even in the West, and for the non-West these ideals never enjoyed saliency. Unlike democracy, and even human rights, where abundant non-Western antecedents exist in a variety of cultural forms, the notion of citizenship seems comparatively specific to Western civilization and thus represents a somewhat "provincial" focus for an inquiry into political identity if conceived inter-civilizationally or globally. The future of citizenship, which is indeed a Western preoccupation these days, partly connected with the decline and changing role of the state, is a favorite topic, but is characteristically addressed as a matter of almost exclusively *intra-civilizational* concern.[22]

Trends toward post-heroic geopolitics Part of the decline of the state, broadly connected in the United States with the persistence of the so-called Vietnam syndrome, relates to the reluctance of citizens to support state policy by putting their lives and the lives of their children at risk. This is a complex phenomenon with many contributing causes, including the declining significance of territorial expansion as an ingredient of power and influence, thereby making warfare less central in the context of geopolitics. This post-heroic style of warfare diminishes the need to excite the passions of the citizens in order to carry out foreign policy, but relies on high-tech weaponry that minimizes the human role.[23] In the setting of the Gulf War, the military architects of victory became momentary heroes, instant presidential possibilities, but the Warhol phenomenon of a quick fade from the limelight of fame occurred.[24]

This post-heroic mode of geopolitics makes the role of the patriotic citizen far less crucial to the operations of the national security state, thereby further marginalizing citizenship at this juncture of world history. The claims on resources for military purposes tend to be rationalized more in relation to the conditions of globalization and thus do not draw on the historical memories and political myths associated with wars of the past that involve the vital narratives of glory and shame that molded the consciousness of a typical citizen. Indeed, under current conditions, the state is likely to encourage popular demobilization, keeping the citizenry apathetic and apolitical, as a means of coping with the displacements and disappointments associated with economic globalization.

The rise of transnational social forces   Connected with the perceived interdependencies of contemporary life, as well as the opportunity for affordable linkages and networks, is the rise of transnational social forces as an innovative and variegated type of politics.[25] The level and intensity of involvement by activist individuals, particularly notable in relation to the environment, human rights, feminism, indigenous peoples, and the economic agenda of the South, represents a further withdrawal of energy from traditional domains of citizen action. It also represents an effort to offset the adverse impacts of globalization and a mimicry of its positive techniques of fashioning global arenas for the pursuit of its interests. It is illuminating to contrast these transnational social forces as creating an alternative globalization, globalization-from-below, to offset the co-optation of governments by the market-oriented forces associated with globalization-from-above.[26] Semantically, it is possible to discern in this development either further evidence for the decline of citizenship or the rudimentary elements of an emergent transnational citizenship accompanying the formation of a global civil society. A reluctance to shift the idea of citizenship to a transnational locus is explained by the view that it is still such a weak and irregular type of politics as to be transient or incapable of standing up to a backlash-from-above.

To the extent that transnationalization of identity and participation is happening, a major goal is to provide a regulatory framework to constrain the operation of transnational forces of business and finance. The objectives of activists here include the protection of the global commons, the erection of a global safety net for the poor, the promotion of the agendas of vulnerable constituencies, and the creation of more adequate forms of governance at regional and global levels. Up until now a major arena for these developments has been provided by the United Nations system, in the form of global conferences on social issues, with increasing opportunities for transnational associations of various kinds to participate. The Copenhagen UN Social Summit in 1995 was the peak of formal influence achieved by these transnational forces, providing a quasi-official endorsement of the search for a social agenda to balance the economic agenda of market forces. The leading market-oriented governments did their best to ensure that the Social Summit did not mount radical criticisms of economic globalization and was largely successful. Two consequences ensued: first, a sense of confusion arising from the uncritical mixing of market and social logics (the latter directed especially at employment and poverty) that was evident at the conference and in its formal documents; secondly, an unannounced, yet unmistakable, resolve by market-oriented governments to avoid in the future making available such anti-globalization arenas.

The clear implication is that the future of transnational activism on behalf of the social agenda of public goods is unlikely to be able to avail itself of the state-centric auspices and arenas of the United Nations. Whether equally effective forms of transnational activism can be established will depend on whether the assault on the traditional methods and objectives of citizens can be successfully recast. The label "transnational citizen" is not deserved unless the means exist for effective participation. So far, it seems premature to proclaim the existence of a transnational "citizenry."

Economic Globalization and Conjectures about the Future of Citizenship

Despite threats to the modernist role of citizenship as a consequence of the decline of the territorial sovereign state and the strength of global market forces, the potential contribution of citizenship to the safeguarding of democracy and the realization of human rights remains an important basis for hope about the future. The idea of citizenship as the basis for rights and duties in relation to the state continues to provide a legitimate grounding for oppositional and reform politics being pursued in a variety of national settings. The citizen is entitled, among many other things, to expect that the government and its political leaders will adhere to law, including those international obligations that pertain to the ordering of domestic society. And, in fact, globalization is already generating unprecedented interest in the implementation of economic and social rights on a domestic level as part of the human rights package. This is a new move in human rights activism in Western societies, which in the past tended to limit its operational concern regarding human rights to the domain enclosed by civil and political rights. Even NGOs accepted this focus and, in that regard, provided no normative basis to oppose rolling back welfare or to take full notice of those members of the territorial community who were being victimized by the workings of the global market.

Of course, in a situation of growing rivalry for jobs, there emerges a tendency to draw ever sharper lines between citizens and resident non-citizens, denying the latter social protection and full access to opportunities for health, education, and other services. In this regard, unless there is an outreach that incorporates immigrants, invocation of the status of citizenship could serve as one further pretext to impose burdens on the most vulnerable members of a particular society. Thus it is important to couple the entitlements of citizens and their posture of expecting protection against the harm wrought by the global market with a sense of inclusiveness toward the territorial community as a whole.

To achieve effective social protection may increasingly require action at the regional level, giving rise to a more meaningful conception of transnational or regional citizenship than has existed in the past. It may be, for instance, that the austerity decreed by international competitiveness can be resisted only through agreements negotiated at a regional level, as is the case in Europe in the form of the Social Charter. In time, this wider framework of action may take on a global dimension by way of a global social contract to respect economic and social rights. It would be naive to expect such a development in the near future. There exists too much unevenness in working conditions among countries to engender an acceptance of universal standards, although there are some signs of gropings in this direction. One such initiative is the International Labor Organisation proposal of a new international convention to prohibit so-called extreme forms of child labor.[27] But even if standards can be agreed upon, their implementation would be extremely tenuous given current degrees of unevenness in economic circumstances.

Finally, a fundamental shift on the aspirational side of citizenship involves a movement from an emphasis on *space* to an emphasis on *time*. Such a shift corresponds to the decline of territoriality as the foundation for political identity and the seeming exhaustion of government as a source of creative problem solving with respect to fundamental social concerns. It also reflects the impact of economic globalization and the current absence of countervailing ideological and political possibilities, yet the need for alternatives with normative content, both to moderate the cruelest effects of the global market and to give impetus to reformist perspectives. Time becomes, then, the essential component in a search for solutions. Thus, it is necessary to look primarily to the future, rather than to the existing capacities of regional and global institutions or any other existing institutional setting, in the search for a more compassionate politics. The challenge is to construct such a future through the engagement and impact of transnational social forces, eventuating in the emergence of a global civil society worthy of eliciting participation and of grounding a postmodern sequel to the sort of secular, territorial citizenship that emerged with the modern states of the secular West.[28]

11

Toward Normative Renewal

The Quest

Both world wars in this century encouraged world leaders to embark on a deliberate effort to reform world order in fundamental respects. The League of Nations, and then the United Nations, emerged from this encouragement. Both these experiments in the restructuring of relations among states have been impressive if compared to what had existed previously in international political life. Such steps are deeply disappointing, however, if appraised from the perspective of what would have been needed to create on a global scale a mode of governance that corresponded in normative stature (widely shared ethical standards and societal goals) to the most humane public order systems that have been operating at the level of the sovereign state.

The proximate goal of humane governance, then, seems relatively modest, at least at the outset. It is true that the idea of humane governance on any level of social complexity is conceived of as a process, with horizons of aspiration being constantly reestablished with an eye to the improvement of the existing social, economic, and political order from the perspective of a democratically established agenda. Such a quest should not be confused with the Western tendency toward linearity of expectations, which in recent centuries has been materialized in relation to technological innovation and consumerist satisfactions. It may be that in some circumstances normative horizons reflect the ebb and flow of history, with the emphasis placed on sustainability of past achievements or even the restoration of prior levels of humane governance after periods of regression. The idea of progress that has reigned in the West for many years is a misleading invention by optimists.[1] The future is inherently obscure, too complex to fathom and too dependent on the vagaries of human action for good or ill. Such uncertainty underscores human responsibility to achieve the normative potential that is currently perceived; almost everything necessary for human well-being is sufficiently achievable to be worth pursuing. At the same time, there can be no assurances of success, given the existence of countervailing projects and pressures.

Delimiting the idea of humane governance on behalf of the peoples of the world is itself a daunting and inconclusive undertaking. The unevenness of material circumstances, cultural orientation, and resource endowment makes it especially difficult, and even suspect, to universalize aspirations and set forth some image of humane governance that can be affirmed by all the peoples of the world. It seems appropriate to be tentative, inviting dialogue across civilizational and class boundaries as to the nature of humane governance. From such a bottom-up process, areas of overlapping consensus can begin to be identified, and a start can be made on negotiating differences in values and priorities. If successful, this interactive dynamic could in time produce a coherent project, democratically conceived, to establish humane governance for all peoples in the world.

At present, ingredients of humane governance are present that seem to reflect widely endorsed aspirational principles; but so far there has been no legitimation of an overarching project. Moreover, there are factors at work obstructing the effort to establish such a project as a viable undertaking. There is, first of all, the anti-utopian mood that has emerged from the perceived failure of Marxism–Leninism as the leading modern experiment in applied utopics. Secondly, market forces seem mainly organized around the energies of greed and self-interest, and these have come to dominate policy-forming arenas at all levels of social organization. Thirdly, the potency of such forces has been embodied in regional and global structures that have sapped the normative creativity of states, especially by imposing the discipline of global capital on existing structures of governance, as further reinforced through the ideas of neo-liberal economics. Fourthly, this economistic world picture has acquired added force, through being embraced by the leaders of the most powerful states and adopted by the most influential global actors, including the IMF, World Bank, and World Trade Organization. Fifthly, the new assertiveness of non-Western civilizations has challenged the assumption that Western normative projects deserve universal acceptance.[2]

The focus on humane governance is not meant as a repudiation of economic and cultural globalization or of market forces. These powerful elements of the existing global setting provide many beneficial opportunities for improving the material, social, and cultural experience of peoples throughout the world. Beyond this, the tides of history have swept neo-liberal ideas into such a commanding position in this early period of globalization that it would be futile to mount a frontal challenge, especially given the absence of viable alternatives. What is being proposed is more limited. It recognizes that *within* globalization there exists the potential for humane governance, but only if activated by the mobilization of diverse, democratic forces – what I have elsewhere identified as a process that can be associated with globalization-from-below.[3]

The Approach

Without entering into a complex discussion of successful projects of social change, it seems useful to consider two positive examples: decolonization and human rights. Actually, of course, each of these narratives, if fully related, would involve an elaborate and controversial exposition that provided an interpretation of specific as well as general context. Here, my purpose is to show how unlikely aspirations were realized, given supportive changes in underlying historical conditions.

In the case of decolonization, the values of self-determination and the ideology of nationalism had long challenged the legitimacy and stability of the colonial order. The moment Woodrow Wilson's ambiguous program of global reform was launched in the aftermath of World War I, ideas subversive of the colonial order were validated and inspired individuals who were subjects of colonial masters, even though this appears not to have been Wilson's intention. The outcome of the Russian Revolution also provided colonized peoples with a powerful, if dangerous and opportunistic, geopolitical ally in the form of the Soviet Union. World War II both weakened the morale and diminished the capabilities of the main colonial powers. It also created a fluid situation in which nationalist movements perceived opportunities for success that had not existed previously. The story of decolonization is, of course, many stories. Each struggle was distinct, but there were general conditions that resulted in an overall shift in the relation of forces within the wider colonial reality. A new flow of history ensued that could not have been reasonably anticipated even a few decades before it occurred.

The second example involves internationally protected human rights. The legitimacy of human rights as a core aspect of humane governance owes its main modern origins to the French Revolution, but this is quite different from endowing the world community with the capacity to pass judgment on the internal processes of governance of a sovereign state.

Indeed, the social contract that forms the basis of the United Nations is explicit in its undertaking to refrain from interventions in matters "essentially within the domestic jurisdiction" of states.[4] The modern Westphalian system of world order is premised on the idea of territorial sovereignty, which is inconsistent with the sort of external accountability that is implied by the acceptance of an obligation to uphold international human rights standards. So why would states voluntarily agree to a pattern of obligation that erodes their own sovereignty?

The short answer to a complex inquiry is that states generally didn't take seriously a formal commitment to uphold human rights obligations, undoubtedly feeling secure by resisting moves to establish implementing procedures and enforcement mechanisms. These expectations of governments were disturbed by several unanticipated developments: the rise of transnational human rights civil society organizations (that is, NGOs); the invocation of human rights by the West as a major dimension of the cold war; the success of the anti-apartheid campaign; the internal reliance on international human rights demands by movements of domestic opposition, especially in Eastern Europe during the 1980s; the conjoining of support for political and civil rights with the advocacy of economic liberalization in the new geopolitics of globalization.[5]

The relevant point here is that the normative idea associated with the establishment of human rights has gathered political momentum over the years. The implementation of the idea is still far from complete, but its contribution to humane governance is one of the most impressive achievements of the late twentieth century.

In the next section, several normative ideas are identified that seem crucial to the project of seeking to promote humane governance on a global scale. These ideas are selected, in part, because they are *already* embodied in the normative order (that is, validated by international law and morality, which now includes what might be called an environmental ethos[6]). As such, their realization has some claim to inter-civilizational support, and the aspirational element relates only to various degrees of implementation. The enumeration that follows makes no claim to comprehensiveness. It does seek to set forth the normative ideas that have been globally validated, insufficiently validated, and seem central to the promotion of humane global governance.

Dimensions of Normative Potential

Mainly as a result of social struggle, many normative goals have been acknowledged in recent decades, which, if fully realized, would both neutralize the negative aspects of globalization and create positive momentum for progress toward the attainment of humane governance in the decades ahead.[7] But the task is not a simple one. The normative goals have in many instances been reduced by practice and neglect to rhetorical affirmation, lacking in substance and political conviction, and evoking widespread cynicism as to their relevance. The ideas of neo-liberalism that have been attached to the implementation of globalization are generally opposed to any direct undertakings that subordinate economistic considerations to those of human well-being. And, as has been argued in the previous section, the political strength of regional and global market forces has been manifested partly through a reorientation of outlook on the part of leaders at the level of the state, infusing them with a sense of mission based on nonterritorial priorities and the world picture of globalization. As a result, territorial priorities and identities of many citizens are subordinated. This divergence of outlook was evident in the grass-roots reluctance of the peoples of Europe to signing onto the Maastricht Treaty, as compared with elites who were generally much more comfortable with the loss of economic sovereignty resulting from the treaty than were their citizens. This divergence has narrowed some-what as a result of backlash politics in a number of countries, including widespread strikes, the rise of right-wing chauvinistic populism, and the efforts of leaders to reassure citizens about their social and economic prospects within a more regionalized political setting.

With these considerations in mind, it seems important to revisit some normative breakthroughs in law and morality that have been made during this century, which could, if more seriously implemented, con-tribute dramatically to humane governance for the peoples of the planet. Taken as a whole, these nine normative initiatives provide "a plan of action" for global civil society in relation to the goal of humane gover-nance on a global scale.

Renunciation of force in international relations   Even prior to the United Nations Charter, international law in the Pact of Paris (1928) had already codified the idea that states had no legal right to use force except in self-defense. This idea was carried forward in the UN Charter as a central element, the prohibition being expressed in Article 2(4), and the exception for self-defense being delimited in seemingly more restrictive language in Article 51. The right of self-defense was limited to responses to a prior armed attack, and a claim of self-defense was required to be immediately reported for action to the Security Council. The text of Article 51 gives the impression that even in a situation of self-defense the primary responsibility rests with the Security Council, not with the victim of an attack. If implemented, as written, the role of force in international political life would be radically changed, especially to the extent that these ideas about force are linked to the obligation of states in Article 33 to seek peaceful settlement of disputes endangering world peace and security.

As is widely appreciated, this normative promise was never consistently fulfilled. For one thing, the UN was unable to provide the sort of collective security arrangements that would protect a state against threats of aggression. It was unrealistic to expect a threatened state, especially if vulnerable to attack, to wait until an armed attack occurred before exercising its right of self-defense. The circumstance of Israel is illustrative: surrounded by hostile states, and small in size, it is convinced that its security rests on the option to strike preemptively, as it did most spectacularly in the 1967 Six Day War.

A second obstacle to implementation was the extent to which the UN scheme depended on a continuing commitment by the permanent members of the Security Council to base their responses to uses of force on Charter considerations rather than ideological alignments and geopolitical considerations.[8] With the East–West split dominating the political scene, the conditions were almost never present in the Security Council for the sort of response pattern envisioned by the Charter. Furthermore, geopolitical tensions meant that the collaborative arrangements relating to collective security called for in Chapter VII of the Charter were never put into practice except ritualistically, as in the operation of the Military Staff Committee consisting of military representatives of the permanent members.

It has been evident since the end of the cold war that the reasons for non-implementation cannot be explained by geopolitical tensions alone. An additional independent ground is the unwillingness of major states to transfer political control to the UN in situations involving the use of force. The attitude of the US government is both decisive and revealing in these respects. More than ever, its leaders are unwilling to entrust its soldiers or its foreign policy to a UN command structure or to a collective process over which it lacks full control.

Finally, serious threats to the security of states cannot be confined to armed attacks. Claims to use force have been associated over the years with responses to state-sponsored terrorist attacks (the US attack on Libya in 1986 and support for contras in the war against Sandinistas in Nicaragua; Israeli periodic attacks on Lebanon), to threatened proliferation of nuclear weaponry (Israeli attack on Osirak, Iraq in 1981), to acute suppression of human rights and genocidal conduct (Tanzania against Uganda, Vietnam against Cambodia in 1979, US against Panama in 1989).

In some respects, the current situation is very supportive of this long effort to curtail war. Territoriality is far less significant in the new geopolitics, and the role of war is less relevant to the success and failure of many states.[9] The practical rationale for peaceful settlement is stronger than ever. Most political violence in the present world is of an intra-state variety associated with claims of self-determination. The economistic view of state policy exerts pressure to minimize public expenditures, including those for defense. The threats associated with the further proliferation of weaponry of mass destruction, including chemical and biological weaponry, are unlikely to be eliminated unless all states, including nuclear weapons states, join in their renunciation.

Despite these reasons for seeking a warless world, the obstacles remain formidable: entrenched economic and bureaucratic interests in military establishments, distrust of the capacity and objectivity of the UN system, inertia associated with reliance on the state to provide security against adversaries, and persisting unresolved regional conflicts, border disputes, and territorial conflicts involving offshore islands. As well, geopolitical actors, especially the US government, insist on the relevance of force to deter and contain so-called rogue states and to prevent the further fraying of the nuclear non-proliferation regime.

In these regards, only a transnational peace movement is likely to be able to revitalize the long and crucial struggle to minimize war and preparations for war. At the moment, there is no effort in this direction except in relation to transnational initiatives to abolish nuclear weaponry and some intergovernmental efforts to control the spread of nuclear weaponry and to encourage regimes of prohibition with respect to chemical and biological weaponry.

Human rights   As argued earlier, one of the most dramatic normative developments during the last half-century has involved the universal recognition by governments of the binding nature of international human rights obligations. The human rights framework has been set forth in the Universal Declaration of Human Rights, the Covenant on Civil and Political Rights, and the Covenant on Economic, Social, and Cultural Rights. In some sense, the embodiment of human rights standards in international law was quite a dramatic acceptance by governments of encroachments on their claims of supremacy over sovereign territory and sensitive state–society relations. The initial acceptance of such an encroachment was either cynical (authoritarian governments that felt free to disregard external obligations of a general aspirational nature) or superficial (giving lip service to widely endorsed standards of behavior, but without enforcement or procedures for external accountability).

There was no indication that the governments who joined in endorsing the Universal Declaration over 50 years ago thought that they were engaged in a fundamental process of global reform of the sort that would result from an effective process of implementation. The radical nature of the norms agreed upon, and periodically affirmed, can be appreciated by reference to Article 25 of the Universal Declaration, which promises every person "the right to a standard of living" sufficient to satisfy basic human needs, and Article 28, which insists that everyone "is entitled to a social and international order in which the rights and freedoms set forth in this Declaration can be fully realized." Of course, realizing such rights fully would by itself satisfy many of the core expectations of humane governance and seems more utopian than ever in its current remoteness from the realities and outlook of neo-liberalism. At the same time, the obligations have been clearly expressed and endorsed as forming part of international law.

Unlike the situation pertaining to the renunciation of force, geopolitical and transnational democratic factors encouraged the implementation, although unevenly and incompletely, of agreed standards of human rights. First of all, civil society organizations (often still called NGOs, which is quite misleading) arose to gather information about human rights violations and exert pressure on governments to alter their practices; media exposure also turned out to be an important instrument to induce compliance.[10] Secondly, the ideological divisions in the cold war led the West in particular to emphasize human rights violations of Soviet bloc countries. What started as hostile propaganda turned in the direction of potent politics subsequent to the Helsinki Accords of 1975, with the rise of opposition movements in East Europe and with the change of leadership style in Moscow during the Gorbachev years. Thirdly, under the aegis of the United Nations and with the backing of grass-roots efforts, especially in the United Kingdom and the United States, the anti-apartheid movement seemed to be an important factor in pushing the white leadership in South Africa to abandon apartheid by voluntary action. Fourthly, the unevenness of working conditions in the setting of economic globalization encouraged adversely affected social forces, such as organized labor, to call for the furtherance of human rights, as in relation to China or Indonesia. Many of these supportive moves were partially or totally opportunistic, but their effect has been to put human rights firmly on the global political agenda.

These developments are momentous, but many rights remain unimplemented almost everywhere, and many peoples remain exposed to oppressive patterns of governance. As well, cultural patterns in several regions of the world are at odds with basic ideas about human rights, in circumstances that leave even governments that sincerely accept international standards virtually helpless.[11] The will to implement human rights is insufficient to influence larger states, even when the international community is strongly mobilized at grass-roots levels, as has been the case with respect to Tibet and East Timor. And then there are the complex claims about Asian values or Islamic civilization not being adequately incorporated in the process or substance of international human rights, giving governments increased discretion to interpret standards in accordance with particular cultural outlooks. From such perspectives also emerge the view that the implementation of human rights, as distinct from the authority of the norms, is a matter for the sovereign state, and that intervention on behalf of human rights is never justified unless under the auspices of the United Nations, and then is rarely effective especially as viewed in light of the experience in Bosnia and Rwanda in the 1990s. There is also the contention that the assertion of human rights is filtered through the prism of geopolitics in a manner that gives rise to double standards, with some violators being subject to severe sanctions while others are shielded from scrutiny despite their horrifying practices. Finally, there is the argument that the West, including civil society organizations, is interested only in civil and political rights and pays no serious attention to economic and social rights, which are of paramount importance to the majority of people in the world.

Taken as a whole, the record of achievement with respect to human rights is impressive, yet cruelty and abuse remain widespread, and the way ahead on the road to fuller compliance remains formidable. The undertaking is additionally complicated by the inter-civilizational agenda associated with the recent assertion of non-Western ideas and values. The challenge of humane governance involves closing further the gap between promise and performance, which includes taking increased account of those whose victimization has a special character, as is the case with indigenous peoples. What will achieve further gains for human rights is the continuing convergence and spread of civil society initiatives with reinforcing geopolitical trends. There is a danger here that human rights becomes discredited to the extent that the issue is used insensitively as an instrument of inter-civilizational pressure, intensifying conflict and engendering misunderstanding. The institutionalization of protection for human rights within the European Union suggests that a shared political community committed to liberal democratic values is more likely to accept real accountability to external review of compliance than are more heterogeneous and less democratic states – and possibly, more generally, that the most promising way under current global conditions to advance humane governance with respect to human rights is at regional levels of interaction, while leaving the way open for further incremental developments within the UN system. The UN has steadily upgraded its concern for human rights, holding a high-profile global conference on human rights in 1993, and shortly thereafter adding to its formal makeup a High Commissioner for Human Rights.

From the perspective of this chapter the main point is that within standard-setting, fact-finding, monitoring, and reporting efforts of both inter-governmental and civil society there has emerged a framework for the achievement of the sort of human rights culture that is presupposed by the goal of humane governance. Much needs to be done, but the tensions between universality of approach and diversity of cultural values and political outlook are likely to bring disappointment in the near future to both universalists and relativists. At this stage it would be useful to identify overlapping and convergent ideas as regards advancing human rights through extensive inter-civilizational and inter-religious dialogue. It would also improve the overall context for the promotion of human rights if major states, in particular the United States, were to refrain from relying on human rights rationales as pretexts for imposing sanctions on states with whom it has strong ideological differences (for example, Cuba).

Common heritage of mankind   The Maltese ambassador, Arvid Pardo, in the course of a celebrated 1967 speech in the United Nations, made one of the most idealistic suggestions for global reform. Pardo proposed treating seabed resources of the high seas as belonging to the common heritage of mankind, rather than being subject to appropriation by states with the requisite technological and entrepreneurial capabilities to exploit them. This proposal evoked a strong positive response throughout the international community. The common heritage principle carried within itself the possibility of a more equitable distribution of resources situated beyond the limits of territorial authority. It was also capable of extension to the polar regions and to the potential wealth of space. Its potential relevance to the transfer of technology, especially relating to health and food, is obvious. This relevance is reinforced by the treatment of knowledge and information associated with the Internet as a global public good, although combined with commercial control over various forms of data and the classification as secret of other material. The idea of common heritage could also be used, in part, to raise revenues for the UN system, thereby weakening the bondage of the Organization to the priorities of its most powerful members.

But the substantive outcomes have been disappointing so far. The language of common heritage, while retained as a goal, has been virtually emptied of substantive content in the Law of the Seas context, as a result of heavy lobbying by the private sector and gradual adoption of a neo-liberal outlook by Western states, led by the United States and Thatcherite Britain. This process of "normative co-option" whereby a progressive idea is introduced with great fanfare, but then applied in such a way as to deprive it of substantive content, in this instance, makes common heritage subordinate to the operation of global market forces. Such a process contributes to a kind of complacency in which there is the illusion of commitment to human well-being, but without any tangible results. This pattern invites cynicism and leads to widespread despair.

It is important at this stage to view the idea of common heritage critically, but with an appreciation of its potential role in a future world order based on humane governance. It is a normative idea that could be extended in many directions, ranging from the various relations to all areas outside sovereign territory, to the protection of the cultural and natural heritage even if within the territory of a state, to the status of knowledge and technological innovation relevant for human well-being, including the results of biogenetic research. The politics of co-option in relation to common heritage are illustrative of the policy outcome in settings where global civil society is relatively passive and global market forces are mobilized in defense of their interests.

Sustainable development   One of the most creative and influential normative ideas of the 1980s has been that of "sustainable development." It was initially articulated in the report of the Brundtland World Commission on Environment and Development published under the title *Our Common Future*[12] and seemed to merge and reconcile in an organic and practical way the environmental concerns of the North with the developmental preoccupations of the South. The idea of sustainable development underpinned the discourse at the Earth Summit held at Rio in 1992, avoiding the divisive North–South view of the environmental challenge that had been evident in Stockholm 20 years earlier. It also reinforced the tendency of the North to accept the main burden of subsidizing adjustment costs in the South associated with environmental protection, a pattern that had been initiated in relation to efforts to persuade poorer countries to forego technologies that had serious ozone-depleting effects. At Rio a multi-billion-dollar Global Environmental Facility was agreed upon and established to promote sustainable development in several main sectors of activity by facilitating North–South resource transfers.[13] In addition, more than 150 national councils of sustainable development have been established throughout the world since 1992. The UN has created a Commission on Sustainable Development that meets twice a year to follow up on the sustainable development approach adopted at Rio.

But sustainable development, like common heritage, was a slogan, as well as a substantive principle with dramatic normative implications for behavioral adjustment. It was easy to invoke the language without making the changes in practices that would be required if sustainability were to be given appropriate weight. George Bush, then president of the United States, famously announced prior to Rio that "the American standard of living was not negotiable." In effect, if the rich countries were not even prepared to consider some limitations on affluent life-styles, it would be impossible to induce poorer countries to forego short-term developmental opportunities even if environmentally damaging, as in relation to timber production and slash-and-burn forest clearance.

Experience to date has suggested both the importance of the idea of sustainable development in framing the global debate on policy and the limited capacity to ensure tangible effect to the sustainability commitment. Neo-liberal ideas, as elsewhere, tend to prevail, and the funds pledged to support sustainability were inadequate to begin with, and even these levels of financing have not materialized. As a result, many have questioned whether there is any serious effort in relation to sustainability, given the strength of global capital and its insistence on the efficient use of resources, as measured by relatively short-term gains, as well as its visceral resistance to all forms of regulatory restraint imposed on private sector activities.

Sustainable development is a crucial idea in relation to reconciling policy responses to environment and poverty in a world of very uneven economic and social circumstances. There are a series of other normative ideas associated with this perspective, perhaps best summarized in the Rio Declaration on Environment and Development (1992). However, the normative reconciliation, to be genuine and behaviorally significant, needs to be balanced and seriously implemented. Otherwise the political language becomes a trap that disguises policy failure. A major challenge for advocates of humane governance is to identify the means by which to implement sustainable development, practically and concretely on the scale of state, region, and world.

Global commons   Another closely related normative idea that is generally accepted and underlies many of the initiatives taken to advance international environmental goals has been associated with the notion of "global commons." In essence, affirming the existence of a global commons acknowledges the growing insufficiency of relying on states to achieve an acceptable form of global governance acting on their own.

With reference to oceans, polar regions, ozone depletion, climate, and bio-diversity, there is the awareness that only global cooperative regimes with longer-run perspectives can avoid disaster befalling the global commons. Impressive results have been achieved through the medium of "lawmaking treaties" that seek to bind the entire world to act within an agreed framework of rights and duties. These owe a great deal to pressures mounted by transnational civic initiative.

As elsewhere, the results are inadequate, and do not engender hope that enough is being currently done to protect the global commons from further dangerous types of deterioration. A major difficulty, evident in efforts to impose limits on the emission of greenhouse gases has been the unwillingness of the rich countries to bear all the burdens of high adjustment costs and the refusal of poorer countries to divert resources from their goals of achieving economic growth as rapidly as possible. This difficulty is compounded by domestic political pressures that are less sensitive to the importance of the global commons and are thus opposed to taking steps for their protection if the result is higher costs and restrictions on behavior.

Future generations   The acceleration of history, coupled with concerns about carrying capacity, catastrophic warfare, bio-diversity, global warming, and crowding, has given rise to growing concerns about the responsibility of present generations to the future. Such concerns reverse centuries of Western optimism about the future based on a theory of progress, resting on scientific discovery giving rise to a continuous flow of life-enhancing technological innovations and increases in economic productivity. One consequence of such hopeful expectations was the virtual certainty that those born in the future would enjoy a better life on the average than their forebears, thereby relieving the present generation of any responsibility. This normative move to endow the future generation with rights has been incorporated in several important international treaties and enjoys some support as an emergent principle of international law.[14] The overall ethos has been formulated as a Declaration on the Responsibilities of the Present Generations to Future Generations by the General Conference of UNESCO on 12 November 1997.[15]

Of course, the commitment to future generations remains a rather empty commitment in the absence of any tangible impact on behavioral patterns in the present; but it is a normative idea that has been validated and widely endorsed. As such, it provides the basis for fulfilling the temporal dimension of humane governance – that is, assuring that future generations enjoy life prospects equivalent or superior to those enjoyed by present generations. In this manner, the normative idea of sustainability is linked with the human rights of the unborn.

Accountability: the rule of law and personal responsibility   A widely endorsed normative idea is the duty of all governments and their officials to uphold international law, which includes the obligation to conduct foreign policy within the constraints of law. Such a legalist orientation subordinates sovereign discretion to a framework of agreed-upon constraints and procedures. The constitutional structure for this framework is codified in the UN Charter and elaborated in some crucial resolutions of the General Assembly, such as that of the Declaration on Principles of International Law and Friendly Relations among States.[16]

The extension of these ideas to wartime conditions occurred after World War II in the form of war crimes trials against surviving leaders in Germany and Japan. Both applauded for the effort to hold individual leaders responsible, even if they acted under the color of sovereign authority, and criticized as arbitrary expressions of "victors' justice," this principle of accountability in relation to the humanitarian law of war has been revived during this decade in response to atrocities and genocidal conduct in former Yugoslavia and Rwanda. In addition, war crimes trials have been proposed recently in relation to a series of earlier occurrences, including the reign of terror in Cambodia during the years of Pol Pot's rule and crimes attributed to the regime of Saddam Hussein in Iraq. These initiatives have given rise to a strong movement in global civil society, a coalition of hundreds of organizations, to establish a permanent international criminal court, with pressure being mounted on governments to take formal action. Whether this project will reach fruition and, if so, in what form remain uncertain at the close of the 20th century.

Again, as with earlier normative innovations, the record of achievement is not satisfactory. Geopolitical factors still guide the foreign policy of almost all states, with law and morality used as self-serving rationalizations or as the bases of propaganda attacks on adversaries. Legal standards are not applied uniformly by the United Nations, leading to accusations of double standards. Major states reserve for themselves discretionary control over recourse to force. Even in constitutional democracies, such as the United States, it is exceedingly rare to be able to challenge foreign policy as violative of international law; the courts are reluctant to override the executive branch in the setting of external relations, and the authority of Congress is limited to initial authorizations of war and subsequent withholding of appropriations in relation to contested foreign policy, especially in wartime. More fundamentally, the ethos of government in most countries continues to be that a great power is animated by interests and a mission and is sovereign in relation to law when it comes to matters of such vital concerns as security.

Redress of grievances In recent years there have been a myriad of claims associated with events long past. To mention a few: the inquiry into the Nazi origins of Swiss gold during World War II; the abuses by imperial Japan of "comfort women" in Korea, the Philippines, and elsewhere; the effort by Afro-Americans and by Africa to receive reparations for the injustices of slavery and the slave trade; the Armenian effort to exert pressure on the government of Turkey to acknowledge genocidal policies in 1915; the struggle of indigenous peoples in the United States and elsewhere to obtain an apology for past wrongs and some specific forms of relief. What these various undertakings have in common is their insistence that the past, even the distant past, contains unresolved issues of equity that remain open wounds. The call for redress involves various attitudes, including an opportunistic effort to receive monetary rewards, and each initiative must be evaluated.

What is evident, however, is that the surfacing of claims for redress of past grievances reflects a search for intergenerational equity that complements in many ways the rise of support for responsibilities to future generations. The acceleration of history seems to be giving rise to a greater sense of time consciousness with respect to past and future, making such intergenerational concerns part of the subject matter of justice and hence of humane governance.

Global democracy Rooted in the Preamble to the UN Charter is an affirmation of the populist foundations of international institutional authority, expressed in those oft-repeated opening words, "We the Peoples of the United Nations determined to save succeeding generations from the scourge of war" through the action of representatives acting on behalf of governments "do hereby establish an international organization to be known as the United Nations." From this democratic seedling, almost a fortuitous element in the statist world of 1945, has evolved over time as a challenge to a purely statist UN, increasingly presents itself in various formulations as the emergent ideology of global civil society.[17]

The pursuit of global democracy is taking many forms, ranging from the participatory activism of transnational citizens' groups around the world to global conferences under UN auspices that have served as places of conflict and cooperation in the relations between peoples and governments. Proposals for the creation of a Global Peoples' Assembly within the United Nations system is one element in the effort of transnational democratic forces to enhance their role in the global authority structure. The Secretary-General of the UN, Kofi Annan, has given his endorsement to democratizing moves and has even suggested at one point holding a millennial peoples' assembly in the year 2000.

This focus on global democracy remains almost totally a project to be realized in the future. In fact, its ideological emergence and the activism evident in several global settings have caused a statist backlash, a reluctance to extend the consensus supportive of democracy to the global level, including within the United Nations system. Europe is currently a testing ground for the extension of democratic forms to a regional undertaking, with the European Parliament already offering insight into some aspects of "regional democracy" as the foundation of regional humane governance. It seems evident that a coalition of global market forces and geopolitical actors is resistant to all efforts to give coherent political form to the strivings of global civil society. The prospect for global democracy remains the overarching goal of those committed to the pursuit of human governance for the peoples of the world.

Moving Forward

This enumeration of normative ideas incorporates an interpretation of both the functional challenges facing humanity and a view of human betterment that includes leaving room for the expression of cultural and ideological difference. The political prospects for realizing these ideas in practice depend on the strengthening of global civil society and its continuing orientation along these normative lines. Global civil society should not be romanticized as necessarily aligned with the project for humane global governance. There are tensions evident throughout global civil society, as in any other series of political arenas. My contention is that up to this point, and seemingly into the future, those perspectives that have supported the normative ideas being affirmed here have dominated global civil society. But such a conclusion cannot be taken for granted. There are also regressive normative ideas at the grass-roots level that are being organized transnationally, including coalitions associated with anti-immigrant, fascist, and cyber-libertarian positions. In addition, there are a range of what might be called visionary ideas being promoted by individuals, groups, and segments of global civil society. These ideas are radical in content and claim and are not embedded in the operational codes of international law and morality. Illustrative of visionary ideas are "the ethos of nonviolence" as the foundation for security or the "citizen pilgrim" as orienting political loyalty in an imagined political community of the future.[18]

A hopeful outlook as to the future depends on sustaining and deepening the influence of global civil society and collaborating where possible with other political actors, including states and agents of the private sector. In the past such collaboration has been very effective in promoting such general goals as the furtherance of human rights and environmental protection and more particular undertakings such as the prevention of mining on Antarctica or the movement in support of a regime of prohibition on land mines. Often the collaborative process takes the form of a lawmaking treaty that establishes an appropriate regime. Two such collaborations that are now in process involve the campaign to abolish nuclear weapons (an alternative to the geopolitical project to enforce the non-proliferation regime) and the effort to establish a permanent international criminal court.

Another aspect of a hopeful stance toward the future arises from the assumption that there exists widespread human support on a trans-civilizational basis for species survival and for the betterment of material circumstances. Validation of the normative ideas mentioned above lends credibility to the assertion of this shared sensibility, although disappointments with implementation also need to be taken into account. Implementation will involve encounters with opposing ideas and interests that are often linked to powerful social forces in control of influential states and shaping private sector outlooks, particularly ideas bound up with the economistic world picture as expounded by the proponents of economic neo-liberalism. Underlying this concern about these normative ideas is the central Hegelian conviction that ideas matter, and that in the fluid historical circumstances of the present (with states losing some of their control and dominance and other actors arising in various settings), ideas matter greatly.

Finally, that as commentators on global trends and future arrangements, the context is too complex to yield the sort of understanding that could support meaningful predictions. This uncertainty is an encouragement to those in favor of the normative ideas being advocated. The current perception that their realization is blocked by overwhelmingly powerful political forces and countervailing ideas should not be converted into a sense of resignation or cynicism. The future remains open to a wide spectrum of possibilities, including those directly associated with humane global governance. Recent international history, associated with the peaceful ending of the cold war and the successful struggle against colonialism, has confirmed that desirable outcomes occur even when most instruments of assessment have concluded that such results are virtually impossible. In this sense, political and societal miracles happen, but not by waiting – only as a result of commitment and struggle dedicated to the attainment of such goals. The framework of normative ideas that has been depicted and enjoys widespread support throughout global civil society, gives some political coherence to such striving as we near the end of this millennium.

Notes

Chapter 1   Democratizing, Internationalizing, and Globalizing

1   Lester Brown, "The New World Order," in *State of the World 1991* (New York: Norton, 1991), pp. 3–20, at p. 3.

2   The key document is the Feb. 18, 1992, draft of *Defense Guidance for the Fiscal Years 1994–1999*, excerpts of which were published in the *New York Times*, Mar. 8, 1992, p. 14.

3   The idea of "global apartheid" was apparently introduced initially by Gernot Kohler as a participant in the World Order Models Project in the early 1970s, included as a selection with that title published in Richard A. Falk, Samuel S. Kim, and Saul H. Mendlovitz (eds), *Toward a Just World Order* (Boulder, Colo.: Westview Press, 1982), pp. 315–25, but otherwise largely ignored until recently; in the use of the terminology of apartheid, Kohler's earlier analysis is sometimes acknowledged, while at other times an author has apparently hit upon the term independently. In assessing the world economy, Susan George relies on the same metaphor: "The closest political analogy to this post–cold war world is *apartheid*" ("The Deft Question," Paper presented at the 90th Anniversary Nobel Jubilee Symposium, Oslo, Norway, Dec. 8, 1991, p. 16). On the same occasion, without prior coordination, Ali Mazrui built an entire discussion of the role of race and religion in international relations around the metaphor of apartheid, ending his paper with this rhetorical question and response: "Is the twentieth century getting ready to hand over to the 21st century a new legacy of global apartheid? The trends are ominous – but let us hope they are not irreversible" ("Global Apartheid? Race and Religion in the New World Order," ibid., pp. 19–20).

4   A. Makhijani, *From Global Capitalism to Economic Justice: An Inquiry into the Elimination of Systemic Poverty, Violence and Environmental Destruction in the World Economy* (New York: Apex Press, 1992); for a shorter version of Makhijani's views see his contribution, "Global Apartheid and

the Political Economy of War," in Grace Boggs et al., *Conditions of Peace: An Inquiry* (Washington, D.C.: Expro Press, 1991), pp. 178–222.

5   This quotation and others are from Schelling's contribution to a volume on security after the cold war, edited by Graham Allison and Gregory F. Treverton, *Rethinking America's Security: Beyond Cold War to New World Order* (New York: Norton, 1992), pp. 196–210, at p. 200.

6   Ibid., p. 200.

7   PPS 23, dated Feb. 24, 1948, classified Top Secret, and entitled "Review of Current Trends: U.S. Foreign Policy," in Thomas H. Entzold and John Lewis Gaddis (eds), *Documents on American Policy and Strategy, 1945–1950* (New York: Columbia University Press, 1978), pp. 226–8. Kennan's exact words are worth noting: ". . . we have about 50% of the world's wealth but only 6.3% of its population. This disparity is particularly great as between ourselves and the peoples in Asia. Our real task in the coming period is to devise a pattern of relationships which will permit us to maintain this position of disparity without positive detriment to our national security" (pp. 226–7).

8   Daniel J. Kevles, "Some Like It Hot," *New York Review of Books*, Mar. 26, 1992, pp. 31–9, at p. 32; because such a high proportion of the expected population increase is concentrated in the poor countries – estimated as in the vicinity of 95 percent – this ratio of people to resources is likely to grow even more regressive in the years ahead.

9   With the cold war over, controls by the West over the export of militarily sensitive technology have been significantly refocused on the South, and not only on pariah states such as Libya and North Korea. Even India and Pakistan are explicitly included among states to be concerned about, as well as, of course, Iran, Iraq, and China. No worry is expressed about any state in the North, despite the many uncertainties in Eastern Europe and among the states formed out of the former Soviet Union. See Asra Q. Nomani, "West Relaxes Rules on Export of Technologies," *Wall Street Journal*, Nov. 25, 1992, p. 2.

10 See *The Challenge to the South: The Report of the South Commission* (Oxford: Oxford University Press, 1990), pp. 1–2.

11 During the UN Security Council Summit of Jan. 31, 1991, bringing together heads of state of Security Council members on the future of the organ, Nathan Shamuyarira, Foreign Minister of Zimbabwe, made the following comment: "A new world order that does not make a special effort to eliminate poverty and narrow disparities existing between industrialized and developing countries will not be sustainable": quoted in materials prepared by Juan Somavia concerning the World Summit on Social Development, undated.

12 For representative literature see Edward Goldsmith et al., *Blueprint for Survival* (Boston: Houghton Mifflin, 1972); Donella H. Meadows et al., *The Limits to Growth* (New York: Universe, 1972); Robert L. Heilbroner, *An Inquiry into the Human Prospect* (New York: Norton, 1975); Richard Falk, *This Endangered Planet: Prospects and Proposals for Human Survival* (New

York: Random House, 1971); Barry Commoner, *The Closing Circle* (New York: Knopf, 1971).

13 For convenient summaries of the results of the Earth Summit, see Peter M. Haas, Marc A. Levy, and Edward A. Parson, "Appraising the Earth Summit," *Environment*, 34 (Oct. 1992), pp. 7–11, 26–33; and Haas, Levy, and Parson, "A Summary of the Major Documents Signed at the Earth Summit and the Global Forum," *Environment*, 34 (Oct. 1992), pp. 11–16, 34–6.

14 Quoted by Kevles, "Some Like It Hot," p. 32.

15 *The Economist*, Feb. 7–14, 1992.

16 These themes are explored in Stephen Toulmin, *Cosmopolis: The Hidden Agenda of Modernity* (New York: Free Press, 1990).

17 For an assessment of these influences see ibid.

18 For more detailed considerations regarding the emergence and structure of statism via Westphalia, see Antonio Cassese, *International Law in a Divided World* (Oxford: Oxford University Press, 1986); Lynn H. Miller, *Global Order: Values and Power in International Politics*, 2nd edn (Boulder, Colo.: Westview Press, 1990), pp. 19–72; R. A. Falk, "The Interplay of Westphalia and Charter Conceptions of the International Legal Order," in C. E. Black and R. A. Falk (eds), *The Future of the International Legal Order*, vol. 1 (Princeton, NJ: Princeton University Press, 1969), pp. 32–70.

19 For broad conceptual analysis that richly documents this assertion, see the numerous writings by David Held on this theme of the extensions of democracy, especially his article "Democracy: From City-States to a Cosmopolitan Order?," in David Held (ed.), *Prospects for Democracy* (Cambridge: Polity Press, 1993), pp. 13–52. His interpretations have influenced my thinking about the role of democratic theory within and beyond the state in many ways.

20 Cf. suggestive article by David Kennedy, "The Move to Institutions," *Cardozo Law Review*, 8 (1987), pp. 841–988.

21 In Burns H. Weston, Richard A. Falk, and Anthony D'Amato (eds), *Basic Documents in International Law and World Order*, 2nd rev. edn (St Paul, Minn.: West, 1990), pp. 423–5.

22 It is true that some of the more sophisticated proposals for radical restructuring included a concern for equity and human rights, but mainly as deemed necessary to gain the support of governments that were poor. See Grenville Clark and Louis B. Sohn, *World Peace through World Law*, 3rd edn (Cambridge, Mass.: Harvard University Press, 1966).

23 The cosmo-drama in the singular is an abstraction that is experienced nowhere; what are experienced in a wide array of variations are concrete embodiments of these tensions among contending sources of authority and power; yet both the abstract, by its generalizing account of sameness, and the concrete, by its specifications of difference, inform "the reality." This formulation is indebted to R. B. J. Walker, *One World/Many Worlds* (Boulder, Colo.: Lynne Rienner, 1988); Richard Rorty, *Contingency, Irony, and Solidarity* (Cambridge: Cambridge University Press, 1989).

24 "Captive nations," including Palestine and Kurdistan, seem prepared also to accept autonomy arrangements on an interim basis, in light of their inability to attain Westphalian sovereignty.

25 Invoking, perhaps unfairly, the Vietnam era image of the American officer who, when asked about the destruction of the village of Ben Suc, responded, "We had to destroy it to save it."

26 Robert B. Reich, *The Work of Nations: Preparing Ourselves for 21st Century Capitalism* (New York: Knopf, 1991), p. 311.

27 Arguably nuclear weapons were and are a comparable test, although there is more controversy in this area; realists contend that nuclear weapons produced "the long peace" of the cold war and that the denuclearization of Europe would be a serious mistake. Compare here John Lewis Gaddis, "The Long Peace: Elements of Stability in the Postwar International System," *International Security*, 10 (1986), pp. 99–142, and John Mearsheimer, "Back to the Future: Instability in Europe after the Cold War," *International Security*, 15 (1990), pp. 1–56, repr. in Sean M. Lynn-Jones (ed.), *The Cold War and After: Prospects for Peace* (Cambridge, Mass.: MIT Press, 1991), pp. 141–92, with Robert Jay Lifton and Richard Falk, *Indefensible Weapons: The Political and Psychological Case against Nuclearism*, 2nd updated edn (New York: Basic Books, 1992).

28 *Time*, Feb. 17, 1992, pp. 60–8; a map on p. 64 grades countries according to their degree of contribution on the basis of thousands of metric tons of CFCs and halons released annually.

29 For an account of the regulatory response, see Richard Elliot Benedick, *Ozone Diplomacy: New Direction on Safeguarding the Planet* (Cambridge, Mass.: Harvard University Press, 1991).

30 Andrew Dobson, *Green Political Thought* (London: Unwin Hyman, 1990); also Robert C. Paehlke, *Environmentalism and the Future of Progressive Politics* (New Haven, Conn.: Yale University Press, 1989).

31 During the cold war, with exceptions, the geopolitical stalemate resulted in the marginalization of the UN in its peace and security roles; whether the ending of the cold war will mean that peace and security will be refracted by way of a unipolar world remains to be seen; such was the evident US government hope during the Gulf crisis, but the UN is hardly mentioned in the more recent Defense Guidance document (see n. 2).

32 *Common Responsibility in the 1990s*, Stockholm, Prime Minister's Office, Apr. 22, 1991, p. 36.

33 Such a commission, under the joint chairmanship of Ingvar Carlsson and Shridath Ramphal, was established in mid-1992, with a small secretariat located in Geneva.

34 For reflections on cultural tendencies see William Irwin Thompson, *The American Replacement of Nature* (New York: Doubleday, 1991); the phrase in the text is his, see pp. 61–2.

35 For instance, emphasizing the damage done to the environment by the tactics of both sides during the Gulf War. See Glen Plant, *Environmental Protection and the Law of War* (London: Belhaven, 1992).

36   The cassette and xerox copier played major empowering roles during the Iranian Revolution, eventually disabling the Shah's formidable military and paramilitary capabilities.

37   See James N. Rosenau, *Turbulence in World Politics: A Theory of Change and Continuity* (Princeton, NJ: Princeton University Press, 1990).

38   Joseph A. Camilleri and Jim Falk, *The End of Sovereignty? The Politics of a Shrinking and Fragmenting World* (Aldershot: Edward Elgar, 1992).

Chapter 2   Co-opting the Sovereign State

1   For Bull's criticisms see *An Anarchical Society: A Study of Order in World Politics* (London: Macmillan, 1977); the criticisms are directed against Falk, *This Endangered Planet: Prospects and Proposals for Human Survival* (New York: Random House, 1971) and *A Study of Future Worlds* (New York: Free Press, 1975); for Vincent's most characteristic work see John Vincent, *Nonintervention and International Order* (Princeton, NJ: Princeton University Press, 1976).

2   For the range of earlier proposals of the World Order Models Project, in a series called "Preferred Worlds for the 1990s," see Saul H. Mendlovitz (ed.), *On the Creation of a Just World Order* (New York: Free Press, 1975).

3   "Citizenship and Sovereignty in the post-Westphalian Age," *European Journal of International Relations*, 2 (1996), pp. 77–103.

4   Such an interpretation is strongly argued by Ulrich Beck in "The Reinvention of Politics: Towards a Theory of Reflexive Modernization," in Ulrich Beck, Anthony Giddens, and Scott Lash, *Reflexive Modernization: Politics, Tradition and Aesthetics in the Modern Social Order* (Cambridge: Polity Press, 1994), pp. 1–55, esp. pp. 1–5.

5   For Mearsheimer see "Back to the Future: Instability in Europe after the Cold War," *International Security*, 15 (1990), pp. 1–156; repr. in Sean M. Lynn-Jones (ed.), *The Cold War and After: Prospects for Peace* (Cambridge, Mass.: MIT Press, 1991), pp. 141–92. For more theoretically oriented Waltzian analysis see Barry Buzan, Charles Jones, and Richard Little, *The Logic of Anarchy: Neorealism to Structural Realism* (New York: Columbia University Press, 1993); Hidemi Suganami, *On the Causes of War* (Oxford: Oxford University Press, 1996).

6   For an application of the liberal perspective to the current international agenda see the report of the Commission on Global Governance published under the title *Our Global Neighborhood* (Oxford: Oxford University Press, 1995). For a critical assessment of this report and its liberal orientation see Richard Falk, "Liberalism at the Global Level: The Last of the Independent Commissions?," *Millennium*, 24 (1995), pp. 563–76; for the argument that the liberal option was ended by the events of 1968 and after see Immanuel Wallerstein, *After Liberalism* (New York: New Press, 1995), esp. pp. 1–7.

7   R. B. J. Walker, *Inside/Outside: International Relations as Political Theory* (Cambridge: Cambridge University Press, 1993); but see normative

theorizing in Drucilla Cornell, *The Philosophy of the Limit* (London: Routledge, 1992).

8 For Huntington's reconsidered position see *The Clash of Civilizations and the Remaking of the World Order* (New York: Simon & Schuster, 1996); for a more inclusive view of inter-civilizational relations on the basis of a legitimate world order see Falk, "False Universalism and the Geopolitics of Exclusion: The Case of Islam," *Third World Quarterly*, 18/1 (1997), pp. 7–23.

9 Samuel Huntington, "The Clash of Civilizations," *Foreign Affairs*, 72 (1993), pp. 22–49, at p. 22.

10 For the published text of this lecture see Huntington, "Economic Power on International Relations," Research Program in International Security, Monograph Series, 1 (Princeton, NJ: Center of International Studies, Princeton University, 1993); see also Samuel Huntington, "Why International Primacy Matters," *International Security*, 17 (1993), pp. 68–83.

11 See Joseph S. Nye, Jr, and William A. Owens, "America's Information Edge," *Foreign Affairs*, 75 (1996), pp. 20–37, at p. 35 where, near the beginning of the article, it is written that "[t]he one country that can best lead the information revolution will be more powerful than any other" (at p. 20). A companion article, more technical in nature, proceeded along the same lines: Eliot A. Cohen, "A Revolution in Warfare," *Foreign Affairs*, 75 (1996), pp. 37–54.

12 *International Herald Tribune*, May 6, 1996.

13 The normative dimension of the Nye/Lake conviction that American leadership, which is not presented as hegemonic, is a global public good.

14 An excellent depiction of modernism as constitutive of world order is contained in Stephen Toulmin, *Cosmopolis: The Hidden Agenda of Modernity* (New York: Free Press, 1990).

15 See Beck, Giddens, and Lash, *Reflexive Modernization*, for a different appreciation of the restructuring of world order in the present period.

16 For several arguments along these lines see essays in Yoshikazu Sakamoto (ed.), *Global Transformation: Challenges to the State System* (Tokyo: United Nations University Press, 1994); see also Richard Falk, "An Inquiry into the Political Economy of World Order," *New Political Economy*, 1 (1996), pp. 13–26.

17 For a range of views see Martha C. Nussbaum et al., *For Love of Country: Debating the Limits of Patriotism* (Boston: Beacon Press, 1996); Bart von Steenbergen (ed.), *The Condition of Citizenship* (London: Sage, 1994).

18 On interpretations of the Gulf War see Tareq Y. Ismael and Jacqueline S. Ismael (eds), *The Gulf War and the New World Order* (Gainesville, Fla.: University of Florida Press, 1994); Victoria Brittain (ed.), *The Gulf between Us: The Gulf War and Beyond* (London: Virago, 1991); John Gittings (ed.), *Beyond the Gulf War: The Middle East and the New World Order* (London: Catholic Institute of International Relations, 1991).

19   See especially David Rieff, *Slaughterhouse: Bosnia and the Failure of the West* (New York: Simon & Schuster, 1995); also Susan L. Woodward, *Balkan Tragedy* (Washington, DC: Brookings Institution, 1995); Richard H. Ullman (ed.), *The World and Yugoslavia's War* (New York: Council on Foreign Relations Press, 1996); see also the illuminating paper by Mahmood Mamdani, "From Conquest to Consent as the Basis of State Formation: Reflection After a Visit to Rwanda," unpublished paper, dated Feb. 1996.

20   John Gerard Ruggie, "At Home Abroad: International Liberalisation and Domestic Stability in the New World Economy," *Millennium*, 24 (1995), pp. 507–26; see also Stephen Gill, "Globalisation, Market Civilisation and Disciplinary Neoliberalism," *Millennium*, 24 (1995), pp. 399–423.

21   Hendrick Spruyt, *The Sovereign State and Its Competitors* (Princeton, NJ: Princeton University Press, 1994), p. 185.

22   For discussions of a people-oriented approach to security, specified as "human security," see the various volumes of the *Human Development Report*, published annually since 1990 under the auspices of the United Nations Development Programme, but especially the 1994 volume, *Human Development Report 1994* (New York: United Nations, 1994), pp. 1–107; see also Majid Tehranian and Laura Read, "Human Security and Global Governance: The State of the Art," Prospectus for a Collaborative Research Project, Toda Institute, Honolulu, Hawaii (1996).

23   For a spirited assessment, yet somewhat exaggerated along these lines, see Jean-Marie Guihenro, *The End of the Nation State* (Minneapolis: University of Minnesota Press, 1993); a more careful and convincing analysis along similar lines is to be found in Joseph A. Camilleri and Jim Falk, *The End of Sovereignty? The Politics of a Shrinking and Fragmenting World* (Aldershot: Edward Elgar, 1992).

24   A balanced account of the decline of sovereignty is offered by James N. Rosenau in "Sovereignty in a Turbulent World," in Gene M. Lyons and Michael Mastanduno (eds), *Beyond Westphalia? State Sovereignty and International Intervention* (Baltimore, Md.: Johns Hopkins University Press, 1995), pp. 191–227.

25   For theoretical background see Walker, *Inside/Outside*.

26   Robert H. Jackson, *Quasi-states: Sovereignty, International Relations and the Third World* (Cambridge: Cambridge University Press, 1990).

27   Mark Dery, *Escape Velocity: Cyberculture at the End of the Century* (London: Hodder & Stoughton, 1996), pp. 226–319; see also Kevin Kelly, *Out of Control: The Rise of Neo-Biological Civilization* (Reading, Mass.: Addison-Wesley, 1994).

28   My discussions of these structural aspects of world order can be found in Falk, note 1, and more recently in Falk, *On Humane Governance: Toward a New Global Politics* (Cambridge: Polity Press, 1995), and "Environmental Protection in an Era of Globalization," *Yearbook of International Environmental Law*, vol. 6, 1995 (1996), pp. 3–25.

29   Zygmunt Bauman, *Imitations of Postmodernity* (London: Routledge, 1992), p. xiv.
30   For two important and quite different recent efforts in this direction see Martha C. Nussbaum, "Patriotism and Cosmopolitanism," in Nussbaum et al., *For Love of Country*, pp. 2–17, 131–44, and David Held, *Democracy and the Global Order: From the Modern State to Cosmopolitan Governance* (Cambridge: Polity Press, 1995), esp. pp. 219–86.

Chapter 3   On the Political Economy of World Order

1   Elsewhere I have discussed meeting the challenge of genocide. See Richard Falk, "Meeting the Challenge of Genocide in Bosnia: Reconciling Moral Imperatives with Political Constraints," in Charles B. Strozier and Michael Flynn (eds), *Genocide, War, and Human Survival* (London and Lanham, Md.: Rowman and Littlefield, 1996), pp. 125–35.
2   Michael Mandlebaum, "The Reluctance to Intervene," *Foreign Policy*, 95 (1994), pp. 3–18, at p. 17.
3   The World Order Models Project (WOMP), a transnational collaborative undertaking that is independent of governments and of international institutions, has since the late 1960s based its proposals for reform on such a foundation of widely shared values, a presumptive global ethos, although formulated abstractly and without resolving inner tensions among values, thereby allowing much scope for interpretation; see Richard Falk, *A Study of Future Worlds* (New York: Free Press, 1975), pp. 11–39.
4   Measures of relative military capabilities are of little interest these days as compared to the cold war era and previously, and much more attention is paid to comparative economic surveys as issued by the IMF and UNDP each year.
5   Samuel P. Huntington, "The Clash of Civilizations," *Foreign Affairs*, 72 (1993), pp. 22–49.
6   For critiques of economic globalism from the perspective of the South, see Walden Bello, *Dark Victory* (London: Pluto Press, 1994) and the special issue of the *Third World Quarterly* on "The South in the New World (Dis)Order," 15 (1994), pp. 4–146.
7   The Seattle locus of "Sleepless in Seattle" and "Little Buddha" is notable when taken together with the emergence there of several of the most influential rock groups of the 1990s.
8   Stephen Toulmin, for instance, associates the modern state with absolutist claims that deny validity to those outside its protective reach. See his *Cosmopolis* (New York: Free Press, 1990), esp. pp. 175–220.
9   For an important critique, see Krishan Kumar, "The End of Socialism? The End of Utopia? The End of History?," in Krishan Kumar and Stephen Bann (eds), *Utopias and the Millennium* (London: Reaktion Books, 1993), pp. 63–80, at p. 70.
10   In this regard, the war was momentarily important in erasing not only the

memory of US defeat in Vietnam but, more profoundly, the apparent reversal of control resulting from the collapse of colonialism.

11 Perhaps other war scenarios will emerge: challenging North Korea's efforts to acquire nuclear weaponry or as an attempt to avoid an ultranationalist Russia under the leadership of Zhironovsky.

12 See the cover story in *The Economist*, "Shamed Are the Peacemakers," Apr. 30–May 6, 1994, pp. 15–16.

13 For suggestive wider interpretation see James William Gibson, *Warrior Dreams: Paramilitary Culture in Post-Vietnam America* (New York: Hill and Wang, 1994).

14 See Nobel Jubilee Symposium essays by K. Subrahmanyam and Ali A. Mazrui, in Geir Lundestad and Odd Arne Westad (eds), *Beyond the Cold War: New Dimensions in International Relations* (New York: Scandinavian University Press, 1993), pp. 57–70, 85–98; see debate between Anthony Lake and F. Gregory Gause III, "Confronting Backlash States," *Foreign Affairs*, 73 (1994), pp. 45–66.

15 For a critique of the realist world view, see Richard Falk, *Explorations at the Edge of Time: Prospects for World Order* (Philadelphia, Pa.: Temple University Press, 1992), pp. 214–27.

16 Suppression of wages and labor organization is the expression of this dynamic, accounting in part for the rapid growth of South and East Asian economies.

17 See the devastating critique of US government behavior, including the systematic and extreme abuse of Haitian boat people, recounted in Paul Farmer, *The Uses of Haiti* (Monroe, M.: Common Courage, 1994).

18 This partly revives class consciousness and partly validates a critique of North–South hegemony.

19 Former Secretary of State James Baker, in an informal visit to Princeton University, April 1994, when asked "What became of the new world order?," responded revealingly: "We explained it wrong. We should have said that our system won the Cold War and now represents what people everywhere want for themselves." That is, the neo-Wilsonian "spin" was fundamentally irrelevant to the post–cold war reality.

20 Even modest proposals to give the UN a peace enforcement capability of its own or to ensure financial independence and solvency or to provide token forms of democratization have foundered in the face of a reconstituted realism.

21 See Robin Broad with John Cavanagh, *Plundering Paradise: The Struggle for the Environment in the Philippines* (Berkeley: University of California Press, 1993).

22 See contributions to Bart van Steenbergen (ed.), *The Condition of Citizenship* (London: Sage, 1994).

23 See the magazine *Wired* for both the creative and the elite dimensions of this new electronically oriented, yet radical, political sensitivity.

24 For early anticipation of such an orientation for policymaking at the level of the hegemonic state, see Robert C. Johansen, *The National and the*

Human Interest: An Analysis of US Foreign Policy (Princeton, NJ: Princeton University Press, 1980).

Chapter 4 A Regional Approach to World Order

1 For elaboration see Richard Falk, *A Study of Future Worlds* (New York: Free Press, 1975); *idem, Explorations at the Edge of Time: Prospects for World Order* (Philadelphia, Pa.: Temple University Press, 1992); *idem, On Humane Governance: Toward a New Global Politics* (Cambridge: Polity Press, 1995).

2 The European focus of several early influential analyses of the end of the cold war reinforced these perceptions of discontinuity. See Jack Snyder, "Averting Anarchy in the New Europe," *International Security*, 14 (1990), pp. 5–41; John Mearsheimer, "Back to the Future: Instability in Europe after the Cold War," *International Security*, 14 (1990), pp. 5–56; repr. in Sean M. Lynn-Jones (ed.), *The Cold War and After: Prospects for Peace* (Cambridge, Mass.: MIT Press, 1991), pp. 141–92. On the problematics of sovereignty see Richard Falk, "Toward Obsolescence: Sovereignty in the Era of Globalization," *Harvard International Review*, 17 (1995), pp. 34–5, 75.

3 Bjorn Hettne, "The New Regionalism: Implications for Development and Peace," (Helsinki: World Institute for Development Economics Research (WIDER), United Nations University, 1994), pp. 4–5; see Robert Gilpin, *War and Change in World Politics* (Cambridge: Cambridge University Press, 1981), for a clear presentation of hegemonic stability as the basis of world order and of its erosion.

4 See Hedley Bull, *The Anarchical Society: A Study of Order in World Politics* (New York: Columbia University Press, 1977); for assessments of post-statal world order see James N. Rosenau, *Turbulence in World Politics: A Theory of Change and Continuity* (Princeton, NJ: Princeton University Press, 1990); Richard Falk, *The End of World Order* (New York: Holmes and Meier, 1983).

5 Consider George Bush's neo-Wilsonian rationale for resisting Iraq: "What is at stake is more than one small country. It is a big idea: a new world order where diverse nations are drawn together in common cause to achieve the universal aspirations of mankind – peace and security, freedom, and the rule of law": quoted in *Round Table* (Summer 1994), p. 5.

6 See Charles Krauthammer, "The Unipolar Moment," in Graham Allison and Gregory F. Treverton (eds), *Rethinking America's Security* (New York: Norton, 1992), pp. 295–306.

7 What made Israel "strategic" is somewhat elusive, but it was so perceived by Western leadership, especially in the United States, and reflected domestic pressures via Congress and the media, as well as calculations about stability in the Middle East.

8 For instance, John Mearsheimer, "Why We Will Soon Miss the Cold War," *Atlantic* (April 1990).

9 But note that what was accepted by Washington for two years as tolerable was either the return of a populist leader like Aristide or the stabilization

of military rule, provided the refugee problem was "handled," even if handling meant forcible repatriation, brutal means to discourage the outflow, and resettlement in already overburdened countries in Central America and the Caribbean. See Joanne Landy, "Born-Again Interventionists," *The Progressive*, 58 (Sept. 1994), p. 23; for a mainstream analysis of hegemonic caution see Michael Mandlebaum, "The Reluctance to Intervene," *Foreign Policy*, 95 (1994), pp. 3–18. For recent assessments that have taken account of the successful restoration to power of Aristide and a peacekeeping presence by US–UN forces see James Morrell, "Haiti: Success Under Fire," International Policy Report (Washington, DC: Center for International Policy, 1995); Richard Falk, "The Haiti Intervention: A Dangerous World Order Precedent for the United Nations," *Harvard International Law Journal*, 36 (1995), pp. 341–58.

10 What is called "Asia's 'Asianization'" in a recent article: Yoichi Funabashi, "The Asianization of Asia," *Foreign Affairs*, 72 (1993), pp. 75–85.

11 Samuel P. Huntington, "The Clash of Civilizations?," *Foreign Affairs*, 72 (1993), pp. 22–49.

12 For elaboration see ch. 3.

13 A relevant datum here is the extent to which nominally socialist or welfare-oriented political leaders are led to adopt unconditional capitalist orientations once in power; Mitterand, Clinton, Mauryama, Blair, and Schroeder are examples, although each adapts in a particular way, reflecting variations in place, time, culture, personality, and political mandate.

14 The distinction between negative and positive globalism is itself a reflection of recent developments, especially the globalist character of the world economy; earlier, globalism, at least on the surface, seemed motivated almost exclusively by idealistic ambitions to overcome war by creating effective mechanisms of collective security, with the eventual objective being the achievement of a disarmed world administered by a government of federative structure – that is, a mixture of the Wilsonian effort to supplant the balance of power approach to stability and the more utopian pursuit of the Kantian notion of "perpetual peace." This latter notion has resurfaced in its weak form in the latter stages of the cold war, and subsequently, as achievable by the spread of market-oriented constitutionalism, premised on the argument that liberal democracies do not go to war with one another. See Michael Doyle, "Kant, Liberal Legacies, and Foreign Affairs," *Philosophy and Public Affairs*, 12 (1983), pp. 205–35, 323–53; Bruce Russett, *Controlling the Sword: The Democratic Governance of National Security* (Cambridge, Mass.: Harvard University Press, 1990), esp. pp. 119–45. This positive globalism can also be criticized as naive, hypocritical, and insufficient. For classic treatment see E. H. Carr, *The Twenty Years' Crisis: An Introduction to the Study of International Relations* (London: Macmillan, 1939); for a more recent argument applied to recent world developments see Henry Kissinger, *Diplomacy* (New York: Simon & Schuster, 1994), esp. pp. 804–35.

15 See *Human Development Report 1994* (New York: Oxford University Press, 1994) for an analysis of antecedent conditions.

16   See Thomas G. Weiss, "UN Responses in the Former Yugoslavia: Moral and Operational Choices," *Ethics and International Affairs*, 8 (1994), pp. 1–21.

17   This revival is also connected with the reappearance of a Russian threat to Europe in the form of a more assertive foreign policy and by way of the rise of ultranationalist challenges to Yeltsin's leadership (the Zhirinovsky factor).

18   For earlier lines of specification see Richard Falk, *A Study of Future Worlds* (New York: Free Press, 1975); *idem*, *Explorations at the Edge of Time: Prospects for World Order* (Philadelphia, Pa.: Temple University Press, 1992).

19   See Dusan Sidjanski, *L'Avenir fédéraliste de l'Europe* (Paris: Presses Universitaire de France, 1992).

20   Kenichi Ohmae, an articulate champion of such regionalism, writes: "Political leaders, however reluctantly, must adjust to the reality of economic regional reality if they are to nurture real economic flows." In effect, such leaders must subordinate claims on behalf of the marginalized sectors of their own societies: "Resistant governments will be left to reign over traditional political territories as all meaningful participation in the global economy migrates beyond their well-preserved frontiers." See Ohmae, "The Rise of the Region State," *Foreign Affairs*, 72 (1993), pp. 78–87, at p. 85.

21   This paragraph owes much to a conversation with Ralph Nader, consumer activist, on Aug. 5, 1994; for a range of views along these lines see the collection of essays by Nader et al., *The Case against "Free Trade": GATT, NAFTA, and the Globalization of Corporate Power* (San Francisco: Earth Island Press, 1993).

22   See Raymond Aron, "The Anarchical Order of Power," *Daedalus*, 95 (1966), pp. 479–502; note that this weakness may disappear under the aegis of negative globalism, which is, as argued in the prior section, one of the features of the WTO dimension of the extension of GATT.

23   There are some alleged exceptions by way of "humanitarian intervention," but none stand close scrutiny as real exceptions; for exposition see R. J. Vincent, *Nonintervention and International Order* (Princeton, NJ: Princeton University Press, 1974), esp. pp. 344–9.

24   See proposals of University of Chicago under the aegis of Robert Hutchins: Hutchins et al., *Preliminary Draft of a World Constitution* (Chicago: University of Chicago Press, 1948).

25   For a sustained argument along these lines see W. Andy Knight, "Towards a Subsidiarity Model of Global Governance: Making Chapter VIII of the UN Charter Operational," paper presented at Annual Meeting of Academic Council of the United Nations System, The Hague, June 1994.

26   For support of this notion of a complementary relationship as an aspect of an effective UN see Boutros Boutros-Ghali, *An Agenda for Peace: Preventive Diplomacy, Peacemaking and Peacekeeping* (New York: United Nations, 1992), pp. 35–8.

27   Among the examples, the following stand out: Russia in "the near abroad,"

the US in most regions, but especially in the setting of the Middle East and Caribbean, France in relation to Francophone Africa, especially Rwanda. See Kevin Fedarko, "Back to the USSR?," *Time*, July 25, 1994, pp. 40–3; an editorial, "Russian Interventions," *Wall Street Journal*, Aug. 8, 1994; Charles William Maynes, "A Workable Clinton Doctrine," *Foreign Policy*, 93 (1993–4), pp. 3–20.

28 See assessment in the context of authorization for the use of force to oust the Haitian military regime: Charles Krauthammer, "Goodbye, Monroe Doctrine," *Washington Post*, Aug. 2, 1994.

29 Compare South Africa in the apartheid period, under comparable pressures at both regional and global levels.

30 See Hettne's overview in "New Regionalism."

31 See evaluation by David Held, *Political Theory and the Modern State* (Stanford, Calif.: Stanford University Press, 1989), esp. pp. 214–42.

32 For assessment of these tendencies as pertaining to citizenship and political identity see Bart van Steenbergen (ed.), *The Condition of Citizenship* (London: Sage, 1994); also treaty provisions reprinted under the rubric "A Citizen of the European Union," in Paul Barry Clarke (ed.), *Citizenship* (London: Pluto Press, 1994), pp. 188–90.

33 Hettne's formulation of "the proper balance" between such ideas and forces being "the crucial issue" does not explicitly signal any particular concern for those social and environmental elements of society that are being most victimized by the phenomena of globalization: "New Regionalism," p. 5. Possibly, this concern could be brought in by way of "regionalism and world order values," but the discussion as set forth, pp. 41–3, does not appear to address such ethical implications, at least not directly.

Chapter 5 The Illegitimacy of the Non-Proliferation Regime

1 Michael J. Mazzarr, "Going Just a Little Nuclear: Nonproliferation Lessons from North Korea," *International Security*, 20 (1995), pp. 92–122, at p. 92.

2 "Arms Control and the U.S.–Russian Relationship," Report of an Independent Task Force (Council on Foreign Relations and the Nixon Center for Peace and Freedom, 1996), at p. 22.

3 Michael Klare, *Rogue States and Nuclear Outlaws: America's Search for a New Foreign Policy* (New York: Hill and Wang, 1995), p. 7. The list of rogue states is varied from time to time, but Klare's list seems accurate in relation to current nuclear weapons concerns; see discussion at pp. 130–68 and the list of "prospective rogues" on p. 134 that includes such countries as India, Pakistan, Turkey, and Taiwan. When the idea of rogue or outlaw states is invoked in relation to terrorism, Syria is sometimes left off, and Sudan and Cuba are added. The identification of pariah states was initiated as a serious political project by Ronald Reagan in a widely noticed speech to the Amer-

ican Bar Association in 1985. For text see Current Policy No. 721 (US Department of State, July 8, 1985).

4 As explained by Klare, *Rogue States*, pp. 26–30; the threat of rogue states, also called "backlash states," is conceptualized as a foreign policy challenge by President Clinton's National Security Advisor, Anthony Lake. See Lake, "Confronting Backlash States," *Foreign Affairs*, 73 (1994), pp. 45–55. For a realist argument that proliferation is stabilizing under certain conditions see John J. Mearsheimer, "The Case for a Ukrainian Nuclear Deterrent," *Foreign Affairs*, 72 (1993), pp. 50–66.

5 For my earlier critiques of the non-proliferation approach see "The Denuclearization of Global Politics," in Richard Falk, *A Global Approach to National Policy* (Cambridge, Mass.: Harvard University Press, 1975), pp. 41–53, and "Nuclear Policy and World Order: Why Denuclearization," in *The End of World Order* (New York: Holmes and Meier, 1983), pp. 185–215.

6 See e.g. Mearsheimer, "The Case for a Ukrainian Deterrent."

7 For a comprehensive analysis premised on a critique of nuclearism see Robert Jay Lifton and Richard Falk, *Indefensible Weapons: The Political and Psychological Case against Nuclearism*, 2nd updated edn (New York: Basic Books, 1992).

8 For discussion pointing to US military dominance in the future see Joseph S. Nye, Jr, and William A. Owens, "America's Information Edge," *Foreign Affairs*, 75 (1996), pp. 20–36 esp. pp. 20–3, 35; see also Eliot A. Cohen, "A Revolution in Warfare," *Foreign Affairs*, 75 (1996), pp. 37–54.

9 See citations in n. 8 for general background thinking. William Lynn, an official at the Department of Defense, gave a presentation in October 1996 at the Woodrow Wilson School, Princeton University, in which he described in detail a shift in Pentagon war strategy as moving from a search for "military superiority" to a quest for "military dominance" (the technological capacity to prevail in plausible war scenarios while enduring only minimal casualties).

10 For discussion see Samuel P. Huntington, *The Clash of Civilizations and the Remaking of World Order* (New York: Simon & Schuster, 1996), pp. 312–18.

11 On this see especially E. P. Thompson, *Exterminism and Cold War* (London: Verso, 1982); Jonathan Schell, *The Fate of the Earth* (New York: Knopf, 1982); see also Mary Kaldor, *The Imaginary War: Understanding East–West Conflict* (Oxford: Basil Blackwell, 1990).

12 For a range of views see Avner Cohen and Steven Lee (eds), *Nuclear Weapons and the Future of Humanity* (Totowa, NJ: Rowman & Allanheld, 1986); George Kennan, *The Nuclear Delusion* (New York: Pantheon, 1982); Burns H. Weston (ed.), *Toward Nuclear Disarmament and Global Security* (Boulder, Colo.: Westview Press, 1984); Robert S. McNamara, *Blundering into Disaster* (New York: Pantheon, 1986); Michael Walzer, *Just and Unjust Wars* (New York: Basic Books, 1977), pp. 251–83.

13 The UN system, including the ICJ, provide a capability for third-party roles, but their operations are dependent on voluntary submission and funding and are not consistently available.

14   Thomas Franck, *The Power of Legitimacy among Nations* (New York: Oxford University Press, 1990), p. 16, emphasis original.

15   See chapter entitled "The Ambivalent Crusade," in Klare, *Rogue States*, pp. 169–203.

16   For discussion of Israel's nuclear weapons program see Seymour Hersh, *The Sampson Option: Israel's Nuclear Arsenal and American Foreign Policy* (New York: Random House, 1991).

17   See Mazzarr, "Going Just a Little Nuclear," p. 93; see also Roger Dingman, "Atomic Diplomacy during the Korean War," *International Security*, 13 (1988/9), pp. 50–91.

18   For text of non-proliferation treaty see Burns H. Weston, Richard A. Falk, and Anthony D'Amato (eds), *Documents on International Law and World Order*, 2nd edn (St Paul, Minn.: West, 1980), pp. 204–6.

19   Article X provides that "Each Party shall in exercising its national sovereignty have the right to withdraw from the Treaty if it decides that extraordinary events, relating to the subject matter of the Treaty, have jeopardized the supreme interests of the country." In exercising this right of withdrawal, the country must give three months' notice and an explanation of its action, but its own assessment appears to be unchallengeable within the scope of the treaty.

20   For representative Third World perspectives see contributions of K. Subrahmanyam and Ali A. Mazrui to the 90th Anniversary Nobel Jubilee Symposium volume: Geir Lundestad and Odd Arne Westad (eds), *Beyond the Cold War: New Dimensions in International Relations* (New York: Scandinavian University Press, 1993), pp. 57–70, 85–98.

21   So-called security assurances have been given to nonnuclear states facing nuclear adversaries. For discussion see Tuiloma Neroni Slade, "1995 Review and Extension of the Treaty on the Non-Proliferation of Nuclear Weapons," *Review of European Community and International Environmental Law*, 5 (1996), pp. 246–52, at p. 246.

22   See especially William M. Evan and Ved P. Nanda (eds), *Nuclear Proliferation and the Legality of Nuclear Weapons* (Lanham, Md.: University Press of America, 1995). For additional helpful legal assessments of nuclear weaponry and doctrines governing use see spectrum of views collected in Arthur Selwyn Miller and Martin Feinrider (eds), *Nuclear Weapons and Law* (Westport, Conn.: Greenwood Press, 1984); see also *The Bomb and the Law: A Summary Report of the London Nuclear Warfare Tribunal* (Stockholm: Myrdal Foundation, 1989); Elliott L. Meyrowitz, *Prohibition of Nuclear Weapons: The Relevance of International Law* (Dobbs Ferry, NY: Transnational, 1990); Nicholas Grief, *The World Court Project on Nuclear Weapons and International Law* (Northampton, Mass.: Alethia Press, 1992).

23   See English language texts of Advisory Opinion on the Legality of the Threat or Use of Nuclear Weapons, *International Legal Materials*, 25 (July 1996), pp. 809–938. Undoubtedly, there will be sustained scholarly controversy on how to interpret the decision. See series of articles under title "World Court says Mostly No to Nuclear Weapons," *Bulletin of the Atomic*

Scientists 52 (Sept.–Oct. 1996), pp. 39–47. For my assessment see Richard Falk, "Nuclear Weapons, International Law and the World Court: A Historic Encounter," *American Journal of International Law*, 91 (1997), pp. 64–75.

24 See Robert Jay Lifton and Eric Markusen, *The Genocidal Mentality: Nazi Holocaust and Nuclear Threat* (New York: Basic Books, 1990).

25 These judges were Christopher G. Weeramantry (Sri Lanka), Abdul G. Koroma (Sierra Leone), and Mohammed Shahabuddeen (Guyana).

26 Important UN resolutions supporting this view include G.A. Resolution 1653 (XVI) (1961); G.A. Resolution 2936 (XXVII) (1972); G.A. Resolution 33/71B (XXXIII) (1978); G.A. Resolution 34/83G (XXXIV) (1979); G.A. Resolution 36/92I (XXXVI) (1981).

27 For text see "Pastoral Letter on War and Peace – The Challenge of Peace: God's Promise and Own Response," in Weston (ed.), *Toward Nuclear Disarmament*, pp. 123–46.

28 See Walzer, *Just and Unjust Wars*, pp. 251–83; see especially Kenneth Waltz, "Nuclear Myths and Political Realities," *American Political Science Review*, 84 (1990), pp. 731–45.

29 Joseph S. Nye, Jr, *Nuclear Ethics* (New York: Free Press, 1986); a cruder rationale for nuclearism is offered in John J. Mearsheimer's "Back to the Future: Instability in Europe after the Cold War," in Sean M. Lynn-Jones and Steven E. Miller (eds), *The Cold War and After: Prospects for Peace* expanded edn (Cambridge, Mass.: MIT Press, 1993), pp. 141–92.

30 For legal approach to this oppositional consensus see Michael Bothe, "Challenging French Nuclear Tests: A Role for Legal Remedies?," *Review of European and Community International Environmental Law*, 5 (1996), pp. 253–8.

31 For indictments along these lines see collection of essays published by JUST (Just World Trust) under the title *Dominance of the West over the Rest* (Kuala Lumpur, Malaysia: Vinlin Press, 1995); also Chandra Muzaffar, *Human Rights and the New World Order* (Kuala Lumpur, Malaysia: Vinlin Press, 1993).

Chapter 6   The Quest for Human Rights

1 Human rights are also associated with protection against cruel and oppressive practices. Non-citizens located within territory are also protected.

2 Internal accountability evolved unevenly, yet cumulatively, in the modern Western transition from royal absolutism to constitutionalism, a process that can be traced back to the Magna Carta, with antecedents in ancient Athens and Rome.

3 For a less rigid view of this dichotomy between domestic and international society, yet still situated firmly in the realist, anti-utopian tradition, see Hedley Bull, *An Anarchical Society: A Study of Order in World Politics* (New York: Columbia University Press, 1977).

4 For the classic formulation see Niccolò Machiavelli, *The Prince* (London: Penguin, M. Bull tr., 1961); for a contemporary perspective see Hans

Morgenthau, *Politics among Nations: The Struggle for Power and Peace* 4th edn (New York: Knopf, 1967); for influential critical assessments of the distorting impact of moralism and legalism on international relations thinking see the main writings of E. H. Carr, George Kennan, Henry Kissinger, and Reinhold Neibuhr; also Robert Cox for an extension of critical realist thinking to encompass the political economy. See Cox, "Social Forces, States, and World Orders: Beyond International Relations Theory," in Robert Keohane (ed.), *Neo-Realism and Its Critics* (New York: Columbia University Press, 1986), pp. 204–54.

5 The evolutionary strengthening of domestic constitutionalism over the course of several centuries and in vastly different national circumstances invariably was the inevitable result of concession to societal pressures and was in this respect essentially involuntary; undoubtedly, the most notable expression of these leaps forward in constitutional protection of individuals within domestic political space occurred in connection with the American and French revolutions. Later extensions of protection to individuals arose out of the labor movement as a defensive reaction to the hardships imposed on workers by the early phases of the industrial revolution. This pattern of implementation from below within domestic space anticipates the main argument of this chapter about the role of transnational social forces in accounting for the unexpected potency of the movement to give international legal status to human right claims and standards.

6 Although the main purpose of these trials was to avoid repeating mistakes made after World War I, when the entire human nation was made to bear responsibility for the last war, there were other goals, as well. One such goal was to document the Nazi terror, especially the Holocaust, both to educate international society about the depravity of Nazi Germany and to take seriously, if belatedly, the human suffering inflicted on the victims.

7 The subversive dimension of the war crimes issue has reemerged recently in a vivid way in connection with the end-game diplomacy of the Bosnian War; the Dayton Peace Accords of 1995 takes the extraordinary step of disqualifying anyone from a position of political leadership in the reconstituted Bosnia if they have been formally indicted for war crimes by the tribunal in The Hague – understood as applicable, at the very least, to the Bosnian Serb leaders Karadzic and Mladic. The same double movement is evident in the push within the United Nations to go forward with proposals for the establishment of an International Criminal Court and resistance to such a formalization of individual criminal accountability. As of now, further stages in such a process are being carried on within the limits set by a geopolitical compromise to the effect that the authority of such a tribunal would be engaged only if the Security Council so decides. Such a procedure brings the veto into play, ensuring the permanent members that neither their leaders, nor those of close allies, could be prosecuted as war criminals. In effect, even if such a court comes into existence, it would in all probability stay clear of any process of general applicability and confine its operation to criminal patterns that occur on the margins of international society.

8   But such an original intention did not determine the destiny of the human rights discourse. Unintended consequences and unanticipated agents of influence exerted various pressures upon human rights as merely declaratory. Thus, the discourse as initiated evolved as a process, becoming an instrument of geopolitical conflict and taking on a more juridical character when the norms of the Universal Declaration were restructured in the form of international treaties: the International Covenant on Economic, Social, and Cultural Rights and the International Covenant on Civil and Political Rights.

9   As human rights evolved in subsequent years, being carried forward by unanticipated currents of pressures, this division between categories of rights hardened, producing a clear encounter between the two leading orientations toward human rights which took the form of breaking the content of the Universal Declaration into distinct covenants; the US governmental attitude was pivotal, treating civil and political rights as already embodied in practice, making any internationalization of the obligations to uphold a matter of redundancy, while viewing economic and social claims as at best hortatory and undeserving of legal protection; as support for the welfare state declined in later years, coming into increasing conflict with the operation of the market and the private sector, these human rights claims were dismissed as unworthy, partly because of their socialist implications.

10 In the United States, any attempted internationalization of human rights has been rigorously resisted at every turn by the right wing, essentially because it seemed to give "enemies" a means by which to challenge aspects of domestic social practice, which was doubly objectionable to these critics: it infringed on both sovereignty and federalism.

11 These differences in outlook and behavior are well depicted in Harold D. Lasswell and Myres S. McDougal, "Diverse Systems of Public Order," in McDougal (ed.), *Studies in World Public Order* (New Haven, Conn.: Yale University Press, 1960); see also Falk, *Human Rights and State Sovereignty* (New York: Holmes and Meier, 1981), pp. 125–52.

12 For a highly critical view of US policies in relation to human rights see Noam Chomsky and Edward S. Herman, *The Political Economy of Human Rights*, 2 vols (Boston: South End Press, 1979); see also Richard J. Barnet, *Intervention and Revolution: The United States in the Third World* (New York: World, 1968); for a spirited normative defense of this US approach see Jeanne Kirkpatrick, an orientation toward human rights that reflected anti-Communist ideology and led to the adoption of the Reagan Doctrine of assisting anti-Communist insurgencies by alleged reference to human rights considerations.

13 The most blatant Soviet interventions in Eastern Europe were Hungary (1956) and Czechoslovakia (1968), but threats of Soviet intervention encouraged Communist regimes to tighten up their authoritarian control and, overall, minimized the space available for implementing human rights of a civil and political character.

14 G.A. Resolution 1514, 1540.

15 This idealist influence was all the more effective in that it was congruent with political myths and traditions in America that retain vitality for a large portion of the citizenry and can be invoked by political leaders at times to reassert the moral leadership and influence of the United States in world affairs, reclaiming a heritage as "a Lockean in a Hobbesian world."

16 Cf. David Held on the deeper significance of this step in *Political Theory and the Modern State* (Stanford, Calif.: Stanford University Press, 1984), pp. 232–4.

17 A strong instance of ideologically tilted ratings for human rights performance was to be found in the annual Freedom House reports, which represented an alignment between official Western views on human rights and a fairly conservative sector of civil society.

18 Bloc barriers were important insulators during the cold war, whereas indifference toward political outcomes of struggles in most Third World countries or Western hostility to Islamic militancy, even if democratically supported (Algerian elections), protected most oppressive states from external pressures, given current global conditions.

19 This was certainly the case with respect to ILO Convention No. 107 (1956), text available in Burns H. Weston, Richard A. Falk, and Anthony D'Amato (eds), *Basic Documents in International Law and World Order*, 2nd edn (St Paul, Minn.: West, 1990), pp. 335–40.

20 As evidence of success by indigenous peoples in promoting their normative preferences and correcting the earlier misunderstandings see ILO Convention No. 169 (1989), text available in Weston, Falk, and D'Amato, (eds), *Basic Documents*, pp. 489–97. For an even stronger expression of indigenous viewpoints see United Nations Draft Declaration of the Rights of Indigenous Peoples, which, as of early 1999, continues to be reviewed by the human rights bureaucracy prior to presentation to the General Assembly for final approval. See tentative text and resolution 1995/32 of UN Commission on Human Rights, *International Legal Materials*, 34 (Mar. 1995), pp. 535–55. It is likely that the outcome of this process will be inconclusive, as states seem likely to resist any move that legally confirms claims of self-determination by indigenous peoples, fearing state-shattering implications.

21 On the right to development see Roland Rich, "The Right to Development: A Right of Peoples?," in James Crawford (ed.), *The Rights of Peoples* (Oxford: Clarendon Press, 1988), pp. 39–54.

22 Such an assessment is provisional and selective. There is some evidence in the mid-1990s of a revival of labor militancy, especially where unions are firmly embedded in the public sector and in basic utilities, as in France, Italy, and Spain.

23 But see the skeptical view of these pressures in Paul Krugman's book *Peddling Prosperity: Economic Sense and Nonsense in the Age of Diminished Expectations* (New York: W. W. Norton, 1995), esp. pp. 245–92.

24 Even on the domestic scene in the United States, the anti-welfare climate of opinion is strong enough to immobilize welfare advocacy constituencies.

See Tamar Lewin, "Liberal Advocates Seem Speechless," *International Herald Tribune*, Nov. 25–6, 1995.

25 For underlying philosophical specification see John Rawls, "The Law of Peoples," in Stephen Shute and Susan Hurley (eds), *On Human Rights: The Oxford Amnesty Lectures 1993* (New York: Basic Books, 1993), pp. 41–82. Rawls's views are set forth as purely a matter of state–society relations. His approach acknowledges that orientations other than liberal can satisfy the requirements of decency embodied in "The Law of Peoples", but he fails altogether to consider whether governments have this option, given external links and constraints associated with the way markets are organized.

26 Xenophobia and hostility to immigration are on the rise, for a variety of reasons, including efforts to shift responsibility for job loss and declining real wages on to immigrants, legal and illegal. One of the striking features of globalization is that, despite its rhetoric of "freedom," the impact on the majority of persons is likely to be a decline in relative and absolute economic security. Such an impact is often discussed as an aspect of the polarizing effects of globalization, but it is also a consequence of liberating capital from the constraints of territorial space, while tying most workers more closely than ever, as well as tightening up indirect modes of mobility by way of immigration, refugee flows, and asylum policies. For an imaginative and persuasive treatment of these themes see chapter by Susan Jonas, "U.S. 'National Security' vs. Regional Welfare as the Basis for Immigration Policy: Reflections from the Case of Central American Immigrants and Refugees," in Kay Castro (ed.), *Transnational Realities and Nation States: Trends in International Integration and Immigration Policy in the Americas* (Boulder, Colo.: Lynne Rienner, 1996). A recent journalistic account reports that construction workers from Mexico's northern border can earn 15 times more by crossing to the United States and that enforcement efforts are increasing to reduce the number of illegal crossings. Sam Dillon, "Enforcement Reduces Illegal Crossings from Mexico," *International Herald Tribune*, Nov. 25–6, 1995. Another aspect of this pattern of economic legitimation and territorial protection in the North and criminalization and intervention in the South is evident in relation to such diverse issues as anti-terrorism, the drug war, and the non-proliferation regime as contrasted with arms sales.

27 The response at the regional level of multilateralism is uneven, but definitely part of the wider story. In Europe, where the preconditions for a rudimentary form of regional democracy were present, at least until the end of the cold war, the claims of the new multilateralism were accommodated by revolutionary means in the human rights area, creating formal institutions that were capable of responding directly to civic grievances, enabled to provide both accountability external to the state and extra-statal procedures of direct recourse. Such possibilities were reinforced, as well, by the existence of the European Parliament. Regional developments outside Europe, aside from initiatives intended to promote economic cooperation, have been minimal.

28 The former assertion is posited as the main position of Richard Rorty in Amnesty Oxford lecture, crediting Gregory Rabassa with the phrase. See Rorty, "Human Rights Rationality, and Sentimentality," in Shute and Hurley (eds), *On Human Rights*, pp. 111–34. The universalist argument is also made in Christopher C. Joyner and John C. Dettling, "Bridging the Cultural Chasm: Cultural Relativism and the Future of International Law," *California Western International Law Journal*, 20 (1989–90), pp. 275–314.

29 Difficult issues of agency and the causal impact of normative ideas are raised by such an assertion that cannot be addressed here. Suffice it to say, socialism owed its effectiveness, as Marx brilliantly perceived, to the prospect of mobilized, potentially revolutionary, industrial labor sectors of society. A limit on this effectiveness, which Marx realized much less clearly, was the weakness of transnational class solidarity as compared to nationalist bonds of solidarity. Human rights as a normative discourse became effective as a result of the convergence of geopolitical factors (ideological confrontation restricted by nuclear stalemate) and the rise of transnational civil initiatives. What is happening in the late 1990s is a softening of both these sets of empowering pressures, creating an impression of drift with respect to the political relevance of the human rights idea.

30 Many of these arguments are advanced in a significant way by Ahmet Davutoglu, *Civilizational Transformation and the Muslim World* (Kuala Lumpur, Malaysia: Mahir Publications, 1994); see assertion, p. 24: "This monopolistic tendency by the hegemonic powers to marginalize other cultures is also an aspect of the globalization of international economics.... Western civilization in its attempts to globalize and impose its hegemonic paradigm, has effectively marginalized other cultures. If this process is not arrested, we may see the inevitable evaporation of other cultures and civilizations."

31 For an essay relying on the terminology globalization-from-above and globalization-from-below see essay by Falk, "The Making of Global Citizenship," in Jeremy Brecher, John Brown Childs, and Jill Cutler (eds), *Global Visions: Beyond the New World Order* (Boston: South End Press, 1993), pp. 39–50.

32 The perspectives of JUST in Penang, Malaysia, are indicative of this orientation. See proceedings of 1994 conference, "Rethinking Human Rights" (Kuala Lumpur), and 1995 Penang workshop, "Images of Islam: Terrorizing the Truth." See book by founder and director of JUST: Chandra Muzaffar, *Human Rights and the New World Order* (Penang, Malaysia: Just World Trust, 1993).

33 The alleged global democratizing trends post-1989 are ambiguous even if South and East Asia are left aside; for most of the countries in Eastern Europe and the countries that have taken the place of the former Soviet Union and Yugoslavia, the democratic commitment is cosmetic at best and may even be reversed or compromised by electoral outcomes. In the Middle East, as well, authoritarian rule flourishes beneath many banners, and even a military takeover may be preferred by the West to the risk of respect for democratic processes that end up handing the reins of government to reli-

gious extremists. Abdel Monein Said Ali, Director of the Al Ahram Center for Strategic Studies in Cairo, was recently quoted as follows on the prospect for forthcoming elections being less than fair: "Democracy in Egypt is not deep-rooted. Belief is still in the state. If you want something done, it is the state who [sic] will do it." John Lancaster, "In Egyptian Elections, Democracy Also May Win or Lose," *International Herald Tribune*, Nov. 28, 1995.

34   See generally, David Held, *Democracy and the Global Order* (Stanford, Calif.: Stanford University Press, 1995); Richard Falk, *On Humane Governance: Toward a New Global Politics* (Cambridge: Polity Press, 1995); David Held and Daniele Archibugi (eds), *Cosmopolitan Democracy* (Cambridge: Polity Press, 1995).

35   Edward Said, *Orientalism* (New York: Pantheon, 1978); proceedings of the JUST conference "Rethinking Human Rights" in Kuala Lumpur, Malaysia, Dec. 1994; Abdullahi Ahmed An-Na'im (ed.), *Human Rights in Cross-Cultural Perspectives: A Quest for Consensus* (Philadelphia: University of Pennsylvania Press, 1992).

36   For constructive assessments that encourage dialogue see John L. Esposito, *The Islamic Threat: Myth or Reality* (New York: Oxford University Press, 1992); Fred Halliday, *Islam and the Myth of Confrontation* (London: I. B. Tauris, 1995).

37   There are special obstacles that arise when the historical memory of inter-civilizational relations is one of abuse on the part of the subordinated civilization. The relations of the West with Islam, Africa, and indigenous peoples disclose different facets of this background, which casts a long shadow of suspicion across efforts at reconciliation. Acknowledgment and apology seem important steps for the dominant side to take, not to erase the memory, but to move it beyond a preoccupation with past grievance. One other approach, taken in relation to Islam, is to overcome existing modes of discrimination that are, in effect, relegating Islam to the status of civilizational subordination. For discussion see Falk, "False Universalism and Geopolitics of Exclusion: The Case of Islam," *Third World Quarterly*, 18 (1997), pp. 7–23.

38   These encounters need to encompass, as well, the claims of indigenous peoples.

39   The current effort to establish an International Criminal Court is illustrative of the likely inability to achieve goals by way of the old multilateralism.

Chapter 7   The Outlook for UN Reform

1   See Alexander Ivankov, described as "a United Nations spokesman," who was quoted as saying "The Bosnian Serb Army is behaving like a terrorist organization": *New York Times*, May 29, 1995, p. 1.

2 For a scathing, yet persuasive, critique of the UN role in Bosnia see David Rieff, *Slaughterhouse: Bosnia and the Failure of the West* (New York: Simon & Schuster, 1995).

3 In this regard, the Khmer Rouge in Cambodia, FRAPH in Haiti, the Bosnian Serbs in Bosnia. For general discussion see Richard Falk, "The Haiti Intervention: A Dangerous World Order Precedent for the United Nations," *Harvard International Law Journal*, 36 (1995), pp. 341–58.

4 For elaboration see Richard Falk, *On Humane Governance: Toward a New Global Politics* (Cambridge: Polity Press, 1995).

5 The UN "success" in Afghanistan involved facilitating the removal of the Soviet Union from the country, a step that, unfortunately, has not produced normalcy or peace for the country.

6 In the UN hostage crisis of 1995, the UN personnel were seized in retaliation for NATO bombing.

7 Limiting expectations will be difficult, given the degree to which the Security Council is subject to the control of its leading members. As argued, it is often useful for these governments to use the UN as a shield behind which to obscure their own low levels of commitment. The UN as so used is abused. To change such irresponsible practices is, in the first instance, an educational task: to convince governments both that it is more important to uphold the reputation of the Organization and public opinion and that the UN needs capabilities commensurate with its responsibilities if it is to be held accountable for disappointing results.

8 The scope of the UN role would have to evolve on a case-by-case basis, keeping in sharp relief the importance of conforming missions to available capabilities. Mistakes might still be made, but they would be seen more clearly for what they are, misjudgments as to means, not ambivalence as to ends. See suggestions along these lines in Brian Urquhart, "For a UN Volunteer Military Force," *New York Review of Books*, June 10, 1993. See also Saul Mendlovitz, with John Fousek, "The Prevention and Punishment of the Crime of Genocide," in Charles B. Strozier and Michael Flynn (eds), *Genocide, War, and Human Survival* (London and Lanham, Md.: Rowman and Littlefield, 1996), pp. 137–52.

9 See Richard Falk, "The Making of Global Citizenship," in Jeremy Brecher, John Brown Childs, and Jill Cutler (eds), *Global Visions: Beyond the New World Order* (Boston: South End Press, 1993), pp. 39–50; David Held and Daniele Archibugi (eds), *Cosmopolitan Democracy* (Cambridge: Polity Press, 1995).

Chapter 8 Resisting "Globalization-from-Above" through "Globalization-from-Below"

1 See two recent reports of global commissions of eminent persons, published as *Our Global Neighbourhood* by the Commission on Global Governance

(Oxford and New York: Oxford University Press, 1995) and *Caring for the Future* by the Independent Commission on Population and the Quality of Life (Oxford and New York: Oxford University Press, 1996).

2   Immanuel Wallerstein, *After Liberalism* (New York: New Press, 1995), pp. 1–8, 93–107.

3   Effectively argued in Smitu Kothari, "Where are the People? The United Nations, Global Economic Institutions and Governance," in Albert Paolini, Anthony P. Jarvis, and Christian Reus-Smit (eds), *The United Nations: Between Sovereignty and Global Governance* (London: Macmillan and New York: St Martin's Press, 1997), pp. 186–206.

4   This position is elaborated in Richard Falk, "An Inquiry into the Political Economy of World Order," *New Political Economy*, 1 (1996), pp. 13–26.

5   For initial reliance on this terminology with respect to globalization, see Richard Falk, "The Making of Global Citizenship," in Jeremy Brecher, John Brown Childs, and Jill Cutler (eds), *Global Visions: Beyond the New World Order* (Boston: South End Press, 1993), pp. 39–50. For a useful and sophisticated overview of globalization-from-below in the context of transnational environmentalism, see Paul Wapner, *Environmental Activism and World Civic Politics* (Albany, NY: State University of New York Press, 1996).

6   For an attempted clarification of world order values and their interrelations, see Richard Falk, *A Study of Future Worlds* (New York: Free Press, 1975), pp. 11–43.

7   A comprehensive and important effort to formulate such a perspective is to be found in the writings of David Held; see his *Democracy and the Global Order: From the Modern State to Cosmopolitan Governance* (Cambridge: Polity Press, 1995), pp. 267–86.

Chapter 9   Global Civil Society

1   For helpful conceptual discussion of these issues of conceptual framing, see Paul Wapner, "The Social Construction of Global Governance," paper presented at American Political Science Association Annual Meeting, Aug. 28–31, 1996.

2   James N. Rosenau, *Turbulence in World Politics: A Theory of Change and Continuity* (Princeton, NJ: Princeton University Press, 1990), pp. 34–7.

3   Marc Nerfin, "Neither Prince nor Merchant: Citizen – An Introduction to the Third System," *IFDA Dossier*, 56 (Nov./Dec. 1986), pp. 3–29.

4   For concise overview see Wapner, "Social Construction of Global Governance"; also R. D. Lipschutz, *Global Civil Society and Global Environmental Governance* (Albany, NY: State University of New York Press, 1996).

5   Richard Falk, "The Making of Global Citizenship," in Jeremy Brecher, John Brown Childs, and Jill Cutler (eds), *Global Visions: Beyond the New World Order* (Boston: South End Press, 1993), pp. 39–50; *idem*, *On Humane Governance: Toward a New Global Politics* (Cambridge: Polity Press, 1995).

6   This normative potential of statism has been most influentially articulated by Hedley Bull, *Anarchical Society: A Study of Order in World Politics* (New York: Columbia University Press, 1977).

7   For a more historically grounded view of globalization see Ian Clark, *Globalization and Fragmentation: International Relations in the Twentieth Century* (Oxford: Oxford University Press, 1997).

8   Paul Hirst and Grahame Thompson, *Globalization in Question* (Cambridge: Polity Press, 1996), pp. 1–17, 170–94.

9   See items listed in n. 5.

10   J. Sachs, "New Members Please Apply," *Time*, July 7, 1997, pp. 11–12.

11   Francis Fukuyama, *The End of History and the Last Man* (New York: Free Press, 1992).

12   Vandana Shiva, "People's Ecology: The Chipko Movement," in R. B. J. Walker and Saul H. Mendlovitz (eds), *Towards a Just World Peace: Perspectives from Social Movements* (London: Butterworths, 1987), pp. 253–70; Bruce Rich, *Mortgaging the Earth: The World Bank, Environmental Impoverishment, and the Crisis of Development* (Boston: Beacon Press, 1994).

13   Donella H. Meadows et al., *The Limits to Growth* (New York: Universe Books, 1972).

14   Edward Goldsmith et al., *Blueprint for Survival* (Boston: Houghton Mifflin, 1972).

15   Falk, *On Humane Governance*; idem, "An Inquiry into the Political Economy of World Order," *New Political Economy*, 1 (1996), pp. 13–26; idem, "Resisting 'Globalization-from-Above' through 'Globalization-from-Below'," *New Political Economy*, 2 (1997), pp. 17–24.

16   Commission on Global Governance, *Our Global Neighbourhood* (Oxford: Oxford University Press, 1995).

17   Daniele Archibugi et al. (eds), *Cosmopolitan Democracy: An Agenda for a New World Order* (Cambridge: Polity Press, 1995); David Held, *Democracy and the Global Order: From the Modern State to Cosmopolitan Governance* (Cambridge: Polity Press, 1995).

18   Walden Bello, talk at Bangkok Conference on "Alternative Security Systems in the Asia–Pacific," Focus Asia, Mar. 27–30, 1997.

19   For example, Mahathir complains about George Soros's financial speculations as jeopardizing Malaysian development successes: "Malaysia PM Mulls Action against Speculators," *Turkish Daily News*, July 29, 1977.

20   Yoshikazu Sakamoto (ed.), *Global Transformation: Challenges to the State System* (Tokyo: United Nations University Press, 1994); Richard Falk, "State of Siege: Will Globalization Win Out?," *International Affairs*, 73 (1997), pp. 123–36.

Chapter 10   Recasting Citizenship

1   See T. H. Marshall's influential formulations in *Citizenship and Social Class* (Cambridge: Cambridge University Press, 1950).

2   Hobbes, of course, most famously and definitively, specified these realities in *The Leviathan*, ed. by Richard Tuck (Cambridge: Cambridge University Press, 1991); for a sophisticated contemporary discussion see R. B. J. Walker, *Inside/Outside: International Relations as Political Theory* (Cambridge: Cambridge University Press, 1992).

3   These responsibilities were discharged internationally by reference to the broader overlapping category of affiliation designated as "nationality," which traditionally engaged the international law doctrine of "diplomatic protection."

4   This distinction is borrowed from Michael Walzer's *Thick and Thin: Moral Argument at Home and Abroad* (Notre Dame, Ind.: University of Notre Dame Press, 1994).

5   Robert Reich, *The Work of Nations* (New York: Knopf, 1991), p. 8; see also Richard Rosecrance, "The Rise of the Virtual State," *Foreign Affairs*, 75 (1996), pp. 45–61.

6   Reich, *Work of Nations*, p. 9. Reich puts the issue more vividly elsewhere in the book: "To improve the economic position of the bottom four-fifths will require that the fortunate fifth share its wealth and invest in the wealth-creating capacities of other Americans. Yet as the top becomes ever more tightly linked to the global economy, it has less stake in the performance and potential of its less fortunate compatriots. Thus our emerging dilemma, and that of other nations as well" (p. 301). One has to wonder about the functioning of democracy if such a large majority cannot come to appreciate its own self-interest or seem unable to generate the political means for its effective promotion. Or is democracy itself a casualty of the discipline of global capital?

7   For elaboration see Richard Falk, "Resisting 'Globalisation-from-Above' through 'Globalisation-from-Below'," *New Political Economy*, 2 (1997), pp. 17–24.

8   Reich, *Work of Nations*, acknowledges that this rootlessness of economic global citizens is an obstacle to the acceptance of his ideas, but he seems nevertheless hopeful that his appeal will be heeded.

9   See Immanuel Wallerstein, *After Liberalism* (New York: New Press, 1995), esp. pp. 252–71.

10 See *The Economist* cover story, "Latin America's Backlash," 30 Nov. 1996, pp. 17–18, 23–6.

11 For an excellent analysis along these lines see Tu Wei-Ming, "Confucian Traditions in East Asian Modernity," *Bulletin of the American Academy of Arts and Sciences*, 1 (Nov. 1996), pp. 12–39. The relationship between "citizenship" and "human rights" as aspects of the decline of the sovereign state will be discussed in a subsequent section.

12 See results of 1996 survey on science and math in *Newsweek* that puts Singapore, Taiwan, and South Korea at or near the top of the educational ladder up through high school preparation.

13 Reich, *Work of Nations*, pp. 311–15.

14 An intellectually formidable effort to provide such an approach can be

found in Herman E. Daly and John B. Cobb, Jr, *For the Common Good: Redirecting the Economy toward Community, the Environment, and a Sustainable Future* (Boston: Beacon Press, 1989).

15 See Gabriel Kolko's insightful renderings in *Century of War: Politics, Conflicts, and Society since 1914* (New York: New Press, 1994).

16 For representative discussions of these developments see Yoshikazu Sakamoto (ed.), *Global Transformation: Challenges to the State System* (Tokyo: United Nations University Press, 1994); also James H. Mittelman (ed.), *Globalization: Critical Reflections* (Boulder, Colo.: Lynne Rienner, 1996).

17 David Held and Daniele Archibugi (eds), *Cosmopolitan Democracy* (Cambridge: Polity Press, 1995); David Held, *Democracy and the Global Order: From the Modern State to Cosmopolitan Governance* (Stanford, Calif.: Stanford University Press, 1995).

18 See here sensitive discussions by Tu Wei-Ming, "Confucian Traditions."

19 Richard Falk, "False Universalism and the Geopolitics of Exclusion: The Case of Islam," *Third World Quarterly*, 18 (1997), pp. 7–23.

20 The literature here is vast and rich, but see Akbar S. Ahmed, *Postmodernism and Islam: Predicament and Promise* (London: Routledge, 1992); more broadly, see Edward Said, *Orientalism* (New York: Pantheon, 1978); Zygmunt Bauman, *Intimations of Postmodernity* (London: Routledge, 1992).

21 The idea of treason is based on the legitimacy of the state demanding partisanship on a territorial basis in the context of international relations.

22 See e.g. Bart van Steenbergen (ed.), *The Conditions of Citizenship* (London: Sage, 1994); also Martha Nussbaum et al., *For Love of Country* (Boston: Beacon Press, 1996).

23 Best articulated by Edward Luttwak, "Post-Heroic Armies," *Foreign Affairs*, 75 (1996), pp. 33–44; also John Mueller, *Retreat from Doomsday: The Obsolescence of Major War* (New York: Basic Books, 1989).

24 Although for other reasons, Colin Powell reemerged as a powerful political player.

25 Well explored by Paul Wapner in *Environmental Activism and World Civic Politics* (Albany, NY: State University of New York Press, 1996).

26 See Richard Falk, "The Making of Global Citizenship," in Jeremy Brecher, John Brown Childs, and Jill Cutler (eds), *Global Visions: Beyond the New World Order* (Boston: South End Press, 1993), pp. 39–50.

27 See Chakravarthi Raghavan, "ILO-Ban All Extreme Forms of Child Labour," Third World Network Features (1996).

28 I have tried to consider these possibilities in Richard Falk, *Explorations at the Edge of Time* (Philadelphia: Temple University Press, 1992); Richard Falk, *On Humane Governance: Toward a New Global Politics* (Cambridge: Polity Press, 1995); see also the ending of Ruth Gordon's excellent article on "failed states" for a suggested orientation toward identity and cross-national relations that is congenial to the position taken here: Ruth Gordon, "Saving Failed States: Sometimes a Neocolonialist Notion," *American Uni-*

versity Journal of International Law and Policy, 12 (1997), pp. 904–74, at pp. 971–4.

Chapter 11   Toward Normative Renewal

1   As is its sibling, the idea of decline and fall leading to inevitable doom, the work of pessimists.

2   Richard Falk, "False Universalism and the Geopolitics of Exclusion: The Case of Islam," *Third World Quarterly*, 18 (1997), pp. 7–23.

3   Richard Falk, "The Making of Global Citizenship," in Jeremy Brecher, John Brown Childs, and Jill Cutler (eds), *Global Visions: Beyond the New World Order* (Boston: South End Press, 1993), pp. 39–50; Falk, "Resisting 'Globalisation-from-Above' through 'Globalisation-from-Below'," *New Political Economy*, 2 (1997), pp. 17–24.

4   This understanding is, of course, written into the UN Charter in the form of Article 2(7), although with limiting conditions. The word "essentially" provides much room for political interpretation and changed attitudes toward sovereign rights. Also, deference to internal sovereignty is overridden by UN action taken to uphold international peace and security.

5   Note that this last element is generally described under the rubric of "human rights" as an element of foreign policy, but that it is a selective and somewhat contradictory notion. Economic and social rights are not only excluded, but are in practice curtailed or opposed as part of the neo-liberal program.

6   The various aspects of the international environmental ethos are best summarized in the Rio Declaration on Environment and Development. For text see Burns H. Weston, R. Falk, and others (eds), *Basic Documents in International Law and World Order*, 3rd edn (St Paul, Minn.: West, 1997), pp. 1112–15, also N. Low and B. Gleason, *Justice, Society and Nature: An Exploration of Political Ecology* (New York and London: Routledge, 1998).

7   My own effort to clarify this overall quest is Falk, *On Humane Governance: Toward a New Global Politics* (Cambridge: Polity Press, 1995); an earlier depiction is Falk, *A Study of Future Worlds* (New York: Free Press, 1975).

8   The 1956 Suez Operation was the only time that geopolitics were somewhat subordinated by the superpowers. This was also true to some extent in relation to the Korean War, although in this instance the explanation is procedural, a fortuitous result of the Soviet boycott of the Security Council at the time for the unrelated reason of protesting the refusal to adjust Chinese representation to the outcome of the civil war after 1949.

9   See John Mueller, *Retreat from Doomsday: The Obsolescence of Major War* (New York: Basic Books, 1989).

10   On the issue of terminology, I have been persuaded to abandon NGO as a term of art by the analysis and arguments of Liszt Vierira, "Civil Society and Globalization," an undated paper, summarizing her book *Cidadania e Globalizacao* (Brazil: Editora Record, 1997).

11   See S. Kothari and H. Sheth (eds), *Rethinking Human Rights: Challenges for Theory and Action* (New York: New Horizons Press, 1989).

12   Brundtland World Commission on Environment and Development, *Our Common Future* (Oxford: Oxford University Press, 1987).

13   See Agenda 21 Plan of Action.

14   See Philippe Sands, "Protecting Future Generations: Precedents and Practicalities," and R. St. J. Macdonald, "Future Generations: Searching for a System of Protection," in E. Agius and S. Busuttil (eds), *Future Generations and International Law* (London: Earthscan Publications, 1998), pp. 83–91, 149–59.

15   Text in *Future Generations Journal*, 24 (1998), pp. 15–17.

16   G.A. Res. 2625 (XXV), 24 Oct. 1970.

17   See Daniele Archibugi and David Held (eds), *Cosmopolitan Democracy* (Cambridge: Polity Press, 1995).

18   For some elaboration see Falk, *On Humane Governance*.

Index